The Only Kid
on the Carnival

THE ONLY KID
ON THE CARNIVAL

An Extraordinary Childhood

A Memoir

Bill Jackson

iUniverse, Inc.

New York Bloomington Shanghai

The Only Kid on the Carnival
An Extraordinary Childhood

iUniverse books may be ordered through booksellers or by contacting:

iUniverse
1663 Liberty Drive
Bloomington, IN 47403
www.iuniverse.com
1-800-Authors (1-800-288-4677)

Because of the dynamic nature of the Internet, any Web addresses or links contained in this book may have changed since publication and may no longer be valid.

The views expressed in this work are solely those of the author and do not necessarily reflect the views of the publisher, and the publisher hereby disclaims any responsibility for them.

ISBN: 978-0-595-51748-0 (pbk)
ISBN: 978-0-595-62015-9 (ebk)

Printed in the United States of America

To those who dream.

CONTENTS

Prologue and Acknowledgements

Ed Emschwiller, the kind and thoughtful dean of Film & Video to whom I reported at CalArts, used a phrase, "It is my understanding...." In other words, he wasn't saying he was right or wrong, just that his perception of something was such and such. This book is my understanding of the events of my childhood: a hilarious, heart-tugging time where everyday was an incredible adventure. Unfortunately, for the sake of the book's cohesion, I had to leave out many worthy stories and the fascinating people involved. I have changed no names nor have I added fictitious characters, although at times I've shuffled time lines to aid the flow of the story. Dialogue is as my memory serves or reflects the character as I remember him or her, and I have adhered to the essence of every occurrence. Some participants in the story may remember themselves and the events differently, and I can assure them that I will buy their book when it comes out.

First thanks go to God, the Ultimate Author, who indeed has blessed me with an extraordinary life.

Next, I thank my wife, Jo, whose love, encouragement, and support contributed immeasurably during the five long years it took to write the final manuscript. The bright light of her allegiance was and is treasured and priceless.

That the book exists at all is my Brother Sam's fault. He urged me to render into print the "Jackson Stories," that, like the teachings of Socrates, had only been handed down by word of mouth. After three attempts to meld the disparate family escapades, what I had was, as they say in Missouri, "a dog from every town." Sam then suggested that the thread to the book should be my relationship with our father. He was dead right, and the "Jackson Stories" became my story.

Brother John and Cousin Jimmy provided valuable anecdotes, and input from my close friends, Neal (Rodge) Torrey and James Morrow, fleshed out many an episode. Maribeth (Torrey) DeHaven, whom I regard as the Treasure of Putnam County, aided tirelessly with names and dates. Uncle Bill Davis, Aunt Avis Davis, and Uncle Cleo Jackson will find some of their delightful input within these pages. An outstanding resource was Unionville historian Duane Crawford's excellent tributes, *In There Own Words*, Volumes 1 and 2. Don (Captain) Cook, Dorothy (Torrey) Bowers, Ray Klinginsmith, Colleen (Pickering) Putnam, Marilyn (Berry) Jarman, Dan (Buddy) Bramhall, Gerald (Sam) Neighbors, and Jim Peek are among those who contributed, probably without knowing it. Heartfelt thanks for the discerning critiques afforded by my knowledgeable writers' group, encircled around our table right to left: Kathy Veiera, Carol Smeltzer, Dr. Bill Linder, Barbara Matte, Nancy Ross, Mary Moses, Peg Bayer, and Charlie Johnson. And thank you to people I will be embarrassed that I forgot.

Finally, here's a big "thank you" to my agent. Since I didn't have one—thank you, me.

PART I

▼

Following the Phantom

CHAPTER 1

▼

THE BOOM, BUMPA-BOOM OVERTURE

Toots, clangs, cymbal crashes. The deep-throated growl of engines. Shouting and laughing, the rumble-hum of the crowd, and buried deep a faint "boom, bumpa-boom, bumpa-boom." An elderly couple shook their heads in dismay at this strange symphony and studied the overhead canvas banner: "Stephens Carnival—The Show of Shows!"

"The city limits sign to hell," muttered Davy. Sadie held his arm tightly as they walked under the banner and into a forbidden world.

Normally on this sultry Missouri evening, summer of 1940, Davy and Sadie Davis would be sitting on the hard wooden benches fanning themselves and nodding "amen's" to the constant calls for repentance given in Unionville's Church of Christ. But tonight, begging God's forgiveness, Davy had driven their Model A sixteen worry-ridden miles to this carnival the posters had said was playing in Lucerne. A few steps beyond the banner, the old couple found themselves in a land of hoopla: wooden horses bounding in circles; rides spinning people senseless; fluffy pink cones of cotton candy; cherubic Kewpie Dolls with frozen smiles; and a bombardment of suspect salesmen touting good fortune for "a dime, one-tenth of a doll-lah."

Davy spotted his daughter's blond hair right away. He couldn't believe she was twenty five; to him she still looked like the girl fresh from high school who'd run off with this winking banjo player from the traveling tent show. Her face sweet and pure, the daughter invited a young couple to sit inside a large, red box.

Davy slipped up behind her and softly said, "Hello, Virginia Lee."

The girl turned, her face lit up, and she plunged into his open arms, hugged him tightly, and then hugged her mother.

"What are you doing here?" she asked, noting that her father's hair was whiter than she remembered, and her mother more weary.

"Wanted to see how you were," Davy said, "… and the family."

Virginia Lee called to the back of the box, "Cecil! Mom and Dad are here!"

A man in his early thirties, dark-eyed and dripping sweat, emerged from the rear of the red box carrying a short strip of pictures in his hand. He nodded to his in-laws and handed the film to a waiting customer, collecting a quarter. Virginia Lee proudly explained that the structure was a picture-taking machine called a Mug Joint.

"Cecil built it himself," she said, beaming her pride.

Davy looked inside the box. On the right was a little peep hole in the wall and on the left was a small bench in front of a painted background. He shook his head slowly and backed away. Cecil invited his father-in-law into the rear partition of the box to see where the film was developed. Sadie stayed near her daughter and at first opportunity told her she needed to eat more. Davy came out with rivulets of sweat streaming down his face, his only comment being that it was "interesting." Then he asked the whereabouts of his five-year-old grandson.

Virginia Lee smiled. "Oh, Bill Ray's out there somewhere. We'll find him, probably on the merry-go-round."

The old couple followed their daughter onto the midway, and the carnies, seeing fresh meat, squawked their spiels like crows hustling a meal. Sadie drew closer to her husband, her eyes searching the crowd.

"Don't worry, Mom, Bill Ray's okay," Virginia Lee said. "Everybody looks after him. He's the only kid on the carnival."

The grandson wasn't at the merry-go-round, and Virginia Lee led her parents deeper into the midway. Davy noticed that the *boom, bumpa, boom* he had heard earlier had gotten louder.

"You! Muscles!" called a man chewing a fat cigar. Slender Davy slowed his walk and squared his narrow shoulders. Holding out a mallet, the man invited him to pound a rubber lump at the base of a tall, wooden tower. He explained that if Davy hit the lump hard enough, a metal weight would shoot up the tower and ring a bell at the top. "Ring the bell; win a cigar, jus' like mine!" The man grinned, juicily working the cigar back and forth in his mouth.

"That's the High Striker," Virginia Lee said. "It's a man's game."

Davy seemed intrigued, but Sadie tugged his sleeve and they moved on.

"Big money! Win big money here!" called a dark-skinned girl in a red blouse left unbuttoned at the top. She swung a black ball on a chain at a bowling pin only three feet away and knocked it over. "Five dollars'll get you ten!" Hardly looking at what she was doing, she swung the ball again, knocking over the pin.

Virginia Lee whispered, "That's the Swinger. It's gaffed." Her parents looked puzzled. "Rigged," she explained. "And if you win, watch out going back to your car."

Sadie shivered and drew closer to Davy.

Continuing on, the daughter said, "Bill Ray always stops by to see Delmar. Delmar's his best friend who runs the Spin 'Til You Win. It's a Hanky Pank." Seeing her parents exchange looks, Virginia Lee hastened to say, "Not 'hanky-panky,' a Hanky *Pank*. That's where you think you're going to win the Flash, uh, big stuff, but you usually win some dinky thing."

As they approached the stand, she whispered, "Delmar's not as old as he looks; I think he was just born tired." They stopped in front of a gaunt, salt-and-pepper haired man behind a counter.

With watery blue eyes looking at everyone and no one, he softly said, "Spin 'til you win. Only a dime, a winner every time." In front of him was a horizontal arrow encircled by thin nails. Delmar spun the arrow. Clickity, clickity, click, a piece of plastic sticking out of the arrow's nose struck against the nails and came to rest. "Ah, see?" he said, quietly looking at Sadie, "number seven. You would've won Shirley Temple."

"Shirley's such a nice girl," said a quivering voice.

Sitting nearby, an old woman wearing a turban knitted a doily that looked like a spider web. She was even skinnier and paler than Delmar, and Davy assumed she was his mother. Neither of them had seen Bill Ray for the last half hour.

Continuing to follow their daughter, Davy and Sadie studied the carnies like they were citizens of a foreign land: bow-tied men in boater-style hats calling through fixed smiles for you to come into the tent and visit Lardella, the four-hundred-pound fat lady. Glum, tattooed roustabouts manned the rides, cursing the sweat in their eyes and the ache in their limbs. Leathery women, cigarettes dangling from bright red lips, brandished hoops, balls, or darts, and invited the men to win one for the "leetle lay-dee."

Now the *boom, bumpa-boom* heard at the entrance sounded even closer, and Davy, nodding, said to no one in particular, "That's a base drum."

Virginia Lee paused at the Ferris wheel. "Bill Ray rides this a lot," she said.

Davy and Sadie tilted their heads back to see the top of this gigantic metal wheel with wooden seats. It had stopped, and kids at the top wildly rocked in place, ignoring the slender restraining bars.

"He rides this by himself?" Sadie asked.

Her daughter pretended not to hear the question.

B*oom, bumpa-boom, bumpa-boom!* Ever louder thundered the hypnotic call, and now the crowd, caught in the beat's irresistible grasp, swept the daughter and her elderly parents down the midway like an unstoppable river current. At the far end loomed a large tent with a platform in front of it. A throng, thirty people deep, cheered and hollered at figures writhing on the platform.

Davy and Sadie stood on tip-toes to see.

Boom, bumpa-boom, bumpa-boom!

Standing on an orange crate, five-year-old Bill Ray Jackson pounded a large base drum with all of his might as two nearly naked women rolled their tummies, humped their hips, and shook their grass skirts like a storm blowing Kansas wheat. Billowing behind the dancers, a huge canvas sign proclaimed: "The Belles of Broadway!"

"Hi, Grandma! Hi, Grandpa!"

Grandma and Grandpa didn't know I was just helping my friends. The *Belles* were the barker's wife and daughter, and most mornings we had cocoa and cookies in their trailer before the marks arrived—"marks" being what the carnies called people from the towns. Anyway, if Grandma and Grandpa were going to worry about anybody, it should've been Mom.

Twice a day a man shot her through the heart.

CHAPTER 2

▼

THE GREAT RAMON

Mom's regular job, besides being Mom, was to pretty-talk people to sit in the Mug Joint and have their pictures taken—ten cents a piece, three for a quarter. Dad developed the pictures in the dark room, which was the back half of the big red box he'd built. All the pictures were black and white, and for an additional ten cents a picture, Mom would tint them, which always drew a crowd—it was like a free show. Dad said folks needed a free show because of the Depression. When I asked what the Depression was, he said that it was a bad thing that had happened when some rich people got greedy and now lots of people were poor.

"Are we poor, Dad?" I asked.

"Did you have something to eat for breakfast?"

"A bowl of oatmeal."

"Then we weren't poor this day," he said.

Dad told Mom to be sure to smile at the farmers, they were the ones who might have a dime for a picture. He said the hard times had the townies pinching pennies for food, but the farmers raised their own, and might have a little fun-money wrapped in an old bandana.

One day a man in the crowd who certainly didn't look like any farmer was watching Mom very closely. He had dark skin and a moustache that curled upwards at the ends, and he wore a wide-brimmed white hat. He stepped to the back of the Mug Joint and tapped on the door.

"I am the Great Ramon," he announced. "I do the Free Act."

Dad stuck his head out, squinting in the bright sunshine.

"Dear sir, my assistant ran off last night with a roustabout. I'm only with Stephens one more week. Could your lady fill in?"

"What's it pay?" Dad asked, wiping his hands on his pants.

"Twelve dollars for two acts a day."

Twelve dollars was a bunch more than what the Mug Joint made in two days.

"What's she have to do?" Dad asked.

"Simple stuff. Smile. Break a light bulb under her cape … and … throw darts at my back." The Great Ramon rushed to say, "I stay at the Lucerne Hotel. Send her to me and I'll go over the act with her."

"I'll talk to her," Dad said, "but I'll let you tell her about the darts."

Mom later told me what happened at the hotel. She said wearing a cape sounded fun, but she couldn't believe Dad would let her go to the Great Ramon's hotel room alone. Dad insisted the man wouldn't try anything; the carnies would string him alive.

Mom wasn't totally convinced, and she knocked on the Great Ramon's door ready to kick him square in his greatness if he made a wrong move.

He didn't.

He invited her to sit in an overstuffed chair by the window. Strewn over the bed were flyers showing him staring from under a turban with wide, intense eyes. He explained the act. She would wear a long, black velvet cape. To the audience he would show a playing card, the Queen of Hearts, place it in her right hand, and have her hold it over her heart. He would then close the front of the cape. Behind her would be a light bulb on a stand, over which he would drape the cape. From a black box on a small table to one side of the stage, he would bring forth a pistol and one bullet. He would get someone in the audience to look at the bullet and declare it real. Then, with slight-of-hand, the Great Ramon would load a blank into the chamber, aim at her heart and shoot. The light bulb would shatter, and the cape would be removed to reveal this. Next he would show the audience where the bullet had passed through the card she held over her heart.

"What's the trick?" asked Mom.

"It's all in your apparel," smiled the Great Ramon. Dramatically flinging open a closet door, he revealed a floor length, black velvet cape. Hidden in the dark silk lining was a sharpened lead pencil. Taking the playing card, she would bring both hands inside the cape; and while he draped the back of the cloak over the light bulb, she would punch a hole in the card with the pencil.

Attached to the lining in the back of the cape was a small trip hammer. Using her free hand, she would hold the trip hammer next to the bulb. The instant the revolver fired, she would squeeze a lever, and the hammer would smash the bulb. He would show the audience the hole in the card, and then would lift the back of the cape to reveal the broken glass.

"You can do all of that, can't you?" asked the Great Ramon.

"I think so," answered Mom.

"Good. Then for the close I strip to the waist, and you throw darts at my back."

Mom bolted for the hallway.

"Wait!" he called. "They don't hurt!"

She stuck her head back in the doorway. "How do darts not hurt?" she asked.

"I don't feel a thing. It's the state I put myself in."

"What state is that, New Hampshire?"

That afternoon, I got as close as I could as the Great Ramon strutted to the center of the stage looking like something in the movies. He wore a jeweled turban, a billowing silky shirt, and shiny black pants. Bowing to a puzzled applause, he then paraded the stage holding up the black velvet cape for all to see.

"Ladies and gentlemen, I display before you the incredible Cloak of Invincibility. When Czar Nicholas II and the royal family were assassinated, it is said that Anastasia, Russia's beautiful, young grand duchess, wore this very cloak, and all bullets aimed at her were rendered harmless. I will now demonstrate before your very eyes the miraculous power of this *cloak of mystery.*"

Mom came on the stage wearing a black one-piece bathing suit with shiny beads stuck on it. Some men whistled. The Great Ramon fitted Anastasia's cloak over Mom's shoulders, then held up a deck of cards and took out one, saying it was "appropriately, the Queen of Hearts." Mom held the card over her heart, and The Great Ramon did everything he'd explained in the apartment.

Then he brought out this really big pistol.

"I shall fire one shot at this lovely lady. The bullet will *pierce* the card, *tear* through her heart, *emerge* from her back, and *shatter* the light bulb. And yet, dear audience, this lovely Anastasia shall remain *alive, unmarked, and unhurt.*"

After he got a guy to say the bullet was real, the Great Ramon made a big fuss about checking the light bulb. Then he walked to the far side of the stage, and with his eyes bugged real big, turned slowly and pointed the gun at Mom. Shouts rang out for him to stop and mothers grabbed their children and rushed away.

"Quiet! Please! I must not be distracted!" thundered the Great Ramon.

The crowd fell silent.

"Bang!"

The shot echoed down the midway. Mom stood silent as a tombstone as the Great Ramon reached into the cape and pulled out the card. Holding it away from him for all to see, he poked his finger through the hole. Then he lifted the back of the cape, revealing the shattered bulb. Everyone stood there, struck dumb, staring at Mom, waiting for her to move.

Seconds passed.

"I cried out, "Are you dead, Mom?"

The audience roared with laughter. I ran to her open arms and she wrapped the cape around me. Laughter turned to cheers. Mom was a hit.

CHAPTER 3

▼

THE CARNIES

Grandpa and Grandma headed for the car, but not before Grandpa took Mom aside and told her that this "Tramp man" was dragging us to degradation, that he was nothing but a dreamer. I heard his loud whisper, and didn't know about the degra part, but Grandpa hit dead right about the dreaming; Dad dreamed a truck load, and I wanted to follow right behind him. It was true we didn't always eat regular. Some days no more than three or four people had their pictures taken, which meant we'd be eating lard gravy on bread again that night. But it didn't matter to me; Dad was taking us on adventures with people who were loads of fun—especially the ones here on this carnival. It even had a king.

Well, Mr. Stephens walked the midway like a king. He had a plump, jovial face and a mouthful of gold-filled teeth usually clenched around an ivory cigarette holder, which made him look like the president did in his pictures. Maybe not entirely. His tummy stuck out, wide suspenders held up his baggy pants, and he wore a cream-colored straw hat—Dad called it a Panama—cocked slightly to the left. About nine in the morning, the king would stroll around checking on his subjects, and when he saw something he approved, he wiggled his cigarette holder between his clenched teeth—so everyone watched for the wiggle.

Along about 10 AM, an hour before the marks would arrive, Mrs. Stephens, looking dressed for tea, emerged from her castle—a gleaming Silver Streak—the top of the line for trailers. She had jet black hair, brightly rouged lips, and a slender neck adorned with strands of white pearls. Preferring not to stroll the midway as her husband did, she usually drove into town in the Stephens' big black Lincoln.

But we saw Mr. Stephens early and often. Each morning as the carnies prepared for a new crop of marks, he marched down the midway reviewing his troops: a grinning bunch of pirates ready to extract any treasure a purse or pants pocket might hold. His review began at the merry-go-round and continued past all of the games, rides, and concession stands, ending with the Ferris wheel and the two tents only the adults could enter: the Girl Show and the Wrestling Tent.

Dad said Mr. Stephens was the only one making any real money, 'cause all the carnies had to pay him for the amount of space they took up on the midway. It must've cost a fortune for the space used by the Girl Show and the Wrestling Tent, but our tiny Mug Joint hardly took up any. Even so, sometimes Dad had to go to Mr. Stephens' big silver trailer and ask him to put our bill "on account." When I asked what "on account" was, Dad said, "It's on account of we don't have any money."

Not far from our Mug Joint was a concession named The Magic Shop. It wasn't much bigger than our red box, but it got lots more customers. Dad called the man who ran it Pitchman. Pitchman dressed real nice, the best on the midway, and his mouth moved faster than a woodpecker's peck.

"Hey! Hey! Whaduya say? It's magic time! Baffling, amazing, eye-popping legerdemain that will amaze your boss, your sweetheart, your wife, your ex-wife, your Great Aunt Tillie!"

When the marks heard Pitchman's spiel, they broke for his stand like pigs to a feed trough. I'd squeeze my way to the front of them, straining to see the magician's mysteries: scarves connecting themselves; tightly gripped sponges multiplying like rabbits; wands sprouting flowers; and my favorite—x-ray sunglasses that revealed what cards the other guy was holding.

One hot afternoon after the crowd had moved on, Pitchman looked up from counting his take and saw me back a ways staring at him.

"C'mere, kid." he said.

I edged a couple of steps forward.

"You're 'with it,' ain't ya?"

"*With it*" meant you were part of the carnival. I nodded yes.

"Yeah, saw you at that Mug Joint your dad built. How'dya like to make some geetus?"

I looked puzzled.

"You know, kid, geetus, money. Wanna make some money?"

He brought out a heavy, white paper folded like an envelope and pulled a quarter from his pocket. "This is the Magic Envelope Trick. You unfold the envelope, place the quarter on the paper, fold it around the quarter, and the quarter disappears. I'll teach you how to do it. Then you can demo the trick for the marks and I'll let you keep the quarter, capiche?" When I didn't answer, he said, "Capiche? Understand?"

I capiched.

He slowly folded the quarter into the envelope, opened it, and showed that the quarter was gone. After the third time I had it. The trick was to fold things just right so that you created a secret pocket for the quarter. When you unfolded the envelope a certain way, the pocket hiding the quarter didn't show. Pitchman patted me on the head and said, "Keep the trick for practicing. You start mañana."

I stood there.

"Tomorrow. Scoot."

I rushed home—home being a small plywood trailer parked about ten feet behind the Mug Joint. There was no running water or electricity, but Dad had installed a propane counter stove for cooking and heating, and a tiny closet with a white, metal potty. Mom and Dad had a small bed at one end of the trailer, and I slept on the collapsible table at the other end. Dad had fixed it so the legs folded under the table, and the table lowered level with the built-in wooden seats along the trailer wall. The seat cushions then became my mattress. Our trailer wasn't as nice as the other carnies', but it was better and warmer than the tent we'd lived in down in Texas, and I'll tell you about that later.

That night I sat on my bed and practiced folding the envelope about fifty times, then showed the trick to Dad and Mom. Mom clapped her hands. Dad only nodded. Later when I was practicing at the table, he leaned over me and said I should slow down, so it'd look like I'd just learned how to do it. Dad knew stuff like that. The next morning I dressed special, wearing my blue cowboy hat and the boots Grandma Jackson had given me even though they'd gotten too small and curled my toes. Then I looked down the midway at Pitchman's Magic Shop. The canvas covering the front was still tied shut. The carnival was a late riser and didn't really come to life until after mid-morning. The clock in our trailer said nine o'clock.

I passed the time playing with my bulldog Golly, so named because "Golly!" was what I said when Mom and Dad showed him to me. That one word expressed both delight and astonishment—delight in getting him and astonishment that his tongue hung out so far he couldn't keep it all in his mouth. Golly loved to chase rats, and would run around on bandy legs sniffing them out, his head low and his tongue dragging in the dust. That dog was thirsty a lot.

The sun wasn't quite overhead when the merry-go-round gave a shudder—its horns and cymbals signaling the wooden horses that the day's race had begun. Answering the tinny overture, a growl rumbled from the Ferris wheel at the far end of the midway. Roustabouts shouted the birth of their work day; and the air filled with the ringing of sledgehammers, the clang of the High Striker's bell, and the excited murmur of the marks as they streamed under the carnival's big banner.

Pitchman emerged from his trailer, shaved and perfumed, sleeves rolled back on his starched white shirt, and sporting a red bowtie. He unfastened the canvas from the front of the concession stand and raised it like the unveiling of a palace.

"Hey! Hey! Whaduya say? It's magic time!"

Again he rattled words so fast you hardly could make 'em out, and the marks, knowing they'd see a show, pushed closer for a good look. I placed myself in the middle of a forest of legs and watched as Pitchman showed three or four tricks; then reached below the counter and brought up the white envelope in one hand and a quarter in the other.

"Here it is, Ladies and Gents, a magical phenomenon, a simple envelope that makes money disappear, a trick that will amaze bank presidents and PhD's, and yet is so simple even a *child* can do it." His eyes scanned the crowd, and then he pointed to me.

"You. Boy. Come up here."

Show time!

I approached the counter, stood on tip toes, and stared like I had never seen such a marvel before as he casually folded the sides of the envelope around the quarter. Then he held the envelope in front of him and said, "How many of you saw me place the quarter in the envelope?"

People mumbled they had.

"Looking at me, he asked, "Did *you*, boy?"

"Yes, sir!" I said, swallowing hard.

He tapped the envelope with his finger and said, "Money is the root of all evil. Be gone!"

He opened the envelope wide and held it for everyone to see, and of course the quarter had vanished. The crowd applauded. Then Pitchman brought out another envelope and another quarter.

"Now, little man, did you see how I did the trick?"

"Yes, sir!"

"Then show these nice folks what you saw."

I placed the quarter on the open envelope and began folding, real fast, then remembered what Dad had said, slowed down, chewed on my tongue like I was concentrating, and slowly finished the job. Holding the envelope high, I tapped it with my finger and said, "Money … go away!"

The crowd laughed. I unfolded the envelope for all to see, and sure enough the quarter was gone. Pitchman sold ten or twelve of the tricks right there, and I went home with my quarter and showed it to Mom and Dad. I was so proud. At five years of age I had my first job.

I was a shill.

As good as Pitchman was, Dad said Big Peck was better. Big Peck looked like W. C. Fields, but taller and with a smaller nose and a bigger belly. His head was round like a pumpkin's, and he wore a yellowish straw boater hat and bright red suspenders. He grinned lots and usually had a wooden match stick poking out of one side of his mouth. When he spoke it was like he was telling you something no one else knew. Dad said Big Peck not only could sell the Brooklyn Bridge, but fifty gallons of red paint to cover it.

Buddy didn't stand a chance. He was a short, chubby, man-child with big blue eyes that believed anything. Sometimes he acted younger than I did. Buddy owned the Penny Pitch with his wife Mickey, a cute young woman with brown hair, bright red lipstick, and short shorts that showed off legs that even a five-year-old could appreciate. It was Mickey who worked inside the Penny Pitch's wooden railing, smiling at the townies and sweeping pennies into the side troughs while Buddy got coffee and kept the floor with the numbers in the squares waxed and slippery.

I was playing fetch one morning with Golly and tossed a stick into some bushes by the Penny Pitch, but Golly couldn't find it, so I went to help him. Buddy was waxing the floor. Big Peck sidled up to the railing, glanced toward the nearby trailer for any sign of Mickey, and motioned with his head for Buddy to draw close. Buddy dropped his waxing cloth and rushed over.

Not noticing me and Golly in the bushes, Big Peck clapped his hand on Buddy's shoulder and leaned near. "Dear comrade," he said in a hushed voice, "I have something of the utmost importance to discuss. Would you join me at the cookhouse for coffee and a conference?"

The word "conference" must've made Buddy's head spin. Nobody ever invited him to a *conference*. He ran after the fat man like a happy puppy. At the cookhouse, Big Peck seated himself and Buddy at the far end of a bench away from the other carnies. Unobserved, Golly and I played dig-a-hole behind them.

After the coffee had been served, Big Peck took a sip and asked:

"Ever seen a two-headed goat?"

Buddy shook his head no.

"Neither have most folks. And they'd pay a lot to see one, don't you think?"

You could see that Buddy was thinking about the two-headed goat real hard. Big Peck took the match stick from his mouth and spoke into Buddy's ear.

"My friend, for just a little green I can get us such a marvel. We can display it in a tent, charge admission, and make a fortune." Big Peck struck the match on the wooden counter and held it in front of Buddy's nose.

"We'll set those farmers afire."

Buddy's eyes grew large.

"Got any money?" Big Peck quietly asked.

"In the coffee can in the closet," Buddy answered without hesitation.

Big Peck gave a wink. "Don't tell the wife."

The carny's carny disappeared for two days, then returned and put a tent up near the far end of the midway. That evening he appeared with a megaphone just inside the carnival's entrance banner and, moving back up the midway to the tent, barked a non-stop spiel that rivaled Pitchman's.

"This way, folks! This way! See nature's most incredible creation. See a marvel beyond belief. Hydra, The Amazing Two-Headed Goat. That's right, my friends, I said *two* heads. Hydra. Not in some high-priced New York museum, not even in the magnificent Barnum and Bailey Circus, but right here on Stephens' Show of Shows. Just twenty five cents, one fourth of a dollar, gets you nose to *noses* with the most astonishing aberration in the history of Mother Nature. Hydra! Hurry! Hurry! Hurry!"

The women hung back, but the men, mostly farmers, had to see this thing, even if it cost money. Big Peck led the excited crowd to a tent that stood in darkness away from the other tents. He instructed Buddy to sell everyone a ticket, but to let no one inside until he gave the word. Starting for the tent, Big Peck spotted Golly and me.

"Want to see Hydra?" he asked with a smile.

"Oh, yeah!" I answered.

"Go inside. You can take tickets."

Wow! I get to see the goat! I ran inside with Golly. You couldn't see much, and before we could spot the goat, Buddy let the crowd in. The farmers entered cautiously, thrusting their tickets at me, trying to adjust their eyes to the darkness, looking at Golly sitting there with his tongue out, wondering if he was the goat. The tent was empty: no stage, no cage, no nothin' except near the entrance this little kid and a dog with its tongue hanging out.

And then they saw it. In the far corner. Two, mangy, very dead stuffed goats, sewn together in the middle, a head at each end. Hydra.

The farmers blew like Vesuvius. They yelled and cussed and kicked Hydra's stuffing all over the place. Golly and I ran outside searching for Big Peck and Buddy, but they were long gone. As we ran for home, I stopped to look back. The farmers had been set afire all right. They were kicking down the tent.

Dad called Delmar "the quiet carny." He didn't squawk a loud, promise-the-moon spiel like the other carnies. Instead, Delmar sat on his tall, wooden stool looking out from his Spin 'Til You Win with sad, blue-gray eyes, and about every twenty minutes, even when no one was around, he softly called:

"Spin 'til you win; a prize every time."

You did win every time, as you did on the other Hanky Panks, but most likely the arrow would stop on a number that won you a dinky thing with a "made in Japan" tag and a guarantee to fall apart before you made it to the parking lot. Delmar had never married, and his mom, who he always called "Mother," sat in a tall-backed wicker chair outside of the stand to Delmar's left. Even skinnier than Delmar, she had pale skin, milky blue eyes, and white wispy hair she tucked under a turban. She talked even less than her son, and when I stopped by she usually just listened, gave a little cackle at what was said and continued knitting.

I loved talking to Delmar, and if a mark came by, we switched to Carny, the secret language of the carnival. I'd learned it listening to my folks. You put an "eee-uhzz" near the beginning of words. I caught on fast when Mom said to Dad, "Let's get some eee-uh-zice (ice) cree-uhzz-eem (cream)."

From day one Delmar informed me that I couldn't have any free spins on his game, but he loved hearing about what I'd been playing. I was big on cowboys, and rode my stick horse up and down the midway defending the High Striker and the Penny Pitch from Indian attacks; eventually arriving at Delmar's to share my latest body count. One day I rode up wearing a Lone Ranger mask and asked Delmar to be Tonto.

"I can't be Tonto," he quietly replied.

"Why not?"

"Because ..." he looked around and leaned closer, "eee-uhzz-I ... wee-uhzare ... mee-uhzask ... tee-uh-zoo."

He smiled and fell silent, and I rode off trying to figure out what the ding dong he'd said.

That night I rode my stick horse down to the grandstand to see the new Free Act. The Great Ramon had moved on, ending Mom's career as target practice for a weird guy with a twirly moustache. The sultry air was hard to breath, so I parked my stick horse and walked to the end of the midway. There was no announcement of the new act. Bounding out of the night, a bony-thin clown in a rubber mask and a skin-tight body suit leaped onstage, jumped high into the air and grasped a pair of suspended metal rings. People mopped their brows and stared slack-jawed as the clown swung above and below the rings, bending his body in unbelievable shapes. He bent his foot behind his head. Now both feet met behind his head. A quick flip upside down, and he rocked like a cradle. Then he snake-slithered through the rings, swung by his ankles, and concluded by turning a complete flip and landing on his feet with his arms outstretched in front of him. The crowd cheered and called for more, but he made a short bow and darted into the darkness behind the stage. The applause died, and the crowd returned to cotton candy and one more spin on the Tilt-A-Whirl.

I ran behind the stage and peered into the darkness. The clown was leaning against a tree sucking great gulps of air into his lungs. He pulled at the rubber mask with both hands and finally snapped it from his head. His face was flushed meat red and covered with sweat, his eyes glassy, and his gray hair pointing to every star in the sky.

It was Delmar.

I couldn't believe it. The Free Show was Delmar. The quiet carny, normally glued like a statue to the wooden stool in his concession tent, had twisted through the rings like a frenzied snake. Delmar smiled, brought his finger to his lips and gave a wink.

"Ee-uz-zour … see-uzz-eekrit."

I nodded and walked back into the bright lights and ballyhoo of the carnival. His secret was safe with me. I wouldn't even tell his mother.

CHAPTER 4

▼

GORILLA MAN

A few weeks later I got brave. I edged past the "Belles of Broadway" to the very end of the midway where the biggest tent always stood—the scary one with the huge painted pictures that told you that inside you'd see crazy-eyed men clenching their teeth and strangling each other. In front of the pictures ran a wooden, ballyhoo platform with a ticket stand to one side. Odd things rested on the platform: a large brown leather megaphone, a big iron radiator, and a heavy lead pipe.

I didn't see Gorilla Man, but I thought I might hear him. He probably was practicing snorting and thumping his chest, getting ready for his jungle scream that made all the marks come running to see what in blazes was going on. I'd been too afraid to watch, but now it was early morning before the carnival opened, too early for the screaming, and he probably was having coffee like regular people. Then I heard it: grunting and clanging from behind the tent. I sneaked down the side and peeked around the corner.

Gorilla Man, naked except for a small, stretchy bathing suit, stood in a bow-legged crouch slamming tent stakes with a sledgehammer the size of a mule's hind leg. Tufts of fur covered his entire body except for his head, which was bare as a bullet.

I watched him sweat and swear, tightening the canvas that had loosened from last night's winds. Silently, I edged around to the front of the tent out of his sight. There in the grass in front of the platform were barbells, some really big, some smaller. I grabbed the smallest with both hands and gave a tug. It didn't budge. I made a face like the men in the paintings above me and yanked as hard as I could. Nothing.

"I betcha wear pink panties."

Gorilla Man towered over me, his big square teeth glistening in the sun.

"I do not! I'm a boy!"

I pulled at the barbell with all my might and fell backwards onto the ground.

He picked up the weight with one hand, bounced it off his bicep and caught it—all in one motion.

"Yep," he smirked, "wears pink panties."

He tossed the barbell onto the ground like a plaything and loped ape-like back to his tent stakes.

His real name was Sealy. No one knew if that was his first name or last. The carnies just called him Sealy—The Gorilla Man. There was no Mrs. Sealy, no friends, he stayed to himself. But he was the biggest attraction on the midway. After that time he teased me, I showed up at his platform for every performance. His wrestling matches played like theater: grunting, roaring battles between good and evil, and he always was the evil. No one, not even Peck Brooks, could draw marks like Sealy.

Come show time, he rushed from his tent, leaped onto the ballyhoo platform, bounded back and forth like a demented ape, grabbed up his megaphone and screamed jungle roars that would tear out a normal man's throat. Then he ran a metal pipe up and down the radiator making a racket that reached the parking lot. He drew marks like a magnet. Eyes wide and mouths open, they flocked to his tent at midway's end, shoving each other to get a closer look at this man-animal leaping about on the platform. When he had gathered his prey, Sealy strode back and forth—chest puffed, hands on hips—and bellowed the town's name. The crowd cheered. Then he pulled "the switcher," said he'd heard that the men of that town were a bunch of sissies. Caught off guard, the crowd quieted. Then he delivered the zinger:

"Yeah, they're bunch of pansies. They'd look better in dresses."

Wives and girl friends giggled; men swore.

"Go on, ladies, lend 'em your lipstick!"

Men roared their anger and shook their fists. Grinning broadly, Sealy brought out a long, thick hemp rope and sweetly asked if anyone might want to choke him with it. *You better believe it.* Hands shot up everywhere. Sealy selected two of the biggest guys in the crowd to come on stage. Standing between them, a foot shorter than either man, he wrapped a white bath towel around his neck, made a loop in the rope, and slipped it over his head. He gave both men an end of the rope and had them pull it taut.

"When I give the signal, you girls pull as hard as you can," he said. "Don't hold nothin' back. I'm gonna count to ten. Then you stop."

At this point you saw the crowd get nervous and the men on the platform frowning, probably afraid they'd squeeze his head off. Sealy laughed at their hesitation, said he knew an ancient wrestling trick from India. He had each man firmly plant his legs, hold the rope taut, and prepare to pull. Sealy set his jaw, hunched his shoulders high, and forced his neck muscles into a bulging mass. He dropped his hands as the signal, and the two big men pulled with all their might. Sealy's strained voice started counting, slowly—his eyes squinted shut, his teeth bared, his face turning red. When he got to "ten," he gasped it and waved his hands. The men dropped the rope. The crowd cheered. Sealy's head had remained intact.

Now Sealy asked the two big guys if they wanted to get into the ring inside the tent and wrestle each other. They usually didn't. He sent them back into the crowd and asked if anyone wanted to go inside and wrestle *him*. After the neck strangling episode, the crowd's anger had subsided. Sealy would make it interesting. He would give five dollars to any man who could pin him in three rounds. This was Depression time—earning five bucks in fifteen minutes was unheard of. Men worked in the fields all week baling hay and didn't make five dollars. Large, raw-boned men, those on the rowdy side, nervously licked their lips and encouraged one another to get into the ring with the Gorilla. Hands went up, and Sealy selected a challenger, brought him onto the platform, and with an infuriating smirk, observed that he must've made a mistake—this had to be the high school homecoming queen. The crowd shook fists and roared indignation. Sealy strutted the stage and called his challenger "limp wrist" and "kissy-poo." When the crowd reached pure frenzy, he tossed his challenger a pair of trunks and sent him into the tent—calling after him to "dress fast so no one will see your pretty underwear." Sealy sold a truck load of tickets. Then he went inside and climbed into the ring. He rarely had to pay the five dollars.

Since I was "with it," I could watch the match for free, but inside the tan canvas walls the dark smell of sweat and the groans of nearly naked men heaving and colliding proved too frightening. I contented myself with Sealy's magnificent pre-match ballyhoo and his proud platform strut after his victory.

The days turned sticky-hot and the crowds stayed home close to their electric fans. Desperate to lure people onto the lot, Mr. Stephens moved the Wrestling

Tent near the entrance across from the merry-go-round so anyone within half-a-mile of the place would be drawn by Sealy's gorilla screams.

This was great. Golly and I loved the merry-go-round, and I watch Sealy's show astride my favorite black stallion. One afternoon the air was so still just thinking made you sweat. Sealy bounded onto his platform, screamed through the megaphone and ran the lead pipe up and down the radiator. A small crowd gathered, but he couldn't get anyone to come up and try to strangle him with the rope. It was too hot for the effort. He did coax one guy to wrestle him, and a few perspiring farmers bought tickets just to get out of the sun. Sealy went inside and began the match, and Golly and I continued our ride on the merry-go-round. The heat made me sleepy, and I was ready for the ride to end, when Sealy's raw voice roared from within his tent. He rushed out and leaped onto the platform. Blood streamed from the top of his head.

"He stabbed me! That pansy tried to kill me!" he yelled.

Wild-eyed farmers burst out of the tent followed by a tall guy in baggy, gray trunks. He had a bowl haircut like that worn by some farmers who never get into town, and he held his head down like he was confused. Blood running into his eyes, Sealy screamed like a wounded ape. Up and down the midway men dropped their baseballs, their darts, their High Striker sledges, and hurried to the Wrestling Tent.

For the first time, Sealy was the good guy, declaring that his opponent had pulled a pocket knife from his trunks and stabbed Sealy in the top of his head. Mopping his wound with a white towel and waving the lurid red blotches for all to see, Gorilla Man demanded a rematch—this time with no knives. The crowd, which by now included every male mark on the lot, cheered approval and couldn't get money out of overalls fast enough. When the last ticket had been sold, the sides of the tent bulged.

I was terrified. Maybe Bowl-Cut had another knife. The merry-go-round was still moving, and I jumped off without Golly and ran for the Mug Joint. Dad saw me jump before the ride had stopped, something I was never to do, and took me to the trailer and really gave me what for. When he paused in his lecture, I sobbed my defense: a guy stabbed Sealy and they were fighting again and maybe the guy had another knife and I got scared and jumped off the ride too soon and ran home. Dad studied me for a moment, and then quietly said:

"Bill Ray, I think it's time to add to your education."

I listened, eyes wide and barely breathing, as Dad revealed my hero's terrible secret: *Sealy always wrestled the same man.* The man got paid to follow the carnival from town to town and volunteer when Sealy asked if anyone wanted to take him on. Without even being there, Dad said he knew what had happened today.

He explained that with ticket sales so slow, Sealy decided to stir things up a bit. He had the man pull a little pocket knife out of his trunks and stick Sealy on top of the head with it. Not deep, just enough to bring some blood. Sealy then ran out to the platform yelling that the man tried to kill him.

"With that blood running down his face, Sealy drew a big crowd, didn't he?" Dad asked.

I nodded.

"So he held a grudge match and sold the tent out. Bill Ray, Sealy wasn't really hurt; it was just a trick to hustle the marks."

I couldn't believe it. My Dad was the smartest man in the world, but I couldn't believe Sealy would do such a thing. Not my hero.

"No, Dad!" I yelled, "you're wrong! Sealy's so strong he doesn't need fakers wrestling him!"

Dad stood quiet a minute and then said, "Well, this is our last day here. When Sealy does his ballyhoo in the next town, see who shows up."

The next two days, a Sunday and Monday, were travel days, and near noon on Tuesday the Show of Shows re-opened in another town miles away. Along about two o'clock the gorilla scream roared from the megaphone, the metal pipe attacked the radiator; Sealy leaped around the platform; two big farm boys came up and pulled on the rope; and finally the challenge was issued. Would any of the sissies out there take him on? Five dollars to the brave soul who could make a pin in three rounds. Anybody? A hand went up.

It was Bowl Cut.

Seeing my troubled eyes as I climbed into bed that night, Dad pretended to read the paper, then put it aside and sat beside me. "Don't feel too bad," he said. "Sealy puts on a good show, and sometimes a good show is the best people can hope for."

I said goodnight and turned my head to the wall.

CHAPTER 5

▼

COMING OFF THE ROAD

At summer's end, 1940, America prepared to enter its eleventh year of the Great Depression. Although my young life was a boy's delight—riding the merry-go-round, peering over the towns atop the Ferris wheel, beating the Girl Show drum—I could see the grownups worried a lot. Pictures in the newspapers Dad got out of trash cans showed hungry-looking people in something called bread lines. Our little plastic radio talked about President Roosevelt's recovery plan—a bunch of letters from the alphabet like CCC, TVA, NRA—but most people were still out of work. In some towns families came to the carnival and just walked around. Dad would have Mom tint some left over pictures, but the few people who gathered would watch, nod approval, and silently walk away.

There were days the midway held no more than a dozen marks in it, and Mr. Stephens would lead his carnies to another town. Dad said for me not to fret. I already knew how to play poker and shoot craps, and I'd fronted for a two-headed goat, and shilled for a magic act. In his view, I was getting a first rate education in how to survive. Mom didn't agree. I would be six in September, and she was determined that I be enrolled in school like regular kids. Dad went along with it, but looked awful glum. I asked Mom why, and she gave a little smile and said Dad had been kicking up dust for a long time, and it was hard for him to come off the road.

I adored my foot-loose father, and I suppose this is a good time to tell you that his name was Tramp. Of course that wasn't his real name. His real name was

Cecil Francis Jackson. He hated "Cecil Francis," thought it sounded like some prissy English lord. For bedtime stories, he didn't bother with *Snow White* and *Hansel and Gretel*; he mostly told me about his adventures when he was young and how because of them the town changed his name.

He was in the eighth grade and walking barefoot to school when he decided he'd like to see Texas. So he hopped a freight train, a style of travel favored by his family. In fact, one time two of his older brothers, Cliff and Cash, were working in a field behind the house; a freight came along—Cash hopped it—and wasn't heard from for six months. It was what the Jackson boys did. Dad just did it more.

He returned from Texas, still barefoot, clothes torn, face covered with mud. The sitters and spitters on the courthouse steps allowed he didn't look any better than a tramp, and the name stuck. Dad liked it. Thought it had an adventurous sound.

Early on he hooked up with Clyde Forbes, a pale, mischievous reed of a boy with eyes as blue as September sky. Tramp, with his perpetual tan and eyes as dark as bar room leather, was Huck to fair Clyde's Tom; and both bolted the confines of school for the freedom of the forest. In this case the forest was a rambling apple orchard northwest of Unionville owned by Clyde's father. Winters, the boys popped home for heat and eats; but the rest of the year they fished, raided gardens, cooked stews, drank beer, smoked roll'ems, and,—when in the need of finances—practiced the fine art of junking.

Junking was scavenging back alleys and vacant lots for tired and forgotten metal, and presenting this precious treasure to junk dealers for so many pennies a pound. However, the boys embellished the art of junking considerably. In the dark of night, they climbed over the junkyard's back fence and, with the deftness of grave robbers, selected choice metals like copper and steel; then next morning they foisted them as newfound gems to a salivating and unsuspecting owner.

By the time Tramp was eighteen he'd found another love—music. Not syrupy *Sweet Adeline* stuff, but body trembling twenties music like *Hard Hearted Hannah, Kansas City Stomp,* and *Jailhouse Blues.* Religious groups called it "The Devil's Music," and the more it made people dance, the more they were going to hell. Henry Ford labeled such music "gross." *The Ladies Home Journal* declared it "appalling." Preachers ranted against its sin. And everyone under forty loved it.

Listening to Paul Whiteman, Duke Ellington, and Louie Armstrong on late-night radio, Tramp's ears told his fingers how to play the music—the banjo first, then guitar, piano, clarinet, saxophone, drums—anything not requiring a strong pucker—because he could never hold a firm "embouchure," which is what musicians called tight lips.

By his twenties, Tramp's good looks and banjo picking landed him a job in what represented big time show business in small town America: the traveling tent show. Preceded by gaudy posters and planted newspaper stories, this theater-in-a-tent rolled into town with its pretty, painted people and transported you to a world far, far away from Jeeter's Feed Store. Such a marvel was The Palmer Tent Show.

Tramp had played in the band pit a few weeks when Mr. Palmer took note of his banjo player's lean good looks and gave him a part playing his son. Tramp rehearsed the few lines he had and waited in the wings that night for his cue. Ah, there it was—*no it wasn't*. Tramp walked into the middle of a love scene with Mr. Palmer about to lay a big smooch on the show's leading lady. Tramp froze, unable to utter a word. He'd ruined the scene. The consummate pro, Mr. Palmer un-puckered, turned from his lady love, and said:

"Ah, there you are, son. Did you get the newspaper?"

Tramp's head shook a vigorous no.

Mr. Palmer rolled his eyes. "Well, perhaps you'd best go get it."

Tramp was off the stage before Mr. Palmer finished his sentence.

And now, after years of our family drifting like seeds in the wind, Mom told Dad it was time to take root—their son needed to be in school. Reluctantly Dad disassembled the Mug Joint, roped it onto the top of the car and told me to make my goodbyes.

Golly and I walked the midway one last time and bade farewell to the most delightfully outrageous people I would ever meet. I had been "the kid," the only kid, and the carnies all had become my uncles and aunts, my best friends, playmates, and confidants. Delmar's pale blue eyes watered and Sealy lowered his shaved head and growled, "Yeah, git out of here. Ya still wear pink panties."

On the way back to Unionville, I lost another dear friend. We'd stopped for gas, and Golly spotted a rat running from the back of the station into a cornfield. He jumped from the open car window and with head low and tongue dragging disappeared into the forest of tall stalks. We searched after him for most of an hour, but never saw him again. I cried like crazy. Dad said that Golly saw we were pursing a new life, so he decided he would, too, and right now he was having a ball chasing rats in the middle of a gigantic cornfield. I stared out the window and hoped there was a nice farm on the other side of all that corn.

This thing called school started in a week, and we moved in with Grandpa and Grandma Davis, who lived down a hill south of the town square. In the field behind the house, my year older cousins Donny Cook and Paddy Joe Davis welcomed me to town with a game called "Prisoner."

"Who's the prisoner?" I asked.

An inch-thick hemp rope appeared from nowhere, and my cousins threw me on my stomach and looped a noose around my neck. Then they forced my arms behind me and tied the rope to my hands and feet so that when I jerked, the noose choked me. Face down in the weeds, I heard their laughter fade followed by the occasional buzzing of bees.

Two hours later, when Dad found me trussed up in the field holding still as a 'possum, he decided I needed to know how to defend myself. Next morning he brought home some boxing gloves and had me put them on and do things he called bobbing, weaving, hooking, and jabbing. For a good hour I hopped around the backyard like a spastic rabbit, pummeling the air as Dad yelled encouragement. Finally he pronounced me ready to test my skills.

Up the hill lived Don Clark Pollock, my age, but shorter and skinnier. Dad called him to the backyard and asked him if he'd ever boxed. Don Clark said no. Dad smiled. He slipped the other set of gloves on Don Clark and walked to the center of an imaginary boxing ring. Cupping his hands like a megaphone, he called out:

"Ladeeeze and gentlemen, for the heavyweight championship of the world, in this corner, the Terror of the Hilltop, Don … Clark … Pollock!"

Then Dad made strange noises like a crowd cheering.

Don Clark, just stared at him.

"And in the other corner, the Beast of the Backyard, Bill … Ray … Jackson!"

Again, the crowd-cheering noise from Dad.

"When the bell rings, come out fighting!"

I swallowed hard, trying to remember all the moves Dad had taught me.

"Clang!" yelled Dad.

I rushed forward and jabbed with my left, hooked with my right, bobbed, weaved, and fired two uppercuts—man, I was throwing some leather! Trouble was, I never landed a punch. Don Clark hadn't come forward. He was still five feet away. Dad yelled for us to move closer, mix it up. No movement from my opponent. I rushed to him, threw lefts and rights, rights and lefts, uppercuts and haymakers—again not a blow landed. Don Clark had stepped back a foot. I was worn out.

I dropped my gloves and stood there panting.

Don Clark studied me a moment, then stepped forward, swung his right arm over his head like a windmill and hammered me square on the top of the head. I sank to my knees. Big tears filled my eyes.

The Terror of the Hilltop shrugged off his gloves and went home.

My boxing lesson was over.

Obviously, I had been taken to a big brick prison for kids. They were all over the place, running and shrieking, with a few sobbing softly and clutching their mother's hand. A bell went off and the larger, older kids automatically trudged inside. The youngest ones, me included, were prodded by our mothers up the cement steps and through the large doors.

Inside, voices and footsteps echoed off hard gray walls and marble floors while female guards, mostly out of uniform, stood by different cell blocks, and the kids, apparently hypnotized, obediently marched inside. Gone were the merry-go-round, the Mug Joint, the Two Headed Goat, the tents, townies, carnies and clowns—this was that big lockup called *school* and it was scarier than a carnival spook house. Mom ushered me through a door marked First Grade. Kids crawled all over the place and some seemed to know each other real well and yelled greetings as if their buddies were two blocks away.

A second bell went off and a small, somber-looking lady guard came in shushing everyone. Mom led me to a desk, reassured me for the hundredth time, then went to the door, waved goodbye, *and vanished.* I looked back to the guard behind the desk. She was smiling. Sort of. Maybe she was gritting her teeth. She said her name was Gladys Gillum. We were to call her *Miss* Gillum.

As the days passed my fears subsided. Miss Gillum taught stuff a while, and then let you go outside to play. She treated your owies and hugged you if you needed your mommy, but never fed you baby talk—no sweetie pie, baby-waby, honey-bunny stuff. I thought she was great.

At first I only knew one kid in the class. He sat in the front of the room with a smug look like he was going to get up and teach. It was Don Clark Pollock, the Terror of the Hilltop, sitting right in front of Miss Gillum like Prince Almighty. Just looking at him gave me a stomach ache.

As the days passed, I got this school thing down pat. First bell, get into the room. Second bell, be in your seat and shut your trap. Third bell, *now* we're serious. No goofing off, no throwing paper wads or quacking like a duck—Miss Gillum's gonna talk and you'd better be listening. If you want to flap your lips, hold up your hand; but it's going to be a long time before you're acknowledged, and by then you won't remember what you wanted to say anyway.

Then there was the part about peeing. It was not encouraged. If you were absolutely sure you were going to erupt like Old Faithful you held up your hand and extended one finger. If you had to do big job, you extended two fingers. It didn't hurt if you made a big face. Actually, I was relieved that we could give signals and not have to blab your business in front of the class. I would've died, because Mom and Dad had strange words for going to the bathroom. Dad called peeing, "taking a leak." That wasn't so bad, but Mom called it, "going taw-taw." In fact, she called your thing your "taw-taw." But only boys had "taw-taws." She never said what girls had. And both Mom and Dad called poop, "grunt," Taking a poop was "going grunt." I couldn't imagine standing up in class and telling Miss Gillum I had to "go grunt." Having to *go* do anything was scary enough, because the restrooms were down in the basement, an ill-lit, echoing tomb where Clovie Stuart, the wrinkled janitor, stayed in back doing God knows what behind that big, dingy door.

There were those, however, who would abuse the finger waving bit. Donald Summers, a tired-looking kid in bib overhauls, had his hand up about five times a day. He'd discovered that two frantically waved fingers could buy you at least ten minutes of freedom. Summers was usually my partner at recess in a game called *Horse,* where you took turns being rider or horse and charged into a swarm of other mounted horses and tried to pull down the riders. Eddie Hibbs, the shortest kid in the class, and therefore always a rider, was best at it, mostly because he grabbed noses, ears, hair, anything he could reach, and squeezed like a python until the other rider jumped off. But Summers was a great horse—he stayed away from Hibbs and charged guys like Delbert Jacobs, who was skinny and hung his head a lot.

Anyway, there was this afternoon when Summers' hand was waving the two-fingered salute like a semaphore flag. The girls started giggling.

Miss Gillum said, "Donald, I just let you leave the room fifteen minutes ago."

Don Clark Pollock snorted.

"It's only twenty minutes to the end of class. You can wait!"

Groaning, Summers sank back into his seat. More giggles. He sat in the back row and I was in the row in front of his. I sneaked a peek over my shoulder. My horse looked stricken, his eyes wide like an animal caught in a trap. Then he started sweating and showing his teeth. When the dismissal bell rang, the room emptied in seconds, but I hung back because Summers hadn't moved from his chair.

"Donald, you may go now," said the teacher.

Summers didn't budge. Exasperated, Miss Gillum clumped across the room and stood in front of him. "Donald Summers, get out of that chair this instant!"

Summers, with the look of the doomed, slowly stood up. Down his pant leg and across the floor tumbled something resembling a Baby Ruth candy bar. The three of us stared at it as if it were prime evidence in a courtroom trial. Ladies and gentlemen, *Exhibit A.*

The next morning just after recess, Summers held up two fingers. Miss Gillum didn't hesitate. She pointed to the door and Summers was gone.

CHAPTER 6

▼

ALL SOLDIERS SMOKE

I remember the day the bad thing happened. I was sorting through my toy box for the tiny Superman rag doll that Grandma Jackson had made me. Dad stood shaving at the small wall mirror in our trailer and Mom was dialing different kinds of music on the radio. It was nearly noon, the first Sunday in December, and she said she wanted some Christmas music. The dial stopped on a man's voice, talking real serious, saying that "the attack reports were true." Dad put down his razor. The voice went on talking like a storm, and most of the words I didn't understand, except for "sneak" and "bombing." Dad listened until the man finished and the music came back on, then he tuned to another man saying all the things the other made said. Finally, Dad turned the radio off. Mom looked real worried.

"What's happened, Dad?" I asked.

Dad stood quiet for a few seconds, "You've heard of the Japanese?"

"Yeah. They made the junk prizes on the carnival."

"Well, they dropped some bombs on our sailors."

At school the next day, Miss Gillum's brow had wrinkles I hadn't seen before, and she didn't bother with spelling and arithmetic. Instead, she said we'd get an early start on Christmas decorations and set us to cutting out green construction paper Christmas trees.

I was pasting the star on top of mine when Clovie Stuart, the janitor, stuck his head in the door and blurted, "President Roosevelt just declared war on the Japs!" Kids started crying. Some yelled questions and others, like me, sat like stone posts. After meeting with the other teachers in the hall, Miss Gillum came back and said school was over for today and we should go home to be with our parents.

Dad was sitting on the trailer stoop smoking a cigarette, and didn't seem surprised that I was home early. I sat down next to him and neither one of us said anything for a while. I picked up a rock, chucked it at a tree and missed. Then I asked, "What's 'war,' Dad?"

Dad drew on his cigarette and let the smoke out slowly, as if trying to think of an answer I'd understand. "Well, war is what happens when one country tries to take another country's gold," he answered.

I looked upwards, searching the mid-afternoon sky for Japanese airplanes. "Do we have any gold, Dad?"

"No," he said, flipping his cigarette away. "Jacksons never have any gold."

Our country's battle filled our lives, and by third grade the boys had formed a small gang that played war as much as it played ball, tag, or cowboy. The gang's leader should've been the county superintendent's son, J.C. Shelton. To me, J.C. mirrored my radio hero, *Jack Armstrong, the all American boy.* J. C. read better, ran faster, counted higher, and belted more home runs than any kid in class. But he was a loner. He didn't make close friends and he didn't like gangs; and when we played war, J. C. walked away.

Who didn't walk away was pint-sized Eddie Hibbs, who looked and acted like Leo Gorcey, the pug-faced actor who played feisty, fist-swinging Muggsy in the *Bowery Boys'* movies. Hibbs' dad was dying in a tuberculosis sanitarium, and the only grownup male in Eddie's life was his grandfather: a gaunt, grizzled, former mountain man who had seen Jesse James shoot a man's nose off in a bar. When one of Hibbs' teachers questioned why he got into so many fights, he said his grandfather told him to "stand up for hisself." Hibbs, a lefty, stood up a lot, usually with his left fist cocked. Whatever we had going on, Hibbs was boss. He's the one who taught me the Four Rules of Recess:

1. The big kids get first dibs on everything.

2. Never be obvious about trying to see the girls' underpants when they're on the swings.

3. Never tattle on the guy who started the fight (the girls always told anyway).

4. Never play on the school grounds with a kid in a grade below yours.

Because of Rule Number Four, older cousin Donny Cook—half of the notorious duo that left me hog-tied face down in the weeds—never played with me or my buddies during school hours. But step off school property and Cook joined the fray, and always as the captain, even of Hibbs.

Saturday afternoons, Cook, Hibbs, and I would be found in one place: the first row of Mr. Summers' Royal Theater devoutly watching Roy, Gene, Hoppy, or the Durango Kid. Tickets were a dime, popcorn a nickel. We'd each buy two bags of popcorn, the first for the cartoon and the second for the main feature. Cook always had popcorn left for the main feature, and would grin at us with big kernels between his teeth to let us know it. Hibbs sometimes made it; but I never did. As soon as we sat down, I would jam one bag behind me and try not to think about it. Fat chance. The bag in hand was devoured before Bugs munched his first carrot, and the second never made it beyond the MovieTone News.

The MovieTone News told us about the War. Laughter over the antics of Curly, Larry, and Moe fell silent as whistling bombs fell to earth and burst into bubbling, gray shock waves that ripped apart buildings and bodies. Ugly, long-snouted cannons thundered incessantly; machine guns rattled; helmeted men with grim faces threw grenades; and boys just out of high school, blood seeping through their uniforms, were loaded onto Red Cross trucks. A defiant Hitler flashed the *heil* salute to his goose-stepping army; Tojo made abrupt head-nods as he reviewed his blank-faced kamikaze pilots; and Mussolini, his jutted jaw exuding arrogance, stood at defiant attention as his arsenal rolled by.

For children, such carnage only could be handled by making it a game. We pretended to be a secret attack unit Cook called The Lucky Strikers. Our battlefield was my neighborhood, behind the Methodist Church, where, for minimal rent, Dad had parked the trailer when we came off the road. Firing stick rifles and lobbing empty beer can grenades, Hibbs and I, along with chubby, younger Charlie Bill Pittman, followed Cook as he mounted countless surprise assaults on the Japs and Nazis. Of course Cook was the captain, with Hibbs the lieutenant, and Pittman and I sergeants. No one was a private.

One day Captain Cook directed The Lucky Strikers on a sneak attack of Hitler's Fortress, which here-to-for had been the Putnam County Courthouse. Jumping in and out of storefront doors, we noisily rat-a-tatted our way toward the town square with Hibbs lugging a gunnysack full of choice empty beer cans. Along the way, we charged into Grabosch's Meat Market and lobbed beer can grenades at the Wiener schnitzel, definitely a German booby trap. Unfortunately, Charlie Bill's mother was at the meat counter buying pot roast at the time. She caught Charlie Bill by the ear and led him home. Cook quickly announced a brave comrade had been captured by the enemy and we'd have to go on without him.

Nearing the Courthouse, we made a particularly heavy assault on Freeborn's café, known for its pies, but better known for the flies that buzzed around them. When we jumped through the front door making machinegun noises, a startled old-timer knocked over his coffee. Jay Freeborn, the portly owner, chased us back outside with a broom. We advanced on the main target, and as we drew within twenty feet of the west side courthouse steps, Cook selected an empty Falstaff can from Hibbs' gunnysack. Cocking his hand for a hefty throw, our leader called, "Come on out, Hitler, you sniveling S. O. B.!" Hitler didn't come out of the glass double doors, but the sheriff, or someone who looked like him, did. The beer can fell from Cook's hand, and our leader led a scampered retreat back across the street to an empty office building. The door was unlocked and we took cover behind a large desk.

The maybe sheriff had not followed us. We lay there panting a moment, and then Cook pulled a surprise.

"Time for a smoke," he said nonchalantly.

"What do you mean?" I asked.

"A smoke. All soldiers smoke. It calms their nerves after battle."

I watched in astonishment as our seven-year-old leader revealed why he had named us The Lucky Strikers. He pulled a pack of Luckies out of his hip pocket, tapped a cigarette out the end, and put it in his mouth. Then with his thumb nail, he ignited a wooden kitchen match, lit up, and immediately released the smoke into the air. Eyes squinting from the smoke, he held the pack out.

"Want one?"

"Sure!" said Hibbs, and he lit up.

Both of them were puffing like locomotives, so I stuck a cigarette in my mouth. Cook handed me a match; I struck it on the back of the desk and held the flame to the end of the cigarette.

"You gotta suck in," Cook said.

I sucked in, inhaled a blowtorch, and staggered around coughing and gasping like an elephant had kicked me in the chest. Cook snickered and took another drag.

"You get used to it," he drawled.

Again, he let the smoke out fast. Hibbs had his cigarette stuck in the corner of his mouth and didn't suck much at all. I tried a short suck and spewed the smoke like a tea kettle. No coughing.

Cook grinned. "Now ya got it."

"Yeah," I gasped, taking another short puff. Then with the cigarette dangling from the corner of my mouth I said, "So, when do we shoot some more Nazis?"

I'd never tasted anything so vile in my life.

CHAPTER 7

▼

RED STREAK

A few days later, Cook changed the game. He showed up at the trailer toting a gray slab of wood about three feet long and two feet wide.

"What's that?" I asked.

"Our racer," he replied.

It was a slab of wood. No way did it look like a racer.

"For the Derby," he continued.

The Derby? The Soap Box Derby? That was all the talk on WHO, the radio station in Des Moines. You built your own car out of a wooden crate, raced it down hill fifty miles an hour, swerved in and out, passed all the other cars, and roared across the finish line to raucous acclamation from all your friends and the president of the United States. The Soap Box Derby was every boy's dream.

I looked at the slab of wood.

"Where are the wheels?" I asked.

"We'll find some. C'mon."

We roamed the alley behind the church and found a rusted Radio Flyer wagon with no tongue. Cook acted like we'd found gold, and sent me to ask Dad for some tools. Dad was taking a nap and was grumpy when I woke him; but when I told him Cook and I were building a racer for the Derby, he perked up and got me a hammer and a saw and some nails. When I returned, Hibbs and Pittman had arrived to play army, and Cook had recruited them to "the Derby project." He was the chief engineer and they were assistant engineers. I didn't get a title.

Cook said that before we began "engineering," our Derby entry would need a name.

"Speedy," suggested Hibbs.

"Rocket," countered Pittman.

Cook announced the name would be Red Streak. It became the job of the untitled member of the team to scrounge some red paint. Pittman said his dad had some in his garage; the two of us fetched it and a couple of brushes and painted the slab. It dried fast, and Cook and Hibbs managed to attach the wheels. Then construction stopped. We stared at our entry to the world famous Soap Box Derby: a red slab of wood with some wheels on it.

"Maybe you can use this."

We looked up and there was Dad with a large, worn steering wheel.

"Wow!" Cook exclaimed, and he sat on the slab and held the steering wheel in front of him like he was driving. But he soon put it down, because none of us had the slightest idea of how to make it steer the wheels. Then a familiar magic took place. Dad brought forth his toolbox and opened the lid. I swear eerie music wafted from within. What he did and how he did it, I could not say. We watched him with uncomprehending eyes as Red Streak eerily took form before us. In the midst of this legerdemain, Dad asked me to hand him a screwdriver. *Screwdriver* sounded strange, so I gave him the strangest looking tool in the box.

"That's the pliers," said Dad in a low voice.

Cook and Hibbs snickered. Pittman bit his lip.

"Screwdriver!" Hibbs said, and smacked it into Dad's hand like he was thrusting a scalpel to a surgeon. I wanted to put the screwdriver up Hibbs's nose.

Throughout the afternoon, Dad wove a miracle, making nuts, bolts, nails, wood, and wire do the impossible. And just before supper time Red Steak was born. No matter that official construction rules had been ignored. No matter that it took all of your strength to turn the steering wheel—Red Streak was our Derby entry. Cook reached into his hip pocket and produced apparel he'd brought for the occasion. a cloth aviator's cap. He pulled it on, adjusted the plastic goggles, and snapped the chin strap. He would make the test drive.

We pushed him the half block to Main Street and faced the Streak west, where the street ran downhill away from the Square—a perfect run. For safety, Dad said we should use the sidewalk, not the street. Cook stared over the steering wheel. The sidewalk was old and cracked. Some sections were separated by wide gaps, others scrunched upwards against each other like the aftermath of an earthquake. It was going to be a bumpy ride.

"Go!" Dad yelled.

We pushed the Streak with all our might. The racer rolled forward and picked up speed. Dad had oiled the wheels well. Cook plummeted down the hill, swerved from side to side, dodged deep cracks, bounced over jutting cement, sped faster and faster, hit at least fifty! At the street intersection, the curb protruded higher than the sidewalk, the wheels hit the rise, and Red Streak was airborne—one, two, three seconds. Then, blam! It crashed, knocking the two front wheels flying and sending Cook over the top of the steering wheel. He lay face down in the street, his body frozen to the pavement. We stood at the top of the hill, staring at the crumpled figure of our driver.

Seconds passed.

Cook jumped up laughing and waved his arms. We rushed to our hero, yelling, cheering, clapping him on the back, clapping each other on the back. We had done it! Not before a crowd of thousands at the big Derby in Des Moines. *Our* Derby. In *our* town. Down *our* hill. Red Streak had won! That old slab of wood had shot down the hill. Had gone lickity split, darted around the cracks, jumped over the juts, and then for a wonderful, miraculous moment took flight! What a day! What a marvelous, glorious day! We gathered Red Streak's remains, pumped our fists into the air, and headed happily to our homes and our suppers.

CHAPTER 8

▼

MUMBLE-PEG, JUKE BOXES, AND JIMMY DURANTE

After we came off the road, Mom worked six days a week as a waitress at Tootie Yount's café on the east side of the Square. Dad played weekends in a honky-tonk band. I didn't think much about how the bills got paid, except I guessed Mom was paying most of them. Dad liked to buy the band a round or two of drinks and didn't bring home much of the evening's take. It wasn't that Dad couldn't work more; he just couldn't get interested in what my friends' parents called *regular* jobs—like clerking at the drug store or waiting tables, which he'd already done.

Well, Dad may not have gone to work from nine to five, but that just made more time for us. Afternoons after school I'd come home to find him sitting on the trailer stoop wearing his brown fedora and the brown leather jacket I loved to smell. It was as if he'd been waiting for me all afternoon—a roll'em dangling from his mouth and his breath hinting of whisky—and he would put aside whatever he'd been whittling and we'd play a game of mumble-peg.

You started by flipping the knife off your knee so the blade would stick in the ground, and with each success the launch site progressed up your body until the last one was off the top of your head. The head one always made me nervous. No protection was allowed, and I remembered the blood oozing from Sealy's bald cranium that day on the carnival. I buffered my head by holding the tip of the blade between my fingers. Dad's head was rock hard. He never held the blade point with his fingers, but he didn't dally making the flip, either.

One afternoon during the game, I told Dad about something that had happened at school that day. Miss Carter, my third grade teacher, had given a written test, and when we were done we brought our paper to her desk to be graded. As usual, J. C. Shelton handed his in first, then a couple of girls, then I went up. Without even checking my answers, Miss Carter marked a big red E for excellent at the top of the page. From the side of her mouth she whispered, "Take this back and keep it on top of your desk."

Wow! Was I teacher's pet? An "E" for excellence and she didn't even look at my answers! I spread my paper out on my desk so I could see it real well, then looked at Miss Carter to confirm if I'd done it right. Her head was buried behind the text book.

Abruptly she looked up and yelled, "Clarence Eckles! You're copying Bill Ray's work!"

The class gasped! Copying was the unpardonable sin!

Clarence sat at the desk to my immediate right. He came from the poorest of families in a poor town and wore clothes that looked like they came from somebody's dead uncle.

"I saw you, Clarence! You sneaked a look at Bill Ray's answers!"

Clarence stammered his innocence, but Miss Carter jerked off her horn-rimmed glasses, stood up, and launched a loud lecture on the shame of copying someone else's paper. She must've said *shame* a dozen times.

Clarence hung his head, and the tears made little streaks down his dirty face. The rest of us turned away unable to look at him; we couldn't even look at each other; most stared at their test paper. I slid mine inside my desk.

As Dad listened to my story, his face darkened. When I'd finished, he said: "Entrapment."

Dad always talked to me like that, like I was an adult. Sometimes I didn't know what he was talking about, but I liked listening to him, because he was smarter than anybody.

"What's that?" I asked.

"'Entrapment' is tempting people to do the wrong thing. Tricking them. Clarence Eckles goes hungry most of the time. He lives with a big family in a little shack. He'll never be the sharpest knife in the box, but his life is bad enough.

Don't be a part of making it worse. If a teacher ever asks you to do that again—*don't!*" Dad wasn't in the mood for any more mumble-peg and went inside the trailer.

The next day at school, I covered my test answers with my arm and rushed to Miss Carter's desk with the paper plastered to my chest. Guess what? I didn't get an "E."

One day, I came home from school and Dad was smoking but not whittling. I could see he wanted to talk.

"Bill Ray, people like music with their beer, right?"

They didn't ask questions like this at school, so I just looked at him.

"So, the answer is juke boxes!" His eyes were dreamy-shiny, a glow they always got when the Phantom had told him what to do. Yeah, the Phantom; that's what I called this wee hours spirit that whispered to Dad sometimes. Dad's listening to the Phantom had taken us on some wingding adventures, and it looked like this latest one had something to do with music machines you put a nickel in.

I'll do it!" Dad said.

"Do what?"

"Put a juke box in every bar in Putnam County.

"Every bar, Dad? Sometimes drunks get mad at the music and kick the machines."

"I'll fix the machines."

Of course he would; Dad could fix anything. "Is Uncle Buck going to loan you money again?" I asked.

"No, Uncle Albert."

Uncle Albert was the name folks gave Albert Cassidy, the man who loaned the money at Farmers Bank. Dad admitted there'd be a problem, though. Bankers didn't think musicians were responsible human beings. So, he probably couldn't get the money even if he were Benny Goodman. Well, Mom wasn't a musician, so Dad sent *her* to Uncle Albert, and a miracle happened—with her waitress job as collateral, she got the loan, and the Phantom's whisper came true. Dad put used Wurlitzers in about every bar in Putnam County—and they got kicked, and he did keep them running.

His territory favored east of Unionville, little towns like Hartford, Livonia, Queen City, and Greentop, and he took me as company when he collected the nickels and made repairs. Collecting the money often took quite a spell, as I sat next to Dad at the bar sipping Pepsi while he told me fascinating stories about famous people ranging from Macedonia's king, Alexander the Great, to Kansas

City's kingpin, Tom Pendergast. To me, Dad knew everything there was to know, and as we traveled along the back roads of northern Missouri, I soaked up his take on life:

Pendergast, the bad boss of Kansas City, wasn't all bad.

Rich people call the shots, poor people call for a shot and a beer.

If you don't learn anything else in math, learn percentages.

FDR had a heart, Hoover didn't.

The best ever Hollywood cowboy was a former New York stage actor, William S. Hart.

Jefferson was our most intelligent president.

Lincoln was our best.

Your best boss is you.

The best car is one that's paid for and runs.

It takes money to make money.

Benny Goodman plays the "licorice stick" better than anyone in the world.

Read and you discover the world.

And the most glorious trip in the world would be floating down the Mississippi on a raft.

Dad had sayings he repeated so often they became old friends:

A fool and his money are soon parted

He was right, dead right, as he sped along; but just as dead as if he'd been wrong. Burma Shave.

You can tell a good workman by his tools.

You'll go to the polls with tears in your eyes (meaning I would still be crying when I was old enough to vote).

My pocket's slicker than an auderslide. (I was out of high school before I realized he'd been saying "otter slide.")

And the one I heard most: *Don't do as I do; do as I tell you to do.*

Expecting the juke boxes to take in tons of nickels, Dad sold our little trailer and moved us next to the high school into a big house that came with a basement, back lot, barn, and a big secret. The big secret was that the place was crawling with bedbugs and cockroaches. And, oh, yes, there were rats in the basement. Not many, Dad explained, just a few. Now eight years old, I was given the job of firing the furnace.

Down in rat city.

"Hit 'em with a shovel," Dad said. "They'll scatter."

The basement exuded pure menace—a clammy cavern of silence with a bare light bulb casting dark shadows across wet, crumbling walls. *What was that movement behind those boxes?*

I didn't investigate.

Outside the house, however, became paradise: a front yard for playing ball; a battered barn and collapsing outbuildings; an abandoned garage with weeds sprouting from the dirt floor; and my favorite of all, bordering the south side of the high school lawn—a small forest of short, tree-like bushes where Cook and I crawled on our bellies through dense South Pacific jungle and shot Japs.

It was our duty. Staring from under bushy eyebrows, Uncle Sam pointed a bony finger at everybody who walked by. In 1943, the *I Want You!* poster glared from store windows all over town. From barrooms to church socials, the talk had been all the same: our boys would send Hitler, Tojo, and Mussolini running for their mamas in six months. That was two years ago. At first just the younger men had been drafted, but the enemy hadn't budged. Uncle Sam upped the draft age to forty. Dad was thirty seven.

Word came that if men helped build the Alpine Highway in Alaska they wouldn't be drafted. In a choice between bullets and mosquitoes, Dad chose mosquitoes. So did Mom's brothers, Joe and Bill. Dad left Mom the phone number for a man who would do repairs on the juke boxes, and she was to make sure each bar had a working machine. Mom sputtered a bunch of questions all starting with, "But, what if …", but Dad gave her the keys and a kiss, and joined Uncle Bill and Uncle Joe on the train bound for Alaska.

The train barely had left the station when Bing Crosby and the Andrews Sisters developed laryngitis, at least on our juke boxes. Fuses blew, sparks flew, and the big, rotating 78's lumbered to a halt. Mostly, the repairman didn't answer the phone. When he did make a service call, he was so snockered he couldn't get the back off the machine. Dad had insisted that every bar have a working juke, so Mom bought rebuilt ones and Uncle Buck muscled them into the bars and brought the old ones home. Within a month our basement was a juke box graveyard.

Meanwhile, Uncle Bill's wife Kate moved in with us, making the house now home to two pretty women in their late twenties and one solemn-faced eight-year-old boy. Aunt Kate was a perky brunette whose mother owned the Victory Bar on the east side of the Square. She and Mom, along with girlfriend Wilma Cullum and her husband Red, often joined Uncle Buck and Aunt Nadine at the Victory Bar. Mom never stayed late. Sometimes Kate did.

In the back of my mind lurked the terrible fear that Dad wasn't coming back. He rarely wrote. When he did, we celebrated. Mom would set out cookies and milk and read the letter out loud over and over, both of us devouring every word. He wrote about cramped cabins, shoveling rock, and mosquitoes. Swarms of mosquitoes. Uncle Joe had slapped him on the back, and when Dad took his shirt off, his cabin mates counted thirty six dead mosquitoes. My favorite letter had a picture. It was of a bear cub taking a poop in the snow. Dad wrote on the picture, "Bill Ray taking a grunt." Man, I was proud! I took it to my third-grade class and passed it around the classroom, but Miss Carter intercepted it and made me put it in my pocket.

Other kids missed their fathers, too. One rain-misty recess the boys were playing dodge ball against the school's back wall. The game got rough, and I tore Gerald Dean Carr's new, yellow rain coat, and he broke out crying. Between sobs, he said it had been sent to him by his father who was in the army. His father hadn't been home for a long time. I felt awful. If someone had torn my picture of the bear, I would've cried a bucketful.

Dodge ball didn't seem fun anymore, and I drifted down to the trees behind the school. Sitting in the drizzle on a stump was this new boy in class, a skinny, mopey-acting kid who was throwing rocks at a tree. Actually, he wasn't new at all; he'd been around since the school year began, but he was so pale and tongue-tied he looked nearly invisible. I picked up a couple of rocks and threw at the same tree.

His name was Roger Torrey—well, *Neal* Roger Torrey—but he didn't use his first name, because he thought it sounded too *proper*. I thought "Roger" sounded pretty high falutin', so if it was just the two of us, I called him "Rodge," and if other guys were around I called him "Torrey." Later he *wanted* his name to sound classy, and called himself "Neal," but I never bought it. We stood in the drizzle and he talked about his stepfather. He painted him pretty grim; said his stepfather worked him powerful hard and beat him sometimes. When Rodge's two older brothers had moved out, they left him a .22 rifle, but his step dad took the gun, sold it, and kept the money. Dad had never taken things from me. He *made* me gifts—a marvelous tin can train, newspaper kites that reached the clouds, the indomitable Red Streak—and now he was stuck in some God forsaken, frozen place digging a highway. While I prayed for Dad to come home, Rodge prayed for his step-dad to leave. I felt bad about the rifle, and vowed to get my new friend another one.

I never did.

But I did help him become visible. I brought him into Hibbs' gang, the power center of the fifth grade; the membership being Hibbs, Pollock, myself, and Buddy Bramhall, a short, freckled kid whose claim to fame was he could spit through his teeth about twenty feet. Rodge joined our ranks at recess and lunch hour as we marched behind Hibbs through every game and roughhouse the playground offered. But *off* school property, I still followed Cook, my older, daredevil cousin, and that's exactly what I was doing when we made the big discovery.

Plunging through early morning fog on our bicycles, Cook and I were heading west out of town on a dirt road, when it appeared out of the mist: an ancient, abandoned structure looming in front of us like a land-locked pier awaiting Noah's Ark. It stood alone in the low clouds, a gray, splintered platform running alongside large, wooden vats. The vats, coated with pungent green brine, smelled vile, and resembled residue from a witch's cauldron. Whatever its history, this weathered ghost immediately became our battleship, and we were under Japanese air attack. Cook climbed to a small platform overlooking the vats, curled his hands like binoculars and called out the position of each swooping Zero. A long plank became my ack-ack gun, and I pointed it heavenward and blasted every Tojo-kissing, son-of-a-you-know-what out of the sky. After I'd blown twenty or more planes back to Hirohito, Cook stared through curled fingers and yelled:

"Kamikaze at three o'clock!"

David Lemon emerged from the fog on a bicycle. Befitting his name, Lemon had a slightly yellowish caste to his skin, at least I thought so. He was a loner, Cook's age, and lived with his grandparents in the back of their "sort of" grocery store. I say, "sort of," because the store existed in a permanent state of decay: perennially dark and musty, its shelves stocked with corn flake boxes and pork 'n bean cans from ten years ago. No one ever tended the counter, and you had to cough real loud before old Mr. Lemon would hear you and slowly emerge from behind a dark curtain to wait on you.

"What are you guys doing?" Lemon called.

"Playing ship," I hollered down.

"Ship?" Lemon climbed up the platform ladder. "This is the Old Pickle Factory. My grandfather told me it shut down in the twenties. Said that farmers used to bring cucumbers, pickle 'em in the vats, and ship 'em to Keokuk."

Cook climbed down from his observation perch. "Yeah, I been here lots of times. Thought I'd bring Jackson this time." He leaned over the nearest vat and spat a big glob.

"Care for a cig?" Lemon asked like he was fifty years old. He brought out a pack of Old Golds. They tasted like they'd been on the shelf of his grandfather's store for fifty years. Smokes dangling from our lips, the three of us joyfully spent the rest of the day avenging Pearl Harbor with thunderous firepower from the mighty U.S.S. Pickle Factory.

The adults had abandoned this relic from another world, and now it was ours. While World War II raged on faraway continents, Captain Cook and I escaped reality by biking again and again to the old factory's wonders, conjuring it into prisons, castles, ships and submarines—creating magic in a mystic harbor far from troubled seas.

Near summer's end, Cook and I took leave of the U. S. S. Pickle Factory to pursue more literary endeavors. Beckoning us was not the library, but Herrick's Drug Store. Inside the front door to the right was the gateway to cultural bliss: the comic book rack. We devoured the pages of every superhero magazine in sight—staggering out hours later with our heads throbbing with *Biffs! Bams! Zaps! Splats! Auurghs! Whonks!* and *Thwacks!* But appearances had to be maintained, so we would buy about one comic in every twenty five we read.

However, the magic of Herrick's encompassed more than comic books. One day as we made for the door bloated with *Batman* and *The Green Hornet*, Cook's bleary eyes focused on two hand puppets at the end of the checkout counter. One was old vaudevillian Jimmy Durante and the other was Bob Hope's brash side-kick, Jerry Colona. Durante had a big funny nose, but Cook liked Colona's black, waxy moustache better. We tried them on and mimicked their voices—I doing a choppy, raspy Durante, Cook doing a fast, falsetto Colona. Mr. Herrick, who was watching us, didn't fuss at all. Instead, he laughed, called over customers to watch; they laughed and asked us to do some more, which gave me a great idea. Cook and I would put on a puppet show, charge five cents a ticket, and make a fortune. Cook went for it, mostly because he liked building things and he would get to build the stage.

We rushed home and talked our mothers into backing our bid for Broadway by springing fifty cents apiece for the puppets. Cook lived on the east side of the Square in a third story apartment, and to get to it you went up a narrow, musty stairway and passed through an immense storage room carpeted with dust. In the middle of this cavern we built the stage. Cook sawed and hammered, and I painted the backdrop—a graveyard where Durante and Colona would meet. I felt like it was my birthday. This was the most fun thing I'd ever gotten to do with Cook.

For the script I went to the best comedy source available: the tiny comics tucked inside Double Bubble gum wrappers. We knew we had the makings of a sure-fire hit, and full of confidence, we agreed to invite all of our friends. Trouble was, I didn't have any friends who had five cents. Cook on the other hand traveled with a better-heeled crowd, and it was to these friends he pitched the show. I didn't get the script finished until an hour before our big Saturday afternoon debut. We climbed behind the stage and donned our puppets for the one and only rehearsal.

"Ladeeze and men who are gentle!" I boomed in a loud announcer voice.

"Boo! That's terrible!"

I stood up and peered out the curtain. It was Miles Dickson, a chubby classmate of Cook's who scowled because he needed glasses. He'd arrived early.

"We're rehearsing the play I told you about," Cook called from behind the stage.

"Yeah," I said. "Come back in about an hour."

"Naw, I wanna watch," said Dickson. "Don't worry, I'll pay the nickel."

"You'll tell everyone the jokes," I objected.

"Naw I won't, not a word," Dickson said.

"Promise?"

"Cross my heart and hope to croak," he grinned, making a big "X" over his heart.

"C'mon, let's rehearse," Cook said impatiently.

An hour later about twenty kids climbed the stairs to our puppet emporium and sat in folding chairs Cook's mom had gotten from somewhere. I couldn't believe the Big Names who were there: B. Sue MacDonald, the doctor's daughter; Patty Comstock, of the Funeral Home Comstocks; Gary Grabosch, son of the best known butcher in town; cousin Paddy Joe Davis, son of Uncle Joe, one of Unionville's most respected businessmen; and a host of Cook's other upper crust classmates. Cook collected their nickels and joined me behind the puppet stage.

"We got a buck, five," he whispered.

I began to sweat. We had B. Sue MacDonald, the doctor's daughter, out there. We donned Durante and Colona, stuck them up behind the curtain, and squinted real hard at the scripts tacked in front of us.

I made my voice as deep as I could and called out, "Ladeeze and men who are gentle!"

A few of the girls giggled.

"Presenting for your entertainment ... a puppet show ... starring Jimmy Dur ... an ... tee and Jerry Cah ... lon ... ah!"

Cooked pulled the curtain and our puppets bobbed up and down in front of the graveyard. Delighted laughter from the audience. We were off to a great start.

"Mr. Colona, it appears we've wandered into a graveyard," I said in Durante's raspy voice.

"Yes, indeed, Mr. Durante," replied Cook in Colona's high staccato, "and if we see any ghosts I'll feed them breakfast!"

A titter from the audience.

"Breakfast, Mr. Colona? And what, pray tell, do ya feed ghosts for breakfast?"

"Ghost Toasties!" shouted a voice from the back of the audience.

The kids turned around in their seats and Dickson gave them all a wave from the back row.

"What would ya feed 'em for lunch?" I asked.

"Boo-loney sandwiches!" Dickson yelled.

Laughter and cheers for Dickson.

The idiot proceeded to give every punch line in the play. What happened to "cross my heart and hope to croak?" At the end, Cook pulled the curtain and we came out for our bows. The audience applauded, murmured appreciation, and headed for the long stairway to the street. B. Sue MacDonald started down, then came back and told us how much she enjoyed the show—especially Miles. She turned to Dickson.

"You were *so* funny! How ever did you know all those jokes?"

Dickson smiled like a dog sucking eggs.

I wanted to kill him.

CHAPTER 9

▼

A STRANGER RETURNS

We could hear it coming. Mom and I stood outside the Lucerne train station and peered down the track. It was the winter of 1944 and I was eight years old. Eight months ago Dad had stepped onto this train and out of our lives, but now he was coming back. I would grab his legs and hug him with all my might; and he and Mom would kiss like Clark Gable and Carole Lombard. And we would go home and he and Mom would sleep in their big bed, and I would sleep in my room close by. The next morning we'd have breakfast and I would tell him about my new friend, Rodge, and about the Pickle Factory and the puppet show. And then we would build kites and go fishing and take long rides in the car just like before.

Mom let out a squeal. There he was, wearing the brown fedora he'd left with and a dark mackinaw. I ran to him and hurled myself into his legs and squeezed for all I was worth. He awkwardly patted my shoulders. Mom rushed to him and they kissed, but not the long, movie kiss I had expected, and as we walked to the car Mom had a puzzled look in her eyes. Dad drove us home, and Mom talked nonstop about stuff she'd probably already written him: how we'd left the house for two days when Aunt Kate's brother-in-law, Dick Dickson, set off poison canisters to kill the roaches. Grandma Jackson was fine, but Great Grandma Neighbors had gone nearly blind. I outgrew my clothes almost every month. She and Kate had gone to a lot of movies. Kate had moved out a month ago. The weather had turned chilly. Finally Mom fell silent; Dad wasn't saying much at all.

When we got home, he walked around the house like he was looking for dead bodies or something. He found some when he went down into the basement and discovered all the dead juke boxes. When he came upstairs, he acted happy that he'd found something to upset him and he railed at Mom about how she was supposed to keep them fixed. Mom tried to explain about the drunken repairman, but Dad just waved her off, pulled a bottle of whisky from his bag and went out back to "see what else was wrong."

The days that followed were awful. Dad hardly spoke and spent all of his time down at the bars with his buddies, which hurt more than his being in Alaska, because now that he could be with us, he chose not to. Night after night, Mom set three places at the table and she and I ate alone. After dinner, Mom did the dishes, I did my homework, and we listened to the radio a while. The one phone in the house was on the wall and had a party system where you picked up the receiver to see if anyone was on the line. If no one was, the operator asked you what number you wanted her to dial. Of course, if someone was talking, you could just quietly listen to their business. Mom knew what bar Dad liked, and about nine o'clock at night, she would call it, but Dad rarely came to the phone. And he never came home until after it closed.

After supper I sat at the big window and stared at the street, watching the road get darker, the street lights come on, and pin points of light appear from the homes on the other side of the field across from our house. Mom sat in the front room pretending to read a magazine, and I would hear her crying softly.

In desperation, I tried to *will* Dad home. Sitting by the window, sitting very still with my eyes closed, I created in my mind his every move from the bar to the driveway. It always started with him getting off his bar stool. Then he said good-bye to his friends and walked to the door. He paused, turned back to the bartender and gave a wave. Emerging into the night, he slowly walked the short distance to his car. He opened the car door, slid behind the wheel, shut the door, and started the engine. The car was parked facing east, and he headed down Main Street and carefully made a U-turn at the end of the block where the D-X station was.

Now he drove west across the Square. On his right was the Farmer's Bank, at the corner, Herrick's Drug Store. He moved beyond the Square past the Methodist Church, then down the hill and across the flat by the American Legion Hall. Now up the steep hill to the four-way stop at Kozy Korner, the all-night gas station, and left over the tracks. He was three blocks away. I peered out the window into the darkness and waited. No headlights came up the road.

I went back to the intersection.

He turned left, drove across the railroad tracks, and descended south, passing the small field of weeds where Clarence Eckles' father lived alone in a tar paper shanty. Next was my friend Gerald Neighbors' little house, then Dad drove up the hill to the high school. He was almost home. The high school was on his right, first the main building, then the gymnasium. Finally, he turned into our driveway. I strained to hear the crunch of tires on the gravel.

Silence.

I waited a few moments, and then imagined the whole sequence again, step by step, slowing it down even more, so that if Dad were just starting home, he would catch up. After about the fourth time, my head throbbed, and I left the window and went to bed and fell asleep listening for the crunch of gravel.

What had gone wrong? Before Dad left for Alaska, our house shimmered with laughter and wonderful stories about how he and Mom met; how when they planned to marry, Grandpa and Grandma Davis almost spit nails. All the hard yet wonderful times they shared as newlyweds, and all the adventures we had after I came along.

They had told me about their courtship in bits and pieces, some from Mom, some from Dad. Putting it all together, I had the story. It's a lulu and it starts at Essie's Café.

CHAPTER 10

▼

THE HIGH SCHOOL BELLE
AND THE BANJO PLAYER

The dark man in his twenties settled onto the stool and slid a nickel for coffee across the counter. Essie Jones, gray of hair and mood, placed a cup, no saucer, in front of her customer and poured.

"Black, right, Tramp?" she mumbled.

"Right."

It was mid-September, 1930, and Tramp Jackson, formerly Cecil, had just come off that traveling playhouse, The Palmer Tent Show, where he had played banjo and performed bit parts on the stage. His dark good looks and winking eyes had moved many a country girl to leave love notes for him at the ticket stand.

Tramp sipped his coffee and looked around the room. Essie's Café, with its harsh light and greasy smell, was an unlikely setting for romance. However, Tramp knew that high school girls often stopped at Essie's on the way home from school. Sure enough, at a back table, a group of girls whispered and giggled, but it was the quiet one who caught his eye. She was a blue-eyed honey silently stirring her Coke, her thoughts seemingly far from the banter of her friends. *How old was she? Seventeen? Eighteen? He hoped she was eighteen. Didn't want daddy chasing him out of town.* He shifted toward her, hoping to catch her eye. If she'd look this way, he'd smile and give her one of his winks that made the country girls blush, look away, and look back.

Virginia Lee Davis toyed with her Coke while her girl friends gushed about Jimmy's dreamy eyes and Bobby's wavy hair. Of more interest to the fifteen-year-old was the worldly-looking man sipping coffee at the counter. For the past two years, Virginia Lee had received scads of attention from boys—and some men. Her first date, just last year, was with a man in his twenties who worked in the office of a car dealership. What a snoozer he'd been.

The barnstorming stunt pilot had been more like it. At the edge of town, out of sight of her parents, the pilot invited her aboard his plane. To show off, he took the plane through five loop-de-loops, then flew upside down. But in returning, he came in too low, clipped a telephone line, and made a wobbly, forced landing downtown on Main Street. People burst from the stores like a circus had landed, and the air ace took flight rather than face an irate father.

My, how that man at the counter was smiling. Was that a wink? Virginia Lee turned back to her Coke and her friends, who had taken note of the man's selective attention.

"Dare you to blow him a kiss!" challenged one girl in a loud whisper. The other girls shrieked approval, but Virginia Lee shook her head and stared at her drink. Then, as the group of girls passed by him on the way to the cash register, Virginia Lee paused and pointed at the candy display on the back counter.

"Aren't you going to buy me a box of candy?" she asked.

Doing his best Clark Gable, Tramp crooked an eyebrow, squinted an eye, and growled, "Go on, I'm not your daddy."

Tramp didn't have a car, so he arranged a double date. Arriving at Virginia Lee's house in a shiny, 1929 Model A sports coupe, his friend sat behind the wheel with his girl beside him, and Tramp lounged in the tiny rumble seat. There was no introduction to parents; Virginia Lee burst out the front door and ran to the car.

Seeing that Tramp took up most of the rumble seat, she asked, "Where am I supposed to ride?"

"On my lap, I guess," Tramp replied.

Making a pout, Virginia Lee asked, "What's the movie?"

"On the Sunny Side of the Street."

"Who's in it?"

"Janet Gaynor."

"Oh, I like *her!*"

She climbed into the rumble seat and plopped herself on his lap. It turned out that the movie was in Centerville, Iowa, twenty three miles away. A pretty girl sitting on a man's lap for forty six miles can do things to a man's mind. Tramp sold his banjo and bought a Model A.

Friends reported to Virginia Lee's parents that she had been seen in the company of that man from the tent show—the man called Tramp. Davy and Sadie Davis were pious, hardworking folks. Six days a week you got up at sunrise and worked until sunset. You attended church Sunday mornings, Sunday nights and Wednesday nights. You said hello to everyone you met. You *always* paid your debts and *always* returned things you'd borrowed. And you considered an ice cream at the fair as one heck of a treat.

Davy forbade his daughter to see the man. He was at least seven or eight years older than she—an aging Huck Finn who hopped freights, acted on the stage, and was reported at times to have the dark curse of drink on his breath. No, the man called Tramp was not to come calling.

He didn't. Virginia Lee got boys in high school to call for her as dates, then drive her to prearranged trysts with her Tramp. This ruse worked for an incredible year and a half until she got into an argument with her older sister, Mary Katherine, who petulantly went to mommy and daddy and blew the whistle. That night when Virginia Lee tip toed up the stairs from her date, she opened her bedroom door to find her father sitting sentinel in the darkness in a rocking chair. He wasted no time delivering his ultimatum.

"Stop seeing that Tramp man or I'll take you out of school!"

"But it's only two months to graduation."

"So be it," her father replied.

Virginia Lee threw herself on the bed. "Fine! We'll just get married!"

Davy stood over her. "What kind of house would you live in? He can't even hold a job."

Drawing herself up resolutely, she declared, "Daddy, I love him. I'll live with my Tramp in a tent if I have to."

Davy had been bluffing and his daughter knew it. Virginia Lee graduated from school and openly dated her gypsy man.

Tramp never proposed. Never even said, "I love you." Not ever. He courted by singing love songs to his beloved and kissing her passionately. They mutually assumed they would marry and dreamed of adventures to come. Adventures were scarce in 1931. The Depression was two years old and the street expression was, "Nobody's hirin' nobody." Tramp spent his mornings down at Essie's sipping free refills of coffee and shooting the breeze with the regulars.

A frequent counter companion was Casey Rose, a popular attorney who would become a respected judge. Rose was accustomed to Essie's clientele complaining about no jobs, the price of hogs, and the latest knife fight at the Casa Loma, the beer dive at the edge of town. But this young man called Tramp impressed him. He could talk history, philosophy, literature, and law. When asked where his learning came from, Tramp replied, "The best school going—the library."

Impressed, Rose invited the young man to come by the office anytime and read whatever books he'd like. Tramp took up residence and read many. When he discussed them with Rose, the attorney was so taken by Tramp's intellect that he made and incredible offer:

He would pay Tramp's way through law school.

That night, parked under the stars at the Old City Pond, Tramp told Virginia Lee of Rose's offer. She gave a squeal and hugged him. *Her future husband a lawyer? Oh, her folks would be so proud.*

Tramp stroked her hair.

"I'm not going," he said.

Virginia Lee sat forward. "Not going?"

"Law school takes years. I don't want to be away from you that long."

"But I could visit you at school. You'd come home sometimes."

"Yeah, and you'd be having boyfriends in between."

"I would not!"

Tramp studied her. Blonde. Blue-eyed. Said to be the prettiest girl in Putnam County.

"I'm not going," he repeated.

Virginia Lee dated her vagabond lover for four years, counting the secret trysts, and as her nineteenth birthday drew near, Davy sensed she planned to elope. Knowing his daughter would want his blessing, he played one last card. If Tramp got a steady job, Davy would consent to the marriage. Tramp's brother, Cliff, came visiting from Newton, Iowa, with the news that Maytag's, the appliance factory where he worked, was hiring. Tramp drove the hundred miles to Newton that night and was in the job application line the next morning. He listened as the desperate man in front of him spouted promises to the gruff-faced interviewer that he could do anything, *anything!* Gruff Face said, "We don't have jobs for doing *anything*. Next."

Tramp played it like he was on stage at The Palmer Show. He fished a match out of his pocket, stuck it in one side of his mouth, and nonchalantly stepped to the desk.

"What can ya do?" Gruff Face asked.

Tramp slowly looked around the room like he owned it.

"Specialty stuff," he answered.

"Yeah? Can ya do machine work?"

Tramp showed him his hands. His fingernails were black with grease from changing oil on the Model A the night before.

"Yeah," drawled Tramp. "All kinds."

Tramp started work the next day.

Davy's demand having been met, the two lovers married November 13, 1933, three days after Virginia Lee's eighteenth birthday. The sparse ceremony was in Newton, at the home of a Lutheran minister. The groom slipped a shiny seven dollar ring on his bride's finger; they kissed long and hard, and headed for their honeymoon resort: the one-room apartment where they would live.

The job lasted six months. Tramp came home from work one night and tossed a catalog on the table.

"What's that?" Virginia Lee asked.

"Our fortune," answered Tramp.

Virginia Lee looked closer. The catalog was for household supplies. "We're going to sell soap?" she asked.

"No, look at this." Tramp flipped through a few pages and pointed at a head-line.

"Everybody gets hurt," he read.

"So?"

"So, first-aid kits. The one thing you need whether you're rich or poor. We'll sell 'em door to door from here to Texas. Make more money in two months than Maytag pays in two years."

"But you told the folks...."

"This'll be steady. I told you, people keep getting hurt. I gave my notice at Maytag today."

Virginia Lee slowly sat down on the edge of their bed, her fingers kneading the covers.

"Where are we going to stay? Boarding houses are expensive."

"Wait'll you see the tent I got. Three bucks."

The scene with her father in the bedroom flashed into Virginia Lee's head. She defiantly had proclaimed she would live with her Tramp in a tent if she had to.

Now she had to.

On a chilly April morning in 1934, Tramp and Virginia Lee filled the back seat of Tamp's Model A with first-aid kits. Cramming in a few clothes and the bargain tent, they headed south along the mighty Mississippi. It was to be the most romantic, carefree time of their lives and an adventure best suited for the young. The nights turned bitter cold; even the camp stove at full blaze failed to dispel the numbing chill. Sleep was impossible, and come daybreak they moved their cots outside the tent into the warm rays of the morning sun and slept 'til noon.

The weather turned warm, and when they neared Memphis, Tramp made camp and tested the river's temperature. It was brisk, but not freezing, and he talked his bride into joining him for a swim in the waters made famous by Mark Twain. They rode logs streaming by and laughed and splashed through a game of tag. Then Tramp rolled over on his back to float. Virginia sneaked behind him. She pushed his head under water, taunted him to catch her, and swam away. But Tramp didn't follow. She started back to him, but could make no headway. She had entered the wide, relentless current surging down the Mississippi's middle.

She flailed her arms and kicked her legs. They felt like weights. She called to Tramp, but her mouth filled with water. She choked and gasped for breath. The monster river pulled her, pounded her, swept her along its journey like she was just another log. She was under water. She couldn't breath. Black flashes filled her consciousness. A strong arm came under her and pushed her upwards, freeing her head from the water. Tramp held her up and fought the river. She coughed water and gasped for air.

"Roll over on your back!" he yelled, helping her make the move. "Now relax and float. Don't fight. Relax."

Tramp slowly towed her out of the current and to the shore. They sat huddled on the bank, Tamp holding her close and shaking his head in the realization that he'd almost lost her. When her shivering stopped, they walked back to camp, his arm snugly around her waist. It was only sundown, but they went to bed early that night and renewed their love.

The next morning they spread the joy of first-aid kits.

They hawked these miniature medicine chests door to door and store to store from Missouri to Texas, deciding early that separating covered more ground. At day's end, they met at camp outside of town, and the one who'd sold the most kits bought ice cream. Tramp bought the cones all the way to Fort Worth, but Virginia discovered that she didn't sell much at houses. Women always answered the door. But stores with men behind the counter? Bingo! She dropped residence calls entirely and went straight for downtown. When the purveyors of Band-Aids and iodine headed back north, Virginia Lee bought the ice cream all the way to Unionville.

CHAPTER 11

▼

THE PHANTOM WHISPERS

Fifty dollars. That's what the purveyors of gauze and iodine had to show for their summer's efforts when they returned to Unionville. Tramp and Virginia Lee canvassed the town for jobs, but the Depression had exacted its toll, and the only work remaining was waiting tables. Tramp figured if they had to work that hard, they should own the place. So, with the fifty bucks and a loan from Tramp's brother, Buck, they opened a small café just off the northwest side of the Square. Hamburgers sold for five cents and a slice of Virginia Lee's home-baked apple pie, ten cents. Doors opened at 5:30 AM. and closed at 10:00 PM., seven days a week. For extra income, they rented cots in the back room to coal miners. Dining customers stared at their plates trying to ignore the parade of smelly, grimy men heading for bed.

The romance of the road had taken a sharp detour. Sunrises heralding the day's promise had disappeared—sunrises no longer look so great seen through grainy eyes. Well, Virginia Lee's eyes were grainy; Tramp slept mornings. He played in roadhouse bands at night, slept until noon, and then showed up at the café. At the end of one year, the combination eatery-flophouse showed a net profit of thirty nine dollars. For Virginia Lee, the café's baker-cook-waitress, it had been a long, head-throbbing, feet-aching year for which she was paid not one penny. But there were two things Virginia Lee did get: a new hat and pregnant.

I, Bill Ray Jackson, entered this world September 15, 1935, at 8:05 PM in the back bedroom of a small white house with peeling paint and worn linoleum floors. Mom told of Uncle Buck coming by to see his new nephew. He took one look at my receding chin and said, "Good God! It's Andy Gump!" Andy Gump was a popular comic strip character, an old man with a bald head and no chin. Mom was not pleased.

Dad celebrated the occasion of his first born by launching his own dance band. However, Putnam County's dance crowd kicked up its heels but once a week, Saturday night, which is all the work the band got. After paying the band and buying a few rounds, Dad brought home about three dollars. Mom and Dad ate beans, fried potatoes, and oatmeal. I dined far more elegantly—I had mother's milk.

Five months after my arrival, the previously mentioned Phantom" whispered in Dad's ear. So far, it had directed him to hop freights, join the tent show, and sell those first-aid kits. This time it called him down an even longer road—one that went all the way to California. Perhaps the voice was actually a beery croak down at the bar, because we didn't even have a car. Not to worry. Dad built a car from parts out of junkyards—a car that actually ran. Dad could do that.

With a tank full of gas, food for five days, and fifty dollars from Uncle Buck, we pointed this Chevy-Dodge-Ford-Whatever toward the evening sun. To save fuel, Dad cut the engine as we crested each long hill and coasted down the other side. Come the frosty nights, we slept by the side of the road with me snuggled toasty warm between my parents. Bathing was done in gas station bathrooms, where Mom dipped me into the sink and afterwards washed out my diapers and any other laundry. The car's rolled up windows held the laundry in place, and with shirts, pants, dresses and diapers flapping in the wind, we crossed the western desert like a huge, molting Albatross.

Three days later we ground to a stop at Uncle Clyde and Aunt Maureen's house in Pacoima, California. Uncle Clyde, a high-grade civil service manager for a nearby naval base, had heard sailors from Missouri talking about getting off-duty work at an interior decorator shop. Soon Dad, the banjo-playing gypsy, painted the walls of fancy mansions owned by movie stars. Mom excitedly wrote her younger brother Bill to come out at once, California was the Promised Land.

Sixteen-year-old Bill Davis started hitchhiking with a friend, but in Kansas City his friend was robbed, and he returned home. The police ordered young Bill to go home, also, but the family sent funds to buy a train ticket to Pacoima. Though but a teenager, Bill Davis had a killer smile and the looks of a movie star. A covey of young nuns riding the same train took in his soft blue eyes and wavy blond hair, lost their hearts, and hid him from the ticket taker. When Bill arrived, the unused ticket was cashed, and the family went to Santa Monica Beach where California's magic was celebrated under swaying palm trees with gin, lemonade, and milk.

The magic ended abruptly. The Great Depression finally knocked on the doors of Hollywood's elite and convinced them that the gold speckled paint on that winding staircase may not be as necessary as they thought. Jobs in sunny California dried up, and beaches swarmed, not with tourists, but with the unemployed.

Again the Phantom spoke to Dad. This time it whispered, "Hops."

They were hiring hop pickers in Oregon. Trouble was we didn't have gas money to get there. Dad came up with a novel answer. He sold his jigsaw puzzle car that ran and bought an ancient Nash that didn't. The car that ran brought fifty dollars. The Nash cost twenty five dollars. Dad spent ten dollars for used parts and had the Nash running in two days. Two dollars were spent on beans for the adults and milk for me, leaving thirteen dollars. Two days later we were living near the Willownet River in a tiny picker-shack at a hops field in Independence, Oregon.

Mom took care of me while Dad and Uncle Bill picked from 7 AM to 5 PM. with Sundays off. Pickers were paid at the end of the day by how many full gunny sacks of hops they brought to the collecting wagon. Most wages went right back to the buyers as rent for the shacks they provided the pickers. Dad, Mom and Bill made jokes about going on diets. The diets became way too successful, and soon Dad and Bill would be too weak to work. One Sunday, Dad scavenged the river's shoreline for junk to sell and discovered an abandoned raft. With Uncle Bill baby-sitting me, Mom and Dad paddled the raft to the middle of the river. It was alive with salmon leaping upstream to spawn. Cupping their hands, Mom and Dad flipped meals for several days onto the raft.

Then September blew its chilly breath, the river emptied of salmon, and the fields held no more hops. And something else emptied: the fruit jar holding our savings. Rent and food had taken it all. The Phantom's open road had turned down a rutted detour and disappeared into a thicket of weeds, and Dad decided Unionville hadn't been such a bad place after all. The family tossed every penny from every pocket onto the kitchen table. The total was five dollars, not nearly enough for gas to get us back home, let alone food. Hearing of our plight, two women from the shanty next door left a bushel basket of apples at our door as they departed camp. Mom called out her gratitude to the ladies and made apple butter, which became our sole sustenance for the trip.

To stretch the five dollars as far as he could, Dad pulled a trick on our car that was absolute alchemy. Trading some of Mom's apple butter for an old fuel tank, he mounted it alongside the Nash's regular tank and rigged an alternate fuel line to it. One tank held gasoline and the other tank held kerosene. Then he tinkered with the sparkplugs and distributor. Early the next morning, we headed east into the mountains. After the engine got hot, Dad flipped a lever and switched fuel lines from the tank with the expensive gasoline to the tank with the much cheaper kerosene. The car backfired like a cannon and belched black soot like a smoke stack on a coal train, but the engine kept running, and we headed home.

While we were still in the mountains, Uncle Bill, now seventeen, took the wheel while the rest of us slept. Missouri hills were mere mounds compared to the towering Rockies of Colorado. Cresting a summit, the car plunged down the other side and rapidly gained speed. Bill jammed the brake pedal again and again, but each time he pulled his foot back the Nash lurched forward ever faster. Smoke filled the car and it wasn't the exhaust. Dad woke up coughing and yelled, "Pull over!" Uncle Bill hit the brakes and the car skidded off the road, struck a boulder, and came to rest against a fallen tree. Dad and Uncle Bill jumped out of the car. The tires were on fire from the heat of the brakes.

"We gotta get some water!" Uncle Bill yelled.

"There isn't any!" shouted Dad. "We have to make some! I'll get this side, you get the other!" Dad unbuttoned his fly and, hose in hand, sent a stream onto the smoking tires. Uncle Bill rushed to the other side and did the same. In the midst of the fire, smoke, and hissing, Mom looked out the window and said with a mock sigh:

"My firemen."

For thirteen days the Nash belched and backfired over the mountains and across the plains, coming to a wheezing stop at an oasis in Omaha—the home of Mom's sister, Rose, brother-in-law, George LeMasters, and their two children, George David and Virginia Katherine. We bathed luxuriously, ate abundantly, and slept like the dead, which we resembled. Three days later Dad borrowed a dollar for gas from Uncle George and pointed the Nash southeast through Iowa towards Missouri. Farmers stood by their precious fields shaking their fists as this smudge pot incarnate rattled by spewing exhaust like a crop duster from hell. As Missouri drew closer, the atmosphere in the car grew giddy—Burma Shave signs turned hilarious; past hardships became jokes to tell; and Mom pressed me to her bosom and hummed a lullaby.

Blam! The left front tire blew. Dad didn't bother stopping. He'd put the spare on in Oregon. He gripped the wheel with both hands and drove on. The jokes stopped and so did the lullaby. Five miles later the left rear tire blew, precariously tilting the car and slowing the speed to half. Still Dad refused to stop. Newton, Iowa, where his brother Cliff lived, was only fifty miles away. Dad hunched over the wheel and hummed a song no one knew. Listing left, sparks flying from shrieking metal rims and black smoke billowing from its rear, the old Nash arrived at Uncle Cliff's like a drunken duck with its tail on fire. There, in a smoldering heap in front of Uncle Cliff's house, the old Nash died. Young Bill hitchhiked ahead, and three days later, Uncle Cliff drove the rest of us home.

While Sadie slept, Davy had repaired to the kitchen to fix a late night snack. He heard something outside. He turned on the living room light and opened the door. The light fell across his youngest daughter, now twenty. She had a nervous smile on her face, and in the darkness a few steps back stood her haggard, twenty-eight-year-old husband. Asleep in his arms was the one-year-old grandson. No one spoke. Virginia Lee gave her father a big hug; he gave his grandson a pat on the head; and the old man led his guests into a back bedroom, and returned to his snack. A man of simple tastes, he sat at the kitchen table and placed a single slice of white bread in a bowl and sprinkled sugar on it. Then he poured a small amount of milk in the bowl and with a spoon began eating his treat. Virginia Lee appeared at the kitchen door.

"Come have some sugar-bread," Davy invited.

"No thanks, Daddy," answered Virginia Lee. She slipped into the chair opposite her father. Davy took another bite and chewed it slowly.

"Well, daughter, how was the great adventure? Did you bring back your fortune?"

Virginia Lee reached into her purse and pulled out a small jar. She placed it in the center of the table.

"This is all we brought back."

Davy opened the jar and sniffed the contents.

"Apple butter? You traveled all the way to California and all you brought back is a jar of apple butter?"

Virginia Lee put her head in her arms and cried.

CHAPTER 12

▼

LEAKY TENT, TEXAS

Plink, plunk. Plink, plunk. Plink, plunk. I woke up to water dripping from the tent roof into overflowing kitchen pans. Lightning flashed, thunder rumbled, and wind circled our little canvas home like a hysterical witch. I burrowed closer to Mom who was snuggled next to Dad; the rain subsided to a light patter, and I drifted off to sleep.

Then the siren went off.

Mom bolted upright. "Cecil! What's that?"

"Someone's escaped," mumbled Dad.

"Escaped? Escaped from where?" asked Mom.

"The insane asylum," Dad answered.

"The insane …? Oh, my God! Cecil, do something!"

Dad slipped out of the tent and returned with a hammer. He poked it under his pillow. "It'll be all right," he said and went back to sleep. Mom did not lie back down and neither did I. After a while the siren's wail fell silent. Mom and I watched the tent entrance, straining to hear any warning movement outside our flimsy fortress. The only sound we heard came from inside the tent—Dad's snoring.

We were stranded in Texas. To be precise, in a picnic area at the edge of a national forest near a little town called Rusk. The insane asylum was just down the road. Dad had spotted its gray, crumbling retention walls buried back in the trees when we passed by yesterday. We hadn't stopped at the picnic site to enjoy its bucolic pleasures. We had stopped because that's where we ran out of gas. And food. And money.

The spring following our return from our big trip west, Dad again heard the Phantom's familiar whisper, and we followed county fairs across the Midwest. With funding from Uncle Buck, Dad and Mom ran the cook house: the food tent feeding both carnies and townies. The cook house opened at six in the morning and closed after ten at night, a work shift the Phantom had failed to mention. Dad, weary of days and nights behind his grease-popping grill, studied the carny stands around him. Most of the game stands were outright dishonest, or at best, misleading. However, the picture-taking booth, called a Mug Joint, gave the marks something for their money: spend a dime, get a picture.

One morning while sipping coffee at the cook house, the Mug Joint's owner voiced aloud that he needed someone to develop film for him. Dad wiped his hands on his apron and came out from behind the grill.

"My wife can do that job," Dad said.

"I can?" Mom asked from behind a wash tub of dirty dishes.

The man cast a doubtful look at Mom. "You'd have to learn to mix chemicals."

Dad edged onto the stool beside the man. "She made great grades in school, especially in chemistry."

Mom stared at Dad.

"Well, okay," said the man, "we'll give it a try." He nodded at Mom. "Come over in an hour and I'll show you the ropes." He plunked down a nickel for his coffee and left.

"Cecil! I never even took chemistry!" Mom hissed.

"That's okay. Just come back and tell me everything he tells you."

Which she did, and that next spring Tramp Jackson with his wife and three-year-old son played the Midwest fairs with his self-built Mug Joint. Mom took the pictures and Dad developed them, and the work was far easier than the cook house. When fall's cold breath ended fairs in the Midwest, Dad took us father south. But the Depression had hit the South harder than the North; the fairs got smaller and so did the take. If the townies spent any money at all, it was for the Ferris wheel, which took them high above their troubles; but no one wanted "smile pictures" pretending things were good. Soon there wasn't enough money in the savings jar to get us back to Unionville. The carnies said that people spent more money at the Lufkin, Texas, fair than most fairs around. It started in two days. Dad thought there was enough gas in the car to get there.

There wasn't.

The gas tank went dry about forty miles north of the target, and we coasted off the road and into a picnic area. A sign indicated the saw mill across the road owned the spot, so Dad got permission from the mill to stay overnight.

We left half a year later.

Dad got part time work at the saw mill, "part time" meaning very little. The first day, Dad worked an hour stacking lumber into a pile higher than his head; the foreman came by, said that'd be all they needed that day, paid him a quarter, and sent him home. Dad walked a short distance down the road to a dilapidated general store run by a dilapidated old man named Spurger. Mr. Spurger, a talker, spotted Dad as fresh meat, and launched into several long stories, and at the conclusion of each he would turned to his hired colored boy and say, "Ain't that right, Billy?" Billy always allowed as it was, but as the stories droned on, the boy grew tired and announced he was going to take a nap. He paused on the stairway and said, "Mister Spurger, if you wants to prove anything else, you jus' wake me up." Dad took advantage of the break and with his quarter bought three eggs, a loaf of bread, and a quart of milk, and hurried home.

The purchase made for a sumptuous meal, but most days the only thing on our table was turnips picked from a huge field next to our tent. The farmer selling the turnips only charged colored people five cents an armload, saying they felt better if it wasn't charity. One evening he stopped by to talk with Dad and saw that Mom had sliced a baked potato three ways for our supper. After that, we got all the turnips we could carry for nothing.

When winter set in, Dad built a wood-burning stove out of a rusty metal barrel, stuck on a discarded stove pipe, and thereby installed indoor heating in the tent. When Mom came down with the flu, Mr. Spurger's wife came by offering to do the laundry. No, it wouldn't be a lick of trouble; Mom was to lie back and get well. Mom gratefully accepted the offer, motioned toward the basket of dirty clothes, lay back on her pillow, and rested her eyes.

Mrs. Spurger proved as blabby as her husband. She settled on the floor at the front of the tent and proceeded to chatter about every relative she had and some that other people had. Suddenly there was a sharp "sput!" Mom's eyes flew open. Mrs. Spurger spoke a few more sentences and gave another "sput!" Mom rose up to find Mrs. Spurger emphasizing her remarks by spitting snuff juice the length of the tent, each expectorated missile fired expertly into the small opening at the base of the stove.

Christmas Day I received my most unforgettable toy. Dad built me a shiny, silver freight train using a big coffee can for the engine and six pork and bean cans, five for freight cars and the last painted red for the caboose. With a long string, I pulled my prize over the Texas terrain certain that my father had given me the best present a boy could have. Christmas dinner was a treat, too: fried baloney, the first meat we'd had in weeks.

By January the creek had frozen and so had the tent. We had to have warmer housing and it would take a miracle to get it—and to prepare for the miracle, Dad worshiped as he knew best. He went junking. Somehow he scrounged two wheels, an axel, metal framing, a trailer hitch, and some end rolls of linoleum. Odd-shaped discards were brought back from the saw mill. From cars abandoned in the creek, he disassembled parts, sold them to the junkyard, and bought nails, screws, and other building essentials. Then, hammer in hand, he performed his magic. He built a house trailer from scratch.

That spring the saw mill hired Dad enough for gas money back to Unionville. Dad had learned his lesson: no more chasing fairs. No more southern starvation. We would confine ourselves to the relatively stable Midwest, which led us to the carnival years at the beginning of this story. We came off the road for me to go to school, and Dad put juke boxes in all of the bars. When World War II broke out, he chose battling mosquitoes instead of Germans and helped build the highway in Alaska with Uncle Bill and Uncle Joe.

And when he came back something terrible had happened to him.

CHAPTER 13

▼

HEROES RETURN; LOVED ONES DEPART

Dad stepped off the train a stranger. A bone-chilling wind blew that day in February, 1944, and appropriately so, for Dad had been mysteriously upset with Mom about more than the un-repaired juke boxes in the basement. He stayed out nights drinking heavily, and I dropped off to sleep long before he came home. But I guess Mom waited up, because that November 18th, John Joe Jackson, weighing nearly seven pounds, ended my reign as the only child. John one-upped me by being born in a hospital instead of a back bedroom, but he, too, was dubbed a cartoon character. Uncle Buck had called me Andy Gump. When baby John was presented to the family, the nurse had wetted his hair down and parted it in the middle—however, a few rebellious strands refused to recline. Grandpa Davis said his new grandson looked like Dagwood Bumstead. Again, Mom was not pleased.

Much happened in brother John's first year. America panicked when its father-president, Franklin Delano Roosevelt, died of a stroke. FDR had led us to victory over the Germans, but the Japanese refused to surrender, and as the war continued more and more of our servicemen died. My two favorite uncles were overseas—Uncle Cleo, Dad's younger brother, served in the army and Uncle Bill had joined the navy after returning from Alaska. Would the Japs kill them before giving up? New president Harry S. Truman ended the war and the worry. He dropped two bombs of unbelievable devastation on Japan. Our boys were coming home.

Uncle Bill looked like a walking train wreck. He had been back a week when he stumbled through our front door still in uniform. His navy blues were wrinkled and dirty like he'd slept in them a month and his once white sailor cap was a yellowish brown from spilled beer and who knows what. Mom sat him at the table and poured him some coffee. His face was unshaved and haggard, his hair matted, but it was his eyes that looked the worst. His famous, luminous, pool-blue eyes were an agony-ridden red, bleary from booze, crying, and no sleep. I hovered just outside the kitchen door as Uncle Bill stared down at the table and poured out his grief:

Aunt Kate had not waited for him. She had gotten lonely and spent a lot of time down at the Victory Bar, her mother's saloon. Tall, toothy Keith Steele, a Victory regular who had failed the draft physical, provided lots of attention. Uncle Bill had wondered why her letters grew fewer and less loving. On the way home from the Lucerne train station, his friends told him why. Kate had been running around with Keith Steele for months.

I ran out the front door crying and headed to the old barn in back, where I slumped in a far, dark corner sobbing my anger. How could any woman not wait for my Uncle Bill? This was the guy who at sixteen had captivated a train load of young nuns. I'd been to the Royal and seen the movie heart throbs, and there wasn't another man in all the world more charming, decent, and good-looking than my Uncle Bill. Aunt Kate must've gotten really lonely.

Then it came to me. Dad had been so different when he came back from Alaska because someone had written him about Aunt Kate's fooling around. That's why he'd been so sullen and had all but set up a cot at the tavern—he thought Mom had been fooling around, too. She hadn't; I would've known. Mom would've been getting all gussied up and coming home late or not at all. And the only man who came visiting while Dad was gone was Aunt Kate's pharmacist brother-in-law Dick Dickson—and his gassing the house with bug bombs didn't make for much of a romance.

Uncle Cleo walked through the front door smiling. He looked like a soldier on an army poster: pants with a razor crease; collar starched; tie neatly in place; cap at a jaunty angle. He had served in northern Germany dodging sniper fire while he laid telephone wire so generals could talk to one another. It had been a time of frozen fox holes, hunger, and exhaustion, but here he was, smiling a window wide and bearing gifts: two souvenirs from his great adventure, and they were both for me.

The first sent my mind whirling. It was a German officer's dress sword with a swastika crowning the handle. I immediately strapped the scabbard to my side and drew the sword. My imagination took flight. I had wrested the sword from the German captain who had captured me. He went for his Luger. Swish! Thrust! Got him! He lay in a pool of....

"It's not a toy," Dad said, interrupting my demise of the captain. "It's for looking at, right Uncle Cleo?" Uncle Cleo nodded, but gave me a wink that Dad didn't see. Then Uncle Cleo brought out a second gift: a German officer's pearl-handled .44 dress pistol. What a cannon. It was so heavy it took two hands to hold it out in front of me. The bullet chambers were huge. Dad brought out a 4.10 shotgun shell and it fit except for the cap. There were no bullets, which was well enough, because my fingers weren't strong enough to pull the trigger, and besides, the recoil would've knocked me to Kansas.

Wow! A German officer's sword and pistol. I had to show these beauties off. Dad shook his head, but I pleaded to at least show one friend the sword. He said okay, but I had to have it back in fifteen minutes. Cook, Hibbs, and Torrey all lived too far away, but Gerald Neighbors, a shy, big-eyed classmate of mine lived north down the hill. Lots of my friends said "ain't," but Gerald said "hain't," as in "I hain't allowed to go to the show." As I approached the back of his house, I stopped several feet short of the door, remembering his leathery, old father who looked at you like he was about two seconds from whacking you with a strap. I called from the middle of the backyard, and when Gerald came out I proudly patted the prize belted to my hip. He looked at the sword and when he saw the swastika his big eyes got bigger, and I swelled up about to burst. I knew Dad said not to, but I couldn't help myself; I drew the sword and brandished it over my head like I was Hot Stuff Almighty.

"S.S. troops!" I shouted and charged into the garden and whacked down a dozen corn stalks.

"Get the hell home!"

Gerald's father banged out the back screen door waving a broom like a club. I scrambled up the hill, and then stopped. I had dropped the sword. I looked back and Gerald's father was in the middle of the yard shouting and jabbing the broom in the air. After more cussing and shaking his fist, he went back into the house. A few moments later, Gerald rushed to the corn stalks, retrieved the sword, and placed it just beyond the edge of his father's property. Then with steps of lead he went back into the house. I rushed down, swooped up my precious gift and ran for home. As I neared the front door, I sheathed the sword and entered quietly. Dad and Uncle Cleo were at the kitchen table drinking beer and telling stories. Without a word, I went to my bedroom and tucked my treasure under some long underwear in my bottom dresser drawer.

Most days, that winter of 1945—my fourth grade year—I walked my new friend Rodge home from school on my way to carry in coal for Grandma Jackson. Roger Torrey lived by the tracks behind the power plant. Each time we entered his house, his mother, Gela, a dark, worn-looking woman, stood drenched in sweat, ironing a huge pile of other people's clothes while listening to *Just Plain Bill* on the radio. Some afternoons, Forest Rex, Rodge's always-angry step-father, came home early from driving cab. He'd survey whatever Rodge and I were doing—usually it was drawing pictures—then he'd fire off a bunch of chores for Rodge, and turn a less than pleased look in my direction. I hastened to Grandma's.

Dad had instructed Grandma to only pay me a nickel, but after I'd lugged the two buckets of coal the thirty feet from the coal shed to the house she always slipped me a dime. Grandma Jackson was one of the quietest, sweetest human beings I would ever know. A small lady with skin and eyes dark like Dad's, she had long, beautiful gray hair, which, when undone from its usual bun, fell far down her back. Her voice was soft and delivered not a word of harshness. Her strongest expletive was "Oh, foot!" as in "Oh, foot! I forgot to salt the soup." She took painstaking care of her mother, Great-Grandma Neighbors, who, bent and withered and nearly blind, spent her days chair-bound in the living room with a quilted blanket hugging her legs.

Grandma Jackson took care of me many times during the carnival years, spoiling me with homemade rhubarb pies baked in her black-iron, wood-burning stove. Even better than the pies were the warm, rolled cinnamon strips made from the left over dough. After putting Great-Grandma to bed, she would gather me onto her lap and by the light of the kerosene lamp rock me gently and read the comic page from the Kansas City Star. I loved *Dick Tracy* and *Mutt and Jeff,* but my favorite was *Lil' Abner* with its raw-boned dumb guys from a deep hill-billy country called Dogpatch.

One night she was rocking and reading when a loud knock came at the door. It was never locked, and she sweetly called, "Come in." The door swung open. Three huge, bearded men, completely in black from enormous clodhoppers to wide-brimmed hats, filled the doorway. I jumped off Grandma's lap and ran for the kitchen. *Lil' Abner's* hillbillies had come to get me. Grandma called me back to meet her brothers. Bill, Frank, and Ira lived south of Unionville in a dinky place called Pollock. They had butchered a few hogs and stopped by to leave Grandma some pork belly. Pork belly sounded like something you'd eat in Dog-patch.

When Great Grandma Neighbors died, she'd been living with Grandma Jackson in a little white house so decrepit that a Saint Bernard belch would've blown it down. There the wake was held. It was behind the kitchen door that Dad and my Uncles gathered. I tucked myself next to the iron stove for the ritual I knew to be forthcoming. Beer appeared on the kitchen table and the Jackson tales flowed like the Mississippi. They were funny and true, or close enough, and most were known by all present, which neither deterred nor shortened the telling one whit. The ladies had gathered with Grandma in the little box of a front room in an effort to maintain decorum, but the raw laughter beyond the kitchen door grew boisterous. When a pause came to open more beer, Uncle Buck told this story:

Everyone in Unionville knew the Ruth brothers. Harold, the sensible one, looked after his somewhat backward brother Joe who stuttered. One day some-one told Harold that his brother was getting real thick with a fast girl from Milan, a rough, blue-collar town south of Unionville. Harold rushed to his brother and asked about the rumor. Joe replied that he was so in love that he and the girl were getting married.

"Married?" Joe gasped. "Why, Joe, you idiot, that girl's slept with every man in Milan!"

Joe thought a moment and then said, "Well, M-M-Milan's not a very b-b-big town."

The uncles roared with laughter, not the least being Uncle Cliff, who released a falsetto shriek like a factory whistle. Cousin Mary Walker, a school teacher from Grandma's side of the family, rushed into the kitchen wagging her finger and scolding everyone in the room. Returning to Grandma, she apologized for the males' disrespect of Great-Grandma Neighbors. Grandma patted the school teacher's hand and replied, "Oh, foot, Mary. She's happy the boys are having a good time."

It was harmonized moaning, and I couldn't figure out where it was coming from. The family sat in a big room with a shiny, hardwood floor, and the voices of the Comstock brothers, Jimmy and John Newton, were wailing *Whispering Hope* like there wasn't any. I looked again at the body in the open casket, the first dead person I'd ever seen. It was supposed to be Grandpa Davis, but he looked real different. His body was too still; no smile graced this gaunt face covered with flesh-covered wax, the cheeks and mouth rubbed with rouge in a failed attempt to conceal the ravages of stomach cancer.

It was but two months previous that Grandpa had delighted in holding his newborn grandson, my brother Sam. When Doc Judd stuck his head into Mom's room at the Monroe Hospital and asked the name of the boy he'd just delivered, Dad announced it was Sam Lee Jackson.

Dad, feeling his oats, called out, "Oh, I'm being very worldly. I named my three sons after a colored man, a Jew, and a Chinaman who all used to lived in Unionville. Bill Ray was an old Negro who collected junk; John Joseph was a Jew who owned a men's clothing shop; and Sam Lee was a Chinaman who ran a laundry."

Everyone laughed, none louder than Grandpa. I had loved watching Grandpa laugh—his face would glow and he would nod his head as if to say laughing was the greatest thing in the world. But unlike the wake of Great Grandma Neighbors with its celebration of life from behind the kitchen door, here in Comstock's grandly decorated funeral parlor a hushed duet spoke of heaven's reward in the saddest of voices.

CHAPTER 14

▼

THE SHOESHINE BOY AND BIG JACK

Grandpa had worked hard all of his life, and had he lived a little longer, I think I would have made him proud of me. I know I was. At only nine years of age I had a job reeking prestige: shoeshine boy at Mutt Rouse's Barbershop.

It was Dad who got wind of the job and told me about it. I'd never shined a shoe in my life, but Dad said Mutt probably would teach me if he thought I really wanted the job.

"Oh, yeah!" I said. "Mutt's would be a neat place to work; practically the whole baseball team gets hair cuts there. Ask him if I can have the job."

"No, I'm not the one who's going to shine the shoes," Dad answered. "You need to ask him yourself."

I went down the next morning, a Friday, and looked through the big front window. Mutt and his helper Ed Jones were cutting hair and Mutt was stabbing the air with his scissors, all upset about the previous St. Louis Card's game. I edged into the shop and stood just inside the door until he peered at me over a bushy head of hair and asked, "Son? You want a haircut?"

I shook my head no and stood there like a mope. He clipped some more, then saw me studying the shoeshine chair to his left.

"You want to ask me something?"

"I can learn to do it!" I blurted.

Mutt quit clipping. "You're Tramp's boy, aren't you?" I nodded. He went back to cutting hair, and I figured he'd turned me down. When I started for the door, he looked up and said, "Tell you what, Tramp's boy. I'll buy all your supplies and teach you to shine. As a trade, you sweep up all the hair and fire the wood stove for the water heater. Deal?"

"Deal!"

After closing time, Mutt brought out shoe polish, brushes, rags, and other supplies and showed me how to shine shoes: brush off the dust; dab on the wax; brush again; hold the shine rag at both ends and make that baby fly over the shoes. Finally, apply liquid polish to the outer edge of the soles and heels. I shined Mutt's shoes three times and started on the fourth when he said, "Okay, Bill Ray, come in tomorrow and we'll give you a try." I clapped my hands and started for the door.

"Oh, one more thing," he said. "Folks like a little show. You'll get extra tips if you hum a song and pop the rag once in a while."

I showed up at eight o'clock that Saturday morning, set up all of my supplies, and then sat across from the shine chair. Customers came in, but I took to staring at the floor, too backward to tell them what I was there for. About nine o'clock Mutt pointed his scissors at me and said, "Gentlemen, this is my new shine boy. Trained him myself. If you want a shine, it's only ten cents." A chubby guy in his early twenties had just gotten out of Mutt's chair. He grinned at me and said, "I got a big date tonight and I'd like to impress this girl. Gimme a shine." He climbed into the elevated chair, and I did it just like Mutt showed me, including humming a bouncy version of *In the Mood*. I popped the rag once in a while and when I finished, popped it twice and looked up at my customer for approval. He beamed a smile and lifted his pant legs for a better look. The smile left his face. He was wearing white socks, and I had left a brown circle on them just above his shoe tops. I swallowed and stared at my art work. This guy is going on a date and I had just put what looked like pig poop around his ankles. I looked at Mutt. Mutt looked very unhappy.

But the chubby guy patted my head and said, "That's all right, kid, this girl's into fashion. I'll just tell her brown ringed socks is the latest thing goin'." He grinned and gave me a dime plus a nickel tip for "all the extra polish." Thank God my first customer had a great sense of humor.

Men gathered at Mutt's to talk sports. Want to know why our boys blew it last night? You got the straight skinny next morning at Mutt's. Even years after I shined shoes there, Mutt delighted every male in town by featuring the first television set most of us had seen. A towering antenna on the barber shop roof drew males inside to watch the Saint Louis Cardinals play. Actually, it was more like watching snowmen in a snowstorm. Was that Stan-the-Man Musial at bat? Did he swing? Is he running? Turn on the radio so we can tell what's going on.

Mutt got his name because folks said he looked like the skinny, big-nosed character in the comic strip, *Mutt and Jeff.* His brother was called Fat, because he was. Mutt and Fat used to have a barbershop together, but they were sports nuts and got into horrendous shouting matches while cutting hair. Customers bailed out of their chairs to avoid getting scalped while Mutt and Fat turned purple arguing who was the best golfer, boxer, or baseball player. One day Fat left fuming and moved his haircutting forty miles away to Kirksville. Mutt opened a new shop on the east side of the Square and replaced Fat with a big bathtub.

The tub was housed within a thin plywood cubicle in the back of the shop. For a quarter, a man could enter this sanctuary and bob around in soap bubbles for twenty minutes, an indulgence of great appeal to truck drivers making a pit stop and farmers with no running water on the place. One day, tall, awkward Slim Robinson came in for a bath. Young Slim was a painfully shy bachelor who, if a girl spoke to him, turned tomato red and stared off as if something really important was happening five blocks away. Slim paid Mutt his quarter, went into the cubicle and shut the door. A short while later two ladies bent on saving beauty shop money came into the shop to have their hair bobbed. They sat just a few feet away from the bath cubicle waiting for Mutt's tonsorial attention.

Suddenly, Slim crashed through the cubicle wall and rolled to a buck-naked stop in front of the two ladies, who jumped to their feet and ran shrieking out the door. Later, Mutt would chuckle and say, "Slim slipped on the soap and became my floor show."

Dad always said, "A fool and his money are soon parted." And I proved it by spending most of my shoeshine earnings on Bazooka bubble gum and Captain Marvel comic books. When I ran low of either, a run to Herrick's Drugstore replenished my supply. On my way I'd peer through the Victory Bar's plate glass window to catch a glimpse of my hero, Big Jack Burns, who, at six foot five, was a giant among the elfin citizenry of Putnam County.

Big Jack, a bouncer by occupation, threw bad guys out of the Casa Loma, a rough roadhouse west of town. Hibbs, Torrey, and I thought he was the strongest man alive. I once out superheroed Cook in front of my friends by choosing to be Big Jack over his Superman. Cook, asserting oldest kid rights, always got first pick, which invariably was The Man of Steel, who could fly and beat up everybody. But this day I ingeniously countered Cook by yelling that I was "Big Jack

Burns, toughest man in town!" Hibbs and Torrey cheered my brilliance. Superman was pretend; Big Jack was *real.*

Looking through the window, I saw I was in luck; Big Jack had settled on his usual stool near the far end of the bar and was in quiet conversation with the man on his right. Someone brushed by me and entered the tavern. It was Freddy Aikens, a small, whiny man known for his mooching.

I watched as Freddy took the empty stool on Big Jack's left. Freddy said hello or something. Big Jack gave a nod and turned back to his friend. Freddy kept jabbering at Big Jack. Big Jack ignored him. Finally, Freddy leaned closer and tugged on Big Jack's sleeve. Bad timing. The tug occurred just as Big Jack was taking a sip from his glass and beer slopped all over his lap. The giant set his glass down and stood full height. He grabbed Freddy with both hands, lofted him high over his head and carried him to the front door. Not bothering with the latch, he kicked the door open, walked into the street and threw Freddy onto the pavement. Then Big Jack Burns jumped on little Freddy Aikens with both feet.

Two weeks later, Freddy, wrapped in bandages from head to waist, limped into Mutt's for a shave. Mutt said it was like shaving a mummy.

CHAPTER 15

▼

FIGHTING, FISHING, DRAWING, ACTING

Fifth grade meant fighting. Fight or lose face. It was the code. You could huff and bluff and still not actually fight, but if someone swung at you, you had better swing back or your tough-guy standing crumbled in the catcalls.

One afternoon recess, hot-headed Billy Fowler—Fowler the Scowler—slid into second base and thought I'd tagged him too hard. He came up swinging, so I swung back. He crouched and punched me in the stomach, and I pounded him in the forehead, which banged my knuckles something fierce and had no effect on him whatsoever. Cries of "Fight! Fight!" rang out. All the boys on the school ground encircled us, yelling for blood. Over the top of Fowler's head I saw Miss Hunt plowing through the crowd like a Sherman tank.

Normally, grade school discipline was a male teacher's domain, but Seventh Grade's Rollie Timmons appeared too prissy to command an ice cream social. Not so fifth grade's Miss Hunt, an all-terrain tank who felt no fear. Grabbing Fowler by the scruff of his neck and me by the ear, she dragged us to the office. After barking a lecture, she suggested we apologize to each other. We stared and glared. Miss Hunt's eyes slowly shifted from us to the black metal cabinet in the far corner. We knew what resided behind its doors, the punishment every kid in school knew about: Old Betsy, the long, wooden paddle with the half-dollar holes to increase the sting. Fowler and I immediately exchanged heart-felt regrets over any grievance we may have caused each other.

Despite her Spartan discipline, Miss Hunt had a great sense of humor, often cutting class short to perform her impersonation of Minnie Pearl, the famous Grand Old Opry star. Wearing a lady's hat with the price tag dangling from the back, Miss Hunt would emerge from the cloak room grinning broadly and proclaim:

"Hooooowdy! I'm so proud to be here!"

We were to repeat that catch-phrase throughout our lives.

When the laughter died down from her greeting, Miss Hunt launched into a monologue about her "beau," Red. We all knew that Red Bowman, who liked to tip a few, was her boy friend, and her made-up stories about their dates sent the room full of ten-year-olds into hysterics.

But did this comedic kindness steer us from trouble? Unfortunately not. Within a week of the ball tagging fracas, Fowler, me, and practically every boy in the class, even the proper J.C. Shelton, engaged in a wild, smack-somebody fight in the cloak room. Miss Hunt waded into the frenzy, grabbed ears, noses and necks, and hurled the insurgents into the class room.

Glorious leader Hibbs was swinging both fists like a fighting machine when Miss Hunt came up behind him and grabbed the back of his shirt collar. Hibbs turned with a cocked left, ready to cream his attacker. Luckily for him, he checked the punch. Miss Hunt grabbed him by the ears, lifted him off his feet, lugged him to her desk, and plopped him on top of it like a centerpiece.

You didn't mess with Miss Hunt.

Dad was heading east that spring morning to collect on his juke boxes, which meant he'd be passing by Blackbird Creek; so Rodge and I quickly dug up some night crawlers, grabbed our cane poles, and hitched a ride with him. He let us out at the bridge, saying he wished he could join us, and I believed him. He'd taught me how to "lazy fish," and we'd done a lot of it. Dad didn't believe in racing around lakes in a boat and thrashing the water with store-bought lures. You fished on a bank sitting under a shade tree; casually dropped in a line with a plump night crawler on a hook; and then maybe watched your bobber when you weren't watching doves dart though the trees or imagining faces in fluffy clouds.

The Blackbird's banks were muddy from recent rain and Rodge and I slogged a good fifty yards from the bridge before we found an area dry enough for bank fishing. The treasure in Blackbird was its bullheads, kind of a midget catfish. We selected individual spots separated by a dense clump of trees and tossed in our lines. After about an hour without a bite, I got bored and heaved a big mud clump into the water.

"Help! Rodge! I can't swim!" I yelled.

Rodge charged through the trees like a bug-eyed rhinoceros.

"April Fool!" I yelled, and laughed like crazy.

Rodge growled, "It's not April!" and bulled back through the trees.

Giggling at my cleverness, I returned to watching my bobber. After a few minutes, there was a big *ka-splash* on the other side of the trees.

For a couple of seconds there was no sound. Then quietly:

"Bill ..."

"What?"

"I've fallen in."

"Yeah, sure. Just face it Torrey, you got fooled."

More silence, then:

"Bill ..."

"What?"

"... I really did. I fell in the creek."

"Oh, can it, Torrey. I gotcha good. Man, you shoulda seen your face."

"No, listen ... I can't swim."

"Of course you can swim. Everybody can swim."

"I never learned, Bill. You'd best get over here. I'm ... going under."

I threw my pole down.

"Okay, but if you're not drowning, you're gonna wish you were!"

I pushed through the trees and there was Rodge, bubbling like a hippo, his eyes just above the water. I grabbed a fallen tree limb and poked it toward him. He grabbed on with both hands and I pulled him onto the bank.

"Why didn't you yell?" I yelled. "Why didn't you thrash around?"

Rodge looked sheepish.

"Well, I was told that if you thought you were drowning you should stay calm."

"Not like a petrified 'possum for cripe's sake! You gotta get people's attention!"

"Oh."

He hung his clothes on a tree limb, and by noon they were dry, and we had three bullheads on the stringer.

"Wish we could eat 'em here," I said.

Rodge's eyes brightened.

"We can. My grandfather just lives about a mile from here. I'll hike over, grab a skillet and stuff and be back in no time."

When he got back, I'd caught another bullhead. In minutes we built a fire, cleaned the fish, seasoned them with salt and pepper, and had them floating in a skillet of popping grease. When they were brown and crispy, we sat in the cool shade of the trees and with our teeth slowly pulled the tender meat from the bones, chewing and smiling and wiping grease from our chins in pure happiness.

On this Missouri spring afternoon, lounging by the bubbling water of Blackbird Creek, with birds warbling overhead, and the tender white meat of catfish dissolving in our mouths, we were two ten-year-old boys who couldn't imagine life could get any better.

At age eleven, Rodge and I discovered we really liked to draw, so we decided to become the first sixth graders ever to draw a world-famous comic strip. However, drawing together proved to be a problem. Rodge drew highly detailed *Prince Valiant*-looking scenes and I drew dumb-simple *Little Lulu* stuff. The combination of styles looked like we cranked the strip out at the local bar. So, we settled on drawing separate strips at the same time.

For our first efforts, we drew real people we knew. For my first choice, I selected grumpy Jay Freeborn, the owner of a local, fly-infested restaurant. He was a caricaturist's delight: fat and bald, with wire-rimmed glasses topping an enormous nose, and a moustache bristling like a hair brush. No matter what else happened in the strip, he always served pies swarming with flies.

Rodge drew a prissy, well-tailored man with wavy black hair and a pencil-thin moustache. For the artist's protection, the character remained unnamed, but any one could see that Rodge was drawing Rollie Timmons, seventh grade's fussy, bone-skinny teacher.

The comic strip *Joe Palooka* inspired my next creation. Palooka was an improbable hero, a boxing champion who hated to hit people, even said, "tch, tch," when he knocked them out. My boxer couldn't wait to hit people; in fact, he was deaf and came out swinging before the bell rang. Most folks in Unionville pronounced the word "deaf" as "deef," so I named him "Deefy;" and when he charged his opponents too early, his handlers called him back, so I made his full name "Deefy Comeback." I was so proud of myself.

Our sixth grade teacher, Miss Hill, an angular, dark haired lady of artistic bent, directed all the school's stage productions with the help of her friend, Mae Hunt. Faye Hill was married, but we always called her "miss." On this one particular day she glided into class beaming as if she'd just invented ice cream.

"Class!" she exclaimed, "Last night I had the most marvelous idea. Want to know what it was?"

"Yes, Miss Hill," responded Maribeth Torrey—Maribeth was one of Rodge's cousins and always knew the right answers.

"Thank you, Maribeth. Class, this is so exciting; our next stage performance will be created entirely by ..." here she flung her arms open wide, "... *you!*"

Breathing stopped. Bodies slumped in chairs, even Maribeth's.

"Does anyone have any ideas?" she gushed, scanning the room. Girls examined their pencil boxes. Boys slid to the floor. But not this boy; my hand waved like the start flag at the Demolition Derby.

"Bill Ray, you have a suggestion?"

"Yes. A play about Deefy Comeback!"

"Deefy who-what?" Miss Hill's nose crinkled noticeably.

Giggles from the class.

"Deefy Comeback, a cartoon character of mine. See, he's a fighter who's what people called 'deef.' He's always coming out before the bell rings, and his trainers yell, "Deefy! Come back!"

"How terribly quaint," Miss Hill said.

Seeing her interest, I rushed on, making up the play as I went.

"It's a championship fight. Madison Square Garden is packed. The ref introduces the fighters: first the challenger, then Deefy, the champ. Deefy starts swinging. They drag him back to his stool. The bell rings, Deefy rushes out, and the other guy knocks him out of the ring. He climbs back in and knocks the other guy out of the ring and wins the fight! It's called ... it's called ... *The Comeback of Deefy Comeback!*"

The class erupted in cheers.

Miss Hill stared at me as if I'd told her that Winston Churchill was going to perform the hula. Nervously her eyes swept the room, but not another hand was raised. She gave a sigh.

"All right, we'll do Bill Ray's Deefy What's-his-name this Friday. Bill Ray, you need to complete the story, cast the parts, and begin rehearsal."

Complete the story? I'd just told it to her.

After school I gathered the guys on the front steps for casting. Of course no one could play the lead like its creator, so I had to be Deefy. Torrey volunteered as announcer and referee; Bramhall and Hibbs agreed to be my corner men; and Pollock and Carr would back up my opponent. I'd hoped that Pollock, he of the notorious wind-mill punch, would be the other fighter, but neither he nor anyone else wanted to lose the fight. I pleaded with them, playing up my opponent like he was another Jack Dempsey. We'd call him Bam Bam O'Toole, 'cause he had dynamite in both fists. Bam Bam would be the toughest fighter Deefy ever faced and—just then I had a spectacular idea—and he would give Deefy a black eye!

"How would he do that?" asked a voice outside the immediate circle. It was Fowler the Scowler.

Thinking fast I said, "Well, when I get knocked out of the ring, I'll stick my head behind the side curtain and Bramhall or Hibbs can smear black shoe polish around my eye. Bramhall and Hibbs murmured approval.

Fowler gave a little grin. "Okay," he said, "I'll be Bam Bam."

That Friday in assembly, Miss Hill announced in the crispest of diction that the presentation would be a one-act play, *The Comeback of Deefy Comeback*, written by the sixth grade's Bill Ray Jackson. Of course I hadn't written a word, hadn't even held rehearsal, because Fowler said he knew his part and didn't need any practice.

The curtain parted, and the audience burst into laughter. I hadn't wanted the girls to see how skinny I was, so I had Fowler and me wear bathing suits over our long underwear. We looked like fight night in Dogpatch. Torrey stepped to center stage and introduced the challenger and then the champion and brought us to the center of the ring. He instructed us to shake hands and, at the bell, come out fighting. While we were shaking hands, Fowler gave me a big wink. *What was that for?* We returned to our corners and I immediately rushed back mid-ring and swung leather. True to the story, my handlers called, "Deefy! Come back!" and dragged me to my corner. The play began beautifully.

Torrey rang a cowbell, and I noticed the first deviation from the script. Fowler rushed across the stage and hit me square on the nose. We wore big, sixteen-ounce gloves, but that smarted. I backed away and gave him a *what's-going-on?* He grinned and threw a roundhouse right that ricocheted off my ear. He wasn't faking the fight at all. The audience cheered and stomped as Fowler threw a flurry of lefts and rights, which I avoided by peddling backwards. I decided to cut the play a little short and, although he missed his next punch, I toppled backwards, my head coming to rest behind the side curtain with my feet still on stage.

"Shoe polish! Shoe polish!" I hissed.

Hibbs and Bramhall panicked. They couldn't remember where they'd left the can.

Torrey counted, "One! ... Two!"

Bramhall found the polish can on a window sill, but couldn't get the lid off. You needed to stick something in a slot and twist it.

"Three! … Four!" intoned Torrey.

Hibbs fished a nickel from his pocket, but it was too fat to fit in the slot.

"Five!"

Torrey slowed the count.

"… S-s-six!"

In desperation Hibbs pried the lid off with his teeth.

"Seven!" Torrey pounded on the curtain for me to get up.

"… Eight!"

Bramhall scooped out a glob of black polish and smeared it on my right eye.

"Nine! …"

I scrambled to my feet. The audience whooped its delight—the black eye was a hit. Trouble was, the polish wasn't around my eye, it was in it, blinding me, and it stung like Billy Hell. Wham! Bam! Fowler hit me with a left and a right. I waved my right hand over my head signaling that this was the big knockout punch. I threw it. Fowler dodged, laughed, lowered his head, and punched like a trip hammer in heat. I was so busy blocking punches I couldn't throw any.

I looked desperately at Torrey, but he was frozen stupid by the pounding I was taking. Then Hibbs and Bramhall waved at me from the curtain behind Fowler's corner. I lowered my head, put my gloves together, and shoved Fowler across the stage and through the curtain. Hibbs and Bramhall jumped him, took him to the floor and held him there. Having come out of his stupor, Torrey jabbered a fast ten count and raised my hand in victory. The curtain closed, and the audience whistled and stomped and roared, "More! More!"—meaning, I suspect, more shoe polish in the other eye.

Quieting the room, Miss Hill thanked all who had participated in the assembly, her final comment being directed at me. With a feeble smile, she observed that it had been "a most *original* work."

Miss Hill, with a suspiciously endearing smile, asked me to stay after class. When the bell rang, Hibbs and Bramhall snickered, "Teacher's pet, teacher's pet," and smirked their way out the door. Once the room had emptied, she showed me a flyer on her desk about a children's talent contest at the high school auditorium in two weeks.

She tapped the flyer and said, "I want you in that contest."

"As Deefy Comeback?" I asked.

"No-no-no," she said. "Not as Deefy. Someone very different … an old river-boat captain."

"Miss Hill, I don't know anything about rivers or boats."

"You will," she said, and opened a flowery-looking book to a place she'd marked.

"Poetry?" I gasped.

I glanced toward the door. Hibbs and Bramhall probably were outside peeing down their legs.

"I can't get up in front of people and recite poetry." I started for the door.

She clutched my arm.

"It's not poetry, exactly. It's a 'reading' titled *Jim Bledsoe*." She took me by the shoulders and looked at me intently.

"Bill Ray, they may call your father, Tramp, but you can rise above that. You're going to get on that stage and you're going to make people laugh and you're going to make them cry and you're going to win first prize."

Rise above what? Dad being called Tramp didn't seem such a bad thing. But I liked the making people laugh part. So far all I'd done was the Deefy thing, and then it was the goof-ups that got the laughs.

"How do I make people laugh on purpose?" I asked.

She handed me the book. "Memorize the reading as quickly as possible. I'll teach you how to say the words so people will laugh. Start on it tonight, we only have two weeks.

That night in my room I opened the book and read the first line:

Well, no, I can't tell you where he lives, because he don't live, you see.

Good Lord! There wasn't anything funny about that. It's about a dead guy. What had I gotten into? I read the whole thing and it was a sorrowful mess: a captain crashes his steamboat and gets burned up. That's a lot of grins.

Well, after three days I'd memorized the dumb thing and told Miss Hill so; and she began rehearsal first thing after school, facing me toward the empty desk-chairs like they were the audience.

"Ladies and gentlemen," she announced, "Bill Ray Jackson reciting *Jim Bledsoe*."

Embarrassed by how dull the poem was, I powered through it like a buzz saw. When I'd finished, she said:

"You don't think much of the words, do you?"

I looked out the window. "They're okay, but … kinda preachy."

"Not as much fun as Deefy."

"No. They laughed at Deefy."

"They'll laugh at this."

"Naw, the guy dies at the end. Nobody's gonna laugh at that."

"You're right. They'll cry at the end. But along the way, they'll laugh frequently and listen intently to a compelling story. Now, first I want you to recite the reading in an old man's voice."

Great! A character! I wouldn't have to do it like a dumb kid. I thought about the old men that I knew, the ones who were kinda funny. There was Poker Bill, the town barfly, but, naw, I'd have to end every line with a high pitched giggle. That'd get old. Maybe Darryl Freeborn, the brother of the guy who served pies with flies. Darryl always talked real loud like he was running for office, which he usually was, but that'd mean I'd have to bellow the whole thing. Then it came to me: *Gabby Hayes*, the raspy-voiced old coot in the Roy Rogers movies. I spoke the first line in a wheezing voice from the back of my throat and through my nose.

"Well, no, I can't tell you where he lives ..."

"Don't say "can't," say "*cain't.*""

Cain't? I couldn't believe it. My teacher was having me mispronounce words.

"Well, no, I *cain't* tell you where he lives, because ..."

"*Whar. Becaze.*"

"... *whar* he lives, *becaze* he don't live, ya see."

"Perfect!" exclaimed Miss Hill. "Now pretend you're chewing tobacco and do a fake spit every once in a while."

"You want me to *spit* while I'm doing this?"

"A *fake* spit."

I remembered the sound Mrs. Spurger made in Texas when she spat into our stove.

"... *becaze* he don't live, ya see ... *sput!*"

"Perfect! Now, when you do the spitting part, make sure you lean into the microphone."

"Microphone?"

"The one that will be on stage," she answered sweetly.

I almost swallowed my fake spit. "Microphones make you sound so *loud*," I protested.

"But it will be of immense help for the spits and when your voice goes soft," she replied.

"I'm going to speak softly?" I asked.

"At the end."

That afternoon, Miss Hill gave me one of the most instructive drama lessons I would ever receive. She brought that whole dead bunch of words to life; took me line by line through every inflection, every pause, every whisper and shout, and, yes, every *sput* in the whole darn thing.

The evening of the talent contest, I watched next door from our porch as contestants and their families streamed into the auditorium. Parents had their darlings dressed in their finest: boys in white shirts and dark ties; girls in gauzy, pastel dresses. I went inside and put on a worn, checkered shirt of Grandpa Davis's and a pair of Dad's dingy khaki pants, rolled up the pant legs, and tied the waist with a rope. Then I glued on the frizzy white moustache and goatee Miss Hill had made for me. She also had given me a sea captain's cap and a bamboo cane. Mom said I looked cute. Dad said I looked like Popeye's grandfather. They both promised to be in the audience, and I so wanted to impress them, especially Dad, since he'd been in the tent shows.

"Stay in character," Dad called as I hurried out the door. Putting weight on my cane, I hobbled to the contest.

The competition's adoring relatives packed the auditorium, which was also the school gymnasium; no one in town had passed up the opportunity to see their little Jimmy or Suzy perform. The stage seemed immense, easily five times larger than the one in grade school, and I would be standing in the middle of it. Alone. A lady official looked at my attire with raised eyebrows and took me to the contestant's waiting room: a kitchen area near the stage.

Sitting next to the sink, I silently repeated the poem and eyed my competition. Now I realized what the raised eyebrows meant. Everyone in the room was a dazzler: the boys, dress-suit handsome and reeking of Rose Hair Oil; the girls, perky-pretty in dresses and bows and bright red lipstick.

And I looked like some old wino you crossed the street to avoid.

Each time the backstage door swung open, it brought sounds from the stage: high, incredibly sustained operatic notes; trumpets machine-gunning through *Flight of the Bumblebee*; furious crescendos from keyboards; and always, always, thunderous applause that seemingly would never stop. I scrunched lower in my chair, wishing I could disappear down the sink; wishing I were a singer or trombone player or anything but a kid reciting a poem.

Then it was time.

The arched-eyebrow lady appeared at the door and beckoned me to follow. Backstage was black as a coal mine, with a sliver of light at the bottom of the curtain that separated you from the audience. I heard three teen-age girls on the other side concluding *Drinking Rum and Coca Cola.* Their husky voices sounded real sexy. When the applause finally ended, the whistling continued until the announcer quieted the crowd.

The announcer was Don Melton, the bald, glib insurance salesman who introduced the acts at the fair.

"Thank you, Melissa, Melinda, and Meribelle," he boomed. "Didn't I hear you girls on the radio last night?"

The crowd tittered.

"And now a change of pace. Here is Bill Ray Jackson with a reading titled *Jim Bledsoe.*"

Thudding my cane in front of me, I shuffled the five hundred miles to the microphone. I looked over the audience for Miss Hill, Mom, Dad, any support I could find, but the spotlight blinded me, and I stood alone facing a black cavern of silent, unseen critics.

The reading told about a rough-living riverboat captain who races his old *Prairie Bell* down the Mississippi against the newer *Moving Star.* The *Prairie Bell* wins, but in the effort its engine bursts into flames and threatens to consume ever crew member aboard. The captain holds his boat against the shore so that the crew can escape; but gives up his life in doing so.

Oh, yeah, this is going to be real funny.

Summoning my best Gabby Hayes, I leaned into the microphone and wheezed:

"No, I cain't tell ya whar he lives, 'caze he don't live, ya see! ... *sput!*"

Laughter.

"Whar ya been fer the last three yars that ya hain't heerd folks tell ... sput!"

More laughter.

I had 'em going; I rolled my tongue in my cheek like I had a real wad.

"... how Jimmy Bledsoe passed in his checks the night of the *Prairie Bell....* *Sput! Sput!*"

Cheers and whistles.

The audience roared delight at every sput, even at lines that didn't have a sput. I followed Miss Hill's instructions explicitly, eventually dropping the sputs and lowering my voice in admiration of the coarse, awkward captain's dedication to his crew. I gained momentum recounting the race, and when the fire burst out I'd hit fever pitch, shouting how the captain nosed the *Prairie Bell* to the shoreline and called:

I'll keep 'er nozzle agin' the bank 'til the last galoot's ashore!"

The audience fell silent.

In a hushed voice I recapped how fancy folks had derided the captain's wayward living ... then, even more softly, and with emphasis, I leaned to the microphone and delivered the final line paced exactly as Miss Hill had instructed:

"... but Christ ain't gonna be too hard ... on a man ... that died ... for men."

Silence.

Not a peep.

Not a nothing.

Then the place blew like a blast furnace. Cheers, whistles, stomps and shouts rocked the building. I shaded my brow and saw tears glistening in the eyes of the people on the front row. *Miss Hill, you wizard, you were right!*

Did I win first prize? No, I didn't. I came in second.

The judges gave first prize to a six-year-old ballerina named Suzy.

When I got home, Dad was tinkling something on the piano. Mom rushed out of the kitchen, gave me a big hug, and told me I'd been wonderful. I beamed and looked expectantly at Dad. He paused, looked toward me and gave a nod; then returned to his playing. A nod was high praise from Dad. I went to bed happy.

CHAPTER 16

▼

THE LOVE LETTER

I blame the whole thing on Torrey. He's the one who got Hibbs and me reading *Tom Sawyer*; well, Hibbs didn't read it, but we told him about it. We didn't have any caves or crazed Indians, but we could do that part about the oath being signed in blood. The main thing was that the oath be important enough to warrant sticking a pin in your finger.

Being in the sixth grade, we settled on the obvious: the oath had to be about girls, about not liking them, I mean. Girls worked this sneaky magic on you. They cast mysterious spells by saying your name real soft, looking at you with big saucer eyes, and batting their eyelashes—sneaky tricks that turned your tongue into a washrag and your feet into suitcases. And after you were all stumbly and mumbly, they sent you off with a little smile so that later you would dream about kissing them … and stuff.

Obviously we had to protect ourselves, so one night when my folks were out, Torrey and Hibbs came over, and we went into my bedroom and formed a new club, The Women Haters' Club. To make it a proper ceremony, I turned out the lights and lit a candle. Torrey spread some parchment-looking paper on the floor, I got some pencils, and the three of us lay down and prepared to write.

"This has to be really well written," I said. I nodded at Torrey. "You start."

Rodge moved his pencil to the parchment and froze.

"Uh, maybe we need to get some help. My cousin, Maribeth, is real good at cursive."

"Maribeth curses?" Hibbs asked.

"Not "curses," "cursive," you know, handwriting. She gets 'Excellent' all the time."

"She gets 'Excellent' in blowing her nose," I said. "Yeah, she'd know some high-falutin' words to use."

"Hold it," Hibbs interrupted. "You guys are talking about getting a girl to write our women hater's oath?"

"Oh, I said, "… see what you mean."

Torrey and I took turns writing how treacherous girls were, and Hibbs just grunted and nodded his head. I read the final line:

"Therefore, because girls are always working their tricky stuff, we hereby swear to have nothing to do with all females forever!"

Hibbs quit making hand shadows on the wall.

"What about our mothers? I like mine."

We agreed we all liked our mothers, so I added, "… except for our mothers."

It was done. In the candle's flickering light, we each pricked a finger with a safety pin, dipped a toothpick in the tiny red puddle we each produced, and signed our names in blood. Mr. Twain would've been proud.

We returned to school the next day smiling and winking at each other, confident that our new armor protected us against any sorcery the girls might pull. Not to worry. They didn't even look at us; they were busy skipping rope and whispering secrets. Days passed without the slightest coo, eye flutter or smile. The club languished and was near demise when tall, bow-in-the-hair Natalie Tutt shocked it to life. She invited me to her birthday party. Playground buzz had it that only the better scrubbed, well-behaved kids made the cut. Then why had I received one of the little engrave cards?

The answer came while I was standing at the urinal in the boys' restroom. Next to me was Gerald Dean Carr, whose sole purpose in life was to know every little hushy secret in the whole school. Out of the side of his mouth, he confided that Natalie had a crush on me. I was dumbfounded. Girls didn't like me. But, there was no denying that she did do that big-eyed thing at me a lot. Very well, I accepted my duty. I informed my fellow women haters that I would attend the party strictly as a spy—reporting back any female bewitchment a foot. Hibbs and Torrey looked at me suspiciously, and Hibbs asked point blank:

"You're not going to do any kissy stuff, are you?"

"Scouts honor," I said, making a small cross on my chest with my finger.

"You're not a scout and you're not Catholic," Torrey said. "Swear it on the oath."

Having been made Keeper of the Oath, I kept it in my hip pocket. I fished it out.

"Put it over your heart," Torrey ordered.

"Promise no kissing, no hugging, no *nothin',* " Hibbs said.

Holding the sacred parchment to my chest, I declared, "In the name of The Women Haters' Club and all that is holy, I swear no kissing, hugging ... or anything."

Hibbs folded the paper and put it under my shirt.

"When you go, pin the oath over your heart."

Natalie answered the door smiling good manners and ushered me into the Tutt's apartment, which to a kid who'd lived in a tent, looked like it came out of Rockefeller's mansion: plush furniture, fancy lamps, velvety curtains. Natalie's mother and father appeared by her side sipping dainty cups of tea. They told me how nice it was that I could attend their daughter's "birth anniversary" and moved on. I held out my present, a dime-store brush and comb in a brown paper sack tied with red yarn. Natalie thanked me and deposited my gift on a dark mahogany coffee table with packages wrapped in shiny red and gold and tied in satin bows. Pointing to soft drinks and cookies on a long table across the room, she excused herself with a smile and went to answer the door.

The place was filled with kids I knew. The boys were at the table devouring cookies, the girls scattered around in little groups, looking like they wanted the boys to drop the cookies and pay some attention to them. I patted my heart. With oath in place, I stood combat ready for any devious ploy they might pull. I joined Pollock and Carr, who were each downing a cookie about every ten seconds, and tried to catch up by eating the big ones.

I maintained in fine stead until I saw her in the far corner—Dorothy, Rodge's other cousin—the one girl at school whose big brown eyes bewitched me right out of my socks. I hadn't told Hibbs or Torrey, but I was convinced she secretly hypnotized me during recess. *Cripes,* she even had me thinking about her during dodge ball! Quickly, I reached inside my shirt and patted the oath.

Natalie's mother announced that Natalie would now open her presents. She opened my present first and made a fuss over how much she needed a new brush and comb. I wanted Dorothy to look at me, so I said in a loud voice that I'd swiped them from the Queen of Sheba. Natalie laughed. So did others. Dorothy didn't. She was busy whispering to her pale girlfriend Patty Davis. During the games, I acted real goofy hoping Dorothy would notice me. When everyone bobbed for apples, I howled like a wolf and stuck my head way under water for as long as I could hold my breath. When I came up with an apple clenched in my teeth, Dorothy and Patty were across the room putting on their coats and telling Natalie what a nice time they'd had.

Devastated, I stared at the door as Natalie closed it. Without a word, without a look, without even acknowledging that I existed, Dorothy had plied her magic and filled my mind. I felt under my shirt for the oath. I found it floating in the apple tank.

Reporting to my fellow women haters, I lied in my teeth, saying nothing of Dorothy's overpowering spell and how I'd walked home wobble-legged and thrashed all night like I was drowning. No, I said that, as expected, all the girls had giggled and wiggled and winked, but I had scorned their silliness and buried myself in the cookies. Then I quickly changed the subject.

"Guess who wasn't at the party," I said.

Hibbs glanced at Torrey and said, "We weren't."

"No, but you guys get invited to parties. You were at Shelton's Halloween party. Who never gets invited to *any* parties?"

Torrey raised a finger. "Clarence Eckles."

Hibbs stuck up two fingers. "Donald Summers."

"Right," I answered. "Summers, Eckles ... *any* Eckles ... Gerald Neighbors, Delbert Jacobs—guys who never get invited because they're poor."

"We're poor," said Torrey.

"Yeah, but they're *really* poor," I said.

Torrey grimaced. "But have you seen Clarence's ears? He's got Victory Gardens growing in there."

Hibbs snorted. "And Summers pooped in class, remember?"

"Well, he couldn't help it," I said. "And what's a little ear dirt or bathroom accident? It's not right these guys don't get invited to things. So, how 'bout this? The club throws a party and invites everyone who never gets invited to anything—no girls, of course.

"No, of course not," said Torrey.

While Mom fixed supper that evening, I asked her about having the party.

"When?" she asked.

"This coming Thursday."

"Your Dad's band is playing out of town Thursday, and I want to be with him. I need you to baby sit your little brothers."

My little brothers: Johnny and Sammy. Johnny, heading toward three, I could play with. However, Sammy, at nine months, had, to my mind, but one purpose in life: fill his britches. I pleaded for a reprieve, reminding Mom that Friday was the last day of school. The party would be a sort of celebration, and Rodge and Hibbs and I wanted to invite guys who never got asked to anything.

"What guys?" Dad asked, coming into the kitchen.

"Oh, Donald Summers, Clarence Eckles, Gerald Neighbors, the, uh, outsiders."

Dad poured some coffee and eased into a chair at the kitchen table. I could tell he was thinking about "the outsiders." I'd said it on purpose. Friends had told me that the businessmen in town considered Dad to be way out. They didn't view his pursuit of bar bands and juke boxes as "regular" work like running a store or selling shoes. No, Tramp Jackson wouldn't be attending any Rotary meetings.

"Well, I'm sure they could use a party," Dad said. "Invitations will be pretty scarce in their lifetime."

Dad had given me an opening and I jumped at it. "Maybe Aunt Nadine could take care of Johnny and Sammy. She loves them!" Dad nodded at Mom; Mom called Aunt Nadine; and Aunt Nadine came through. That Thursday Mom baked two apple pies, made some Kool-Aid, and told me to end the party by ten o'clock.

Hibbs and Torrey arrived before the 6 PM start time, and we each had an early glass of Kool-Aid while we waited on the front porch for our guests of honor. Clarence showed first, shambling up to the porch with that hang-dog smile of his. Both ears glistened spiffy-clean. Summers arrived with stains, but they were on his knees; and Clarence's cousin, Francis, he with the glass eye, rode up on a nifty red bike. However, Keith, his big bully older brother, had to stay home for suspicion of having stolen the bike in the first place. Skinny, pale Delbert Jacobs arrived with his usual wooden Indian face, not even responding when Hibbs chided that Jacobs' arms looked like noodles. Gerald Neighbors got a block from the house before his father hollered for him to get back home.

We gathered in the side yard and ate the pies and downed the Kool-Aid in about five minutes. I'd lost my softball the week before, so I suggested a game of tag.

"Where's the girls?" Summers asked.

"We didn't invite any girls," I answered. "This is for guys."

Jacobs spoke for the first time. "Guys? Who wants to chase guys?"

With that, the outsiders who were never invited to anything went home.

The Women Haters' Club trudged back into the house. It wasn't even dark yet, far too early for the party to be over, so I dug out my two-foot stack of comic books. Hibbs and Torrey flopped onto the living room floor and began reading. I sat down at Dad's wooden desk and stared out the window, disgusted with what a bust the party had been. Rodge and Hibbs dove nose-deep into *Batman* and *Captain Marvel.* "Listen," I said, "tomorrow's the last day of school. We need to celebrate ... do something different."

His attention on the Joker in *Batman*, Hibbs said, "Pull a trick."

"On who?" I asked.

"Some girls," said Hibbs.

"Yeah," said Torrey looking hard at Captain Marvel's sister Mary in her short, red skirt.

Hibbs had hit a bull's eye. A trick on some girls would be the perfect way for the club to end the school year.

"What girls?" I asked.

"Any girls," Hibbs said.

I looked out the window and saw that the street lights had come on. Torrey fished another comic from the pile and said, "My cousin, Dorothy, lives about four blocks away."

Dorothy! My mind flooded with her big brown eyes and long, long eyelashes and silky brown hair and how she smiled and ... No! No! I couldn't think love-stuff about Dorothy! She hadn't even noticed me at the party, like I was invisible or something. Well, I'd show her.

"Dorothy would be perfect," I said. "How about this? My Dad and his buddy Clyde Forbes used to wrap dog-poop in a newspaper, put it on somebody's porch, light the paper, knock on the door and run. Whoever came out would see the fire and stamp on it with their foot."

"That might be a bit overboard," Torrey said.

I thought some more. "Okay, let's write a note to Dorothy and tell her how stuck up she is. We could leave it in a box by her front door."

"Okay," Hibbs said going to *Plastic Man.* "Go ahead and start it."

I got pencil and paper out of the desk and started to write.

"Hold it!" Torrey said. "She'll recognize your handwriting. That big scrawl of yours is a dead giveaway."

I had a flash of genius. "I'll write left handed. I've never-ever written left handed. Nobody'll have a clue. So, what do we say, guys?"

My cohorts were nose deep in comics.

Maybe Dorothy hadn't snubbed me. Maybe she just didn't find me worth noticing. That was even worse. I struggled for a great opening line for several moments, and then pure inspiration hit me. Left handed, I slowly scrawled "Dear Dorothy Strutbutt, as you walk down the street and wiggle your seat ..."

Pure poetry. I read it aloud; Hibbs and Torrey grinned approval and returned to their reading. I continued my masterpiece.

Hibbs looked up and said, "Put something in about her friend, Patty Davis ..."

"Okay."

"... and smarty-cousin Maribeth and pouty-lips Marilyn Berry."

"No, don't put anything in about Marilyn," Torrey murmured in a dreamy voice.

When I'd finished, my left-handed tirade had filled two pages and was signed "Mr. Mystery." I read it back to the others, who, twenty comics into the pile, absently voiced approval of my efforts. I placed the letter in one of Mom's old shoeboxes and tied it with kite string.

There weren't many street lights, and with no moon and an overcast sky, the walk to Dorothy's was near spooky, like sentinels in dark shadows were watching us break the law or something. The lights in her house were off except one in the back, and we darted tree to tree to get as close to the front porch as possible. As the primary author, I had the honor of placing the box, and I cautiously edged onto the porch's wooden stoop trying not to make it creak. I would toss the box lightly so it would land close to the door. A light flashed on. Someone's shadow loomed across the closed living room curtains. I froze, one foot on the stoop, the other on the porch. Panicking, I heaved too hard, and the box thudded against the screen door. I leaped off the stoop, shot past Hibbs and Torrey, and led a frenzied dash back to my house.

We filled three glasses with the last of the Kool-Aid, drank a toast to our cleverness, and Hibbs and Torrey left for home. When my head hit the pillow, the nightstand clock read 9:59, a whole minute before Mom's deadline. The note and Dorothy left my mind, and I fell asleep wondering what the last day of school might bring.

CHAPTER 17

▼

THE LAST DAY OF SCHOOL

I awoke with bright sunshine from the window streaming across my face and squinted at the nightstand clock. Seven forty five! School started in fifteen minutes! I yanked on my clothes and ran out the front door, Mom calling from the kitchen that I needed to eat something. But I was already half way down the block on my bike, standing up to peddle, churning my legs like locomotive wheels. The last bell rang as I shot onto the empty school grounds.

I leaped from the bike and charged inside to the sixth grade door and burst into a room filled with the bedlam and joy of the last day of school. The room immediately fell silent, and everyone stared at me. Everyone. Hibbs, about midway back, looked awful; his skin a haggard yellow, his eyes red-rimmed and weary. Rodge sat in the back of the room; good ol' laugh-at-everything Rodge looked down at his desk unable to meet my eyes. Miss Hill, her face pale as the dead, stood at her desk staring at me as if I, her nurtured pet, had betrayed her with some unspeakable disgrace. As I moved to my desk, Summers, who sat in front of Hibbs, leaned toward me and asked, "What'd you guys do after we left?"

I started to make up something, but Hibbs hissed, "It's no use, Jackson. They know the whole thing."

It was the note! Dorothy had taken the note to Miss Hill!

But Dorothy said nothing, and strangely showed no emotion, no traces of crying, and her eyes always followed the teacher. The other girls stole looks at me and fell into whispers. The boys hunkered into their seats, gloating their guiltlessness. Fowler the Scowler grinned. Pollock smirked. Miss Hill, tilting her chin high, announced that after assembly we would return "… for the handing out of grade cards." She made "grade cards" sound like "prison sentences."

No one sat near me in assembly, like I was Jack the Ripper. Rodge, on stage with a singing group, just mouthed the words; and Hibbs, who played saxophone, stood forlornly ready to play a solo. Barbara McHenry and her cousin, Irene, sat behind me to my right. Barbara leaned closer and, feigning innocence, asked:

"Bill Ray, how far do you live from Dorothy?"

What a detective. I mumbled that I didn't know and put my attention to Hibbs' solo. He played as sorry as he looked, honking and squawking through something that might have been *Caldonia.*

When we returned to the class room, Miss Hill handed out the grade cards in alphabetical order. Of our unholy alliance, Hibbs would be first. She paused when his card came up and in a quiet, pained voice said:

"Eddie, you're to stay after class to discuss your card."

That was it! She was going to flunk the three of us!

Sure enough, she sounded the same death knoll after my name and Rodge's.

Then she announced dismissal, and the Sixth Grade Class of 1947 rushed joyously out the door—except for the condemned three. Miss Hunt silently entered the room and stood by her friend. Brandishing the three remaining report cards, Miss Hill announced that we were going to the office. *The office; home of the black metal cabinet.* And in the cabinet lurked the notorious *Old Betsy,* the huge, penance-wielding paddle with the half-dollar holes that gave your butt red tattoos. But Betsy's wrath would be butterfly kisses compared to the shame of flunking sixth grade. How would I face Mom and Dad? I'd never caused them the slighted anxiety, and now I brought this disgrace.

Like prisoners in a chain gang, Hibbs, Torrey, and I followed the two teachers to the office, a small room, originally intended for one secretary, not a gathering of people. Miss Hill handed the report cards to Miss Hunt and closed the door. We stood uncomfortably close to each other, the teachers towering over their errant wards.

Miss Hill began.

"Early this morning, I received a visit from Dorothy's mother."

Dorothy hadn't tattled to the teacher!

"Her mother preferred not to go to your parents with *this.*"

Miss Hill opened a folder she had brought along and produced the note. "Bill Ray, don't bother denying anything; Eddie and Roger already have confessed that the three of you wrote this filthy trash at a party last night." Hibbs and Torrey looked like they wanted to puke. "And you obviously thought you could fool everybody by writing with your left hand. Well, *Mr. Mystery*," she said, waving the note in my face, "I see these big, sloppy "L's" on everything you write." Placing the pages on the desk, her voice turned to vinegar.

"Bill Ray, the words in this note are … lewd."

"Lewd?" I had written "lewd?" Didn't that mean "dirty?" My mind raced over the note. I hadn't written any bad words. No, wait, maybe one. "Strutbutt." Miss Hill considered "Strutbutt" to be lewd: a dirty word disgracing Dorothy. Why hadn't I just said her seat wiggled?

But the punishment involved more than my writing "Strutbutt." I looked at Miss Hill's eyes. They were wounded, angry. I had been her favorite. She had invested in me a year's worth of encouragement; had tolerated my crazy Deefy Comeback play; and spent hours coaching my performance at the talent show. And to show his appreciation, her pet had written a nasty note to one of her girls. Tears came to Miss Hill's eyes and she turned away. Miss Hunt patted her friend's arm; Miss Hill straightened and then slowly turned toward me with a look that would've withered cactus.

"Bill Ray, are you in love with Dorothy?" she asked.

Aurauuugh! I couldn't breathe. My face flushed and my throat filled with a thousand denials; but all I could croak was a shaky no.

"I think you are. And your note was a horrible way to show it." She moved toward the black metal cabinet. "I called Mr. Bartley, the school superintendent, and he said I should handle this transgression as I see fit." Miss Hill opened the black cabinet door. Hibbs, Torrey, and I frantically looked to Miss Hunt for clemency, but the funny lady who did Minnie Pearl impersonations remained mute. From the cabinet's dark interior, Miss Hill brought forth the supreme punishment. Oh, mother, oh, brother, Old Betsy was big. No one had said the paddle was *this* big. Its short wooden handle swelled into a boat oar riddled with ominous, welt-promising holes. Barely breathing, Hibbs, Torrey, and I returned our eyes to Miss Hill.

"You boys have hurt Dorothy and the other girls terribly. I can either punish you with this …," Miss Hill's fingers tightened around the paddle handle, "… or by telling your parents. Which do you prefer?"

"Old Betsy!" Hibbs blurted. "Just don't tell my mom!"

Torrey and I nodded rapid agreement. Shaming our parents would be much worse than Old Betsy's sting. Torrey's cranky step-father would wallop him terrible. Hibbs' mom, raising him alone, would cry for a week. And Dad always said if I got a lickin' at school, I'd get worse at home. But Mom, oh, Mom would become white and teary-eyed and look at me like I'd disgraced the family, and I couldn't take that.

Hibbs got his first. Thank God we didn't have to take our pants down; we would've died. Miss Hill bent Hibbs over the desk and whacked him ten measured smacks—hard ones with her full weight behind them—ones that made his head bounce. Hibbs grimaced, but made not a sound. Then it was Torrey's turn. Then mine. Following Hibbs' lead, neither of us uttered a whimper. But I almost did. She whacked me the hardest.

Punishment rendered, Miss Hill retrieved the grade cards from Miss Hunt and handed them to us. Our eyes raced to the last line. *Passed!* "You're dismissed," said Miss Hill, wiping a tear from her eye. Giddy with relief, we ran out the school doors and raced to the town square, where, butts still smarting, we gingerly sat on the open stairway at the side of Herrick's Drugstore. When Miss Hill and Miss Hunt approached, we wiggled on the steps like our butts didn't hurt. But the teachers paid no notice. They passed by without acknowledging us in the slightest.

I walked into the house smelling potato soup. Mom was in the kitchen. "How was the last day of school?" she asked, placing two steaming bowls on the table.

"Okay," I quietly answered, shifting uncomfortably on the hard kitchen chair. "Eddie Hibbs played a song on his sax. I think it was *Caldonia.*"

CHAPTER 18

▼

LANA TURNER, THE FIGHT, AND THE FALL OF EDDIE HIBBS

That summer I crossed streets, turned up alleys, and feigned interest in window displays just to keep from coming face to face with Dorothy or any of the other girls mentioned in that nasty note. At home, each time the phone rang I was sure that some blabbermouth was calling my parents to unmask the disgusting child they were raising. However, the biggest threat of exposure proved not to be some tattletale on the phone, but my two little brothers' babysitter.

Jo Ann Cannan, a plumpish girl in my class with a blank look in her eye, babysat on weekends when Mom and Dad were out. She usually acted mousy, but one evening when my younger baby brother Sammy filled his diaper, she dropped a bomb on me.

"Change him," she ordered.

"Are you kidding?" I said. "That's your job."

Her eyes didn't look so blank and she beamed a smirky-smile. "If you don't, I'll tell 'em."

"Tell who, what?"

"Tell your folks about *you know what*," she said, rolling her eyes.

I knew *what*. I plopped baby Sammy on his back and changed that diaper double pronto. After that, every time Jo Ann gave that little eye roll I was on the job, and to my knowledge my parents never found out about their first-born's sixth grade disgrace.

That summer I caddied at the Country Club east of town. "Country Club" sounded a bit high-tone for this bumpy thirty acres with its add-on clubhouse and small cement swimming pool, but it was the pride of Unionville. The annual thirty dollar membership fee bought a certain status. Tramp Jackson didn't have thirty dollars, but he belonged to the club—as the fry cook. He worked the kitchen while Mom and I served the golfers their Sunday morning breakfast. We were allowed usage of the golf course and the pool, but no one ever mistook us for bona fide members. Business men and their families were bona fide members; and even if you merely clerked in a store, you were considered a business man. Men who blew horns in honky-tonks were not.

The club's nine-hole golf course was pure Missouri: hills, trees, and ditches circling a large log cabin with a nailed on, plywood meeting room. The first tee broke you in fast; it pointed straight up hill. The "greens" were not manicured grass, but round plots of sand, and when your ball landed on one of these minia-ture deserts, your caddy dragged a T-shaped pipe across its circumference, mak-ing a smooth path to the hole for your ball. Ditches made up most of the hazards, but heaven forbid if you sliced your drive on Hole Number Six. Then you played your next shot from across the highway in Shields' Junkyard.

Different boys from town served as caddies, but the regulars included Cook and me; Torrey and Bramhall; sometimes Hibbs; and on rare occasion, the three trouble-prone King Brothers. Not all of us showed at the same time, so caddies could be scarce, as was the case one morning when W. E. Ross, the town's most influential merchant, arrived late. All available caddies were taken, but one of the King Brothers was resting himself on a nearby bench. The Brothers were not known for their commitment to employment, but W. E. was too old to carry his own golf bag up the hill, so he asked the reclining King if he wanted to caddy. The boy hummed and hawed and looked toward the swimming pool. W. E. knitted his bushy brows and chewed on his cigar. After a long, awkward silence, Unionville's most prominent businessman leaned down to the boy's eye level, tongue-rolled his cigar to one side of his mouth and said, "Well, now, King, don't rush into anything."

Seventh grade began, and to my dismay, Dorothy had not moved to France. She was everywhere—in class, on the playground, walking with her friends on the way home from school—and I felt like pig puke every time I saw her. But she didn't act hurt, she didn't act anything. She never had paid much attention to me, even before the note. Maybe the truth was that she just didn't think much about me at all. Well, that was better than her thinking I was "lewd."

The Women Haters' Club languished, and out of silent consent by its three charter members it died of neglect. Hibbs returned to bossing recess and Rodge and I created the school's first student newspaper. We could've covered the routine stuff—birthdays or who sang *Way down Yonder in the Paw Paw Patch* at assembly—but we decided to forego the usual school yawners and go directly for tabloid press.

"Mullins Escapes!" shouted our front-page headline. Tow-headed Harvey Mullins, a walking-talking sex manual who had joined us in Fifth Grade, had moved away. Rodge and I wrote a fabricated, but more exciting exit: school authorities had silenced Harvey's naughty tongue by locking him in a dark cell in the school basement. Ever resourceful, Harvey had bribed janitor-guard Clovie Stewart with two pinups of Lana Turner in a tight sweater and escaped to an undisclosed Amish settlement in Iowa.

Over the weekend, Rodge and I hand-lettered three large pages of newsprint covering Harvey's outrageous confinement and ingenious escape. Prominently displayed on page one was a shared drawing of Lana Turner in a sweater. We'd flipped a coin to determine who drew what, and I lost and had to draw the head. That Monday, when the bell rang for morning recess, Rodge ran to the door and held high the first edition of *The Naked Truth*. Then he placed it on a nearby desk; the class swarmed to it, and various classmates read different parts aloud. Snickers, then guffaws, filled the room, and Rodge and I stood by the door beaming our pride.

Skinny, soft-spoken Rollie Timmons, our seventh grade teacher, remained at his desk correcting papers. He'd probably figured out that the time taken to create the newspaper had taken a mighty toll and its first edition would be its last. He was right. Ten minutes into attempting Issue Number 2, we abandoned *The Naked Truth* and tuned the radio to *Jack Armstrong*.

But my rebellion was not yet spent. I had entered the Show-off Age, and interrupted geography lessons by crowing about my world travels on the carnival. I'd decided that sissy man Rollie with his pencil-thin moustache would have to accept my grandstanding no matter what. Wrong. When my mouth refused to rest, Mr. Timmons rose quietly, moved to my side, and clamped his right hand onto my wrist like a pit bull's jaws on a chicken bone. Pain shot to my shoulder, my eyes bulged, and I froze quiet as a tombstone. Rollie slowly bent to my ear and hissed, "Quit … showing … off." With that, he resumed class, and there were no further interruptions.

That lunch hour he gathered all the boys from the sixth and seventh grades in front of the school and instructed them to stand shoulder to shoulder in a big square. With pursed lips he announced that he was providing "an outlet for young male aggression," and instructed each class to choose its best boxer. Without hesitation, the sixth grade selected husky Clark Carter, who was stronger than any kid in school—except maybe seventh grade's Keith Eckles. Eighth graders went to the high school building, so Cook and his buddies were no longer here. Keith was husky *and* fat, a lumbering giant who had been held back a grade or three. Unfortunately, on this day he hadn't bothered to lumber to school.

Carter shucked his shirt and put on a pair of boxing gloves. Holding up a second pair, Mr. Timmons stepped to center ring.

"And who is representing the seventh grade?" he asked.

We searched our own for a challenger. Hibbs? No. Too small. He scrapped better than anyone, but no biting and kicking would be allowed. Shelton? No, Shelton had been our best at anything, but last year rheumatic fever had robbed him of his strength and his ranking. Torrey? No, Torrey always said he was a lover not a fighter. Jackson? I didn't want to lose face; Carter would cream me. The seventh grade boys shifted uneasily and kicked little clouds of dirt. Then I remembered that Carter had gotten sick and had been held back a year, and I almost yelled out, *Carter's really a seventh grader!* But that was a technicality. Truth was we were all scared spitless of him.

"No one?" Mr. Timmons arched his eyebrows.

Carter grinned and extended his gloves to Mr. Timmons for removal.

"I'll fight him."

What misguided soul said that?

"Dale?" asked Mr. Timmons.

The new kid in the class stepped forward. Dale Dixon, short in stature, heavy on freckles, had moved into the east side of town last summer. I met him when we were both at the Country Club looking for golf balls. He was a withdrawn, serious kid in need of some friends. He didn't make many. When school started, few in the class knew his name. They would know it now: Dale Dixon, the pint-sized fearless one who stood up to Carter. Dixon took off his shirt and handed it to Torrey. Torrey made the sign of the cross—our noble gladiator had the build of a skinned Chihuahua. Mr. Timmons laced the gloves on Dixon, stepped out of the ring, and crisply enunciated:

"Clang!"

Dixon shot across the ring and swung a roundhouse right that hit Carter in the Adam's apple. Carter looked puzzled and felt his throat. Dixon charged again and threw lefts and rights, landing a good half dozen before Carter got his big forearms up. No longer smiling, Carter fired his first punch, a straight right to Dixon's forehead that knocked him backwards into the crowd. Carter crouched and moved toward his prey. Dixon didn't wait; he broke through Carter's guard and hit him flush in the mouth. The seventh graders cheered, "Go, Dale, go!" Carter ran his tongue over his upper lip and his eyes narrowed. His left slammed away Dixon's gloves and his right rocked Dixon's head. Dixon staggered backwards; Carter stepped in close and fired a short right to the nose that knocked Dixon flat on his back.

"Clang!"

Mr. Timmons announced the end of the round and the end of the fight. He said that Dixon was to come to the boys' restroom and they would stop the bleeding.

Torrey and I tried to help Dixon up, but he had none of it. He got to his feet, shook free his gloves and, holding his shirt to his bleeding nose, led the seventh grade boys back through the school doors. As we filed behind him, Torrey turned to me and muttered, "We were a bunch of pansies."

When I got home from school, Dad was sipping a beer and playing the piano. He played by ear, and was deep into *Mood Indigo* when I started telling him about the fight—pretty much painting Carter as the big-bully villain. Dad lifted his fingers from the keys. He took a drag on his cigarette and looked at me.

"S'pose you were Clark Carter. What would you have done?" he asked.

"Well, he didn't need to hit him so hard."

"Oh, he didn't? Wasn't the other kid hitting him hard?"

"Well, yeah, but ..."

"Being bigger and stronger doesn't mean you have to be a punching bag. Clark did what he had to do. Besides, you'll be cheering him someday."

"Cheering him?" I protested.

"Yes, cheering him. He's a big kid getting bigger. When he plays football in high school, who do you think is going to be making all those touchdowns?"

Dad proved to be right. Carter did make touchdowns And I did cheer him.

As soon as we turned twelve, most of the seventh grade gang joined the Scouts. Cook had been in a year already, and strutted around in his uniform flashing a "first class" insignia. With a valiant struggle I made "second class," even though all my knots came out grannies and I identified poison ivy by wading into it. Hiking and camping were fun, but what I liked best was Cook's patrol meetings.

He'd picked Hibbs as his assistant—a status I would have died for—and with Torrey, Bramhall, and Pollock aboard, naturally our meetings had nothing to do with tying knots or helping old ladies across the street. A mental lapse by the city fathers allowed us to hold our meetings at City Hall, a small store-front building on the south side of the Square. Normally such gatherings were monitored by one of the member's parents. None of ours volunteered, certainly not Dad; he felt you camped out of doors without joining a club. So, prominent grocer Oren Lee Halley, our scout master, let us meet on our own, issuing strict guidelines on proper procedure. He even bragged on us to other scouts, telling them that Cook's patrol took such great interest in the subject of camping that he had observed its members carrying packs to the meetings.

We met Monday nights, gathering around City Hall's large oaken table in the back room. Solemnly, Patrol Leader Cook called the meeting to order. First came roll call. Any idiot could see who was there, but Assistant Patrol Leader Hibbs had been directed by Scout Master Halley to enter our names in the attendance book. Usually Hibbs just scribbled "All of us." Continuing our scout master's guidelines, Cook asked, "Is there any old business to discuss?"

On cue, Hibbs shouted, "Yes!" tore open his pack, pulled out a large cap gun and began firing. That was it. Guns appeared from all the packs and once again the battle was on: Cook, Hibbs, Pollock on one side; Torrey, Bramhall, and I on the other. Out went the lights and on raged the war; from the back room to the front desk; cap pistols blazing; fearless soldiers yelling, charging, diving for cover. Many were wounded; none ever died. When the hall became a cloud of acrid smoke, we poured out the front door and took our battle into the night, the streets long emptied of any scolding adults. Ah, that was scouting.

One evening when the patrol members arrived, Cook stood waiting outside the building. He'd found the door locked, and Oren Lee had come by and told him we couldn't meet there anymore. Most of us figured that the city fathers had grown upset with all the used rolls of caps, the turned-over furniture, and the place smelling like a dynamite factory. The problem proved to be none of that. It was the safe. The safe stood against the wall in the anteroom with its door ajar because the office secretary long ago had lost the combination. Oren Lee had made us swear on scout's honor to ignore the safe entirely, and we had, except in the heat of battle when it made a good shield. But petty cash kept in the safe had come up missing, and our cap gun battles ended.

Later, Cook told me that the city fathers thought the culprit might be Hibbs. I didn't believe it. Hibbs was feisty, but not a thief. He was my leader. On school grounds, his scrappy, take-no-guff style made him commander of the class, a miniature MacArthur who led us through every rebellion recess could offer. You want to play softball, dodge ball, horse? You cleared it with Hibbs. If he said okay, the game was on—with him as captain of one of the teams and getting first dibs on the best players.

Hibbs' reign as supreme commander continued until one black day near the end of seventh grade. It was afternoon recess, and big bully Keith Eckles, after a month's sabbatical, showed up at school. Hibbs had decided on softball, and, naturally, captained one team, so Eckles took over the other. Gerald Dean Carr, known to "call 'em like he sees 'em," was made umpire. Hibbs' side won the toss and went to bat. Eckles made himself pitcher, and instead of the customary lobs across the plate, really whipped the ball and struck out the first two batters. Hibbs always got a hit, and always batted third, because the shortness of recess made for one-inning games, and he would knock in any other runners on base.

Big Keith delivered the first two pitches like cannon shots, and Hibbs whiffed them both. This was not good. Hibbs was our champion, our ace; he *never-ever* struck out. Big Keith smiled confidently, wound up and fired the third pitch. Hibbs jumped back like it almost hit him, but Carr called, "Strike three."

"Inside!" yelled Hibbs.

"Inside corner of the plate," Carr corrected.

"No. It was a ball. Pitch it again, Eckles," Hibbs ordered.

Eckles grinned. "Three up, three down," he said, and started for the plate.

Hibbs took his batting stance. "Get back and pitch, Eckles,"

Eckles moved closer. "Gimme the bat.

Hibbs swung the bat back and forth. "Pitch the ball!"

Eckles' face darkened. In a menacingly low voice, he said:

"Give me the bat."

Hibbs swung viciously; his eyes filled with tears.

How could this be? Our leader was crying.

Eckles moved closer. "Gimme the bat, Hibbs!" he snapped, reaching out with his right hand. Hibbs swung the bat and caught Eckles on the thumb. Blood gushed from under the nail, but Eckles paid no heed. His beefy hands grabbed for Hibbs' throat.

"Stop it!"

Miss Hunt, Sherman Tank Hunt, stepped between pitcher and batter. No one spoke. The only sound was Hibbs' snuffling.

"Get to the office, both of you!"

Head low, Hibbs trudged toward the school house. Eckles followed, sucking the blood oozing from his thumb and grinning .He'd been to the office lots of times. The boys of the seventh grade watched as Hibbs entered the school door. He looked very small—and he was still crying.

The world had gotten too big for our miniature MacArthur. He led no more.

CHAPTER 19

▼

DAD'S LAST DREAM

The summer of my twelfth year, the Phantom broke from his slumber and whispered yet another dream to Dad, a whopper, the Barnum and Bailey of the whole shebang. Dad would open a nightclub—not another beer dive of which the county had so many—but a classy supper club where you dined on T-bone steak and danced to Kansas City jazz bands. Where might Dad build this dream castle? The Phantom directed Dad to a decomposing beer bar next to a large, cattle auction barn reeking of cow manure.

If you entered town from the west, the Casa Loma greeted you about a hundred yards before the city limits sign. Owned by Slim Robinson—whom you'll remember as the bashful young man who did a naked half-gainer through Mutt Rouse's bathhouse wall—the Casa Loma's customers were mostly the surly unemployed who sat and sipped and swore. For entertainment there was Little Jimmy Dickens on the juke box and the teeth-flying, eye-gouging Saturday night fights proudly presented by the boys at the bar. Sometimes a little knife action was thrown in as added attraction. Big Jack Burns had been the bouncer, but he grew weary of heaving bodies out the door and nobody hauling them to jail. The sheriff was too afraid to come to the Casa Loma.

Undeterred by its history, Dad envisioned a new Casa Loma, a glamorous dine and dance roadhouse finer than anything to ever grace Putnam County. This was a gamble of enormous proportion. Folks in Unionville guarded their money pretty closely; entertainment primarily consisted of movies and beer bars, with the best dinner in town being the chicken-fried steak at Essie's Café. However, Slim welcomed help with the rowdies, and if Dad were the Barnum to bring class to Unionville, more power to him. The agreed price for co-ownership cost Dad everything he got for the juke boxes.

Dad came alive, fairly glowing with purpose, joking and laughing like he did in the carnival days. He and Mom were getting along super, and Mom was so happy to see the old Dad that she smilingly accepted the new living quarters for our family of five: the tiny loft above the Casa Loma bar. Mom and Dad's bed rested against the loft's far wall; baby brother Sam slept in a crib; and three-year-old brother John and I shared a daybed near the stairway. The bar's grease-laden kitchen became our dining area, and our bathing needs took place in the customers' grimy, confining restroom with a toilet and sink that looked like they were being used for the same purpose.

Starting in the large room off the bar, Dad single-handedly constructed a band stage and dance floor; then filled the room with dining tables and unscrewed half of the room's light bulbs for a soft, romantic look. With Mom and me helping, cracks were patched, corners dusted, walls painted, and the wooden bar waxed to a warm glow. The Casa Loma menu featured T-bone steaks and baked potatoes with sour cream and chives. As for booze, the county prohibited anything stronger than 3.2 beers, but if you came to dine you could bring your liquor in a paper sack, casually stow it under the table, and mix it with your Coke or 7 Up. Dad hired no extra help: Slim tended bar; Dad cooked; Mom served as waitress; and I bussed tables. Dad nailed up posters for fifty miles around, and on a sultry Saturday night in August 1947, north Missouri's finest and only nightclub opened its doors.

From the dining room stage, Two-Sax Jack looked over a dark room filled with white faces, gave the downbeat, and his seven-piece, all black band from Kansas City serenaded its audience with *I'll Buy That Dream*. With the soothing strains of jazz filling the night air, anyone with half a brain knew that this had to be the classiest joint within a hundred miles.

Around midnight, Two-Sax—real name something like Hector Jackson—demonstrated how he got his nickname. He'd been sipping out of his paper sack quite a bit, and he shucked his suit jacket, loosened his tie, and stuck a saxophone in each side of his mouth. With a tongue-impaired "Uh, doo, dree," he ferociously honked a one-man duet of *Pistol Packin' Mama*. The crowd went wild. Mesmerized by such artistic accomplishment, I wiped a large puddle of beer onto some poor guy's lap. Not to worry. He was so enthralled with Two-Sax's performance that he just giggled and left me a dollar, the biggest tip I made all night.

After we closed, Dad began cooking the band some steaks and I spread my tips on the kitchen table to count. Two-Sax came in for payment, and Dad had it ready and handed him cash in an envelope. The black man didn't count it, just slipped it inside his jacket and stood there chuckling and bobbing his head, talking to Dad about "how jumpin' the joint had been." I was entranced by his Hershey-bar skin and big Chiclets smile, having never been this close to a darky in my life. Most folks in Unionville called them niggers. Teachers called them Negroes, but my grandparents and Mom called 'em colored. Whatever they were called, none lived in Unionville, and when I was younger I had asked Dad why.

He had told me that years ago "a black buck" was accused of raping the mayor's daughter. The mayor had the man hauled to jail and ordered "every nigger out of town by sundown."

Then the young black man was hanged.

Shortly after that, a law was passed that Negroes couldn't be in town after dark. I had noticed that they weren't encouraged to mosey around *before* dark, either. But the Casa Loma was beyond the city limits sign, so it was all right for Dad to have Two-Sax and his boys there at night, as long as they moved on when their tootin' was done. I'd heard Dad say "nigger" a lot, but tonight he hadn't said it once. When the steaks were ready, he had the band sit at the bar and enjoy the meal. After Two-Sax finished his, he came back into the kitchen and complimented Dad on how good it was. Then, yawning, he asked:

"Hey, Tramp, where can we got some shut-eye in this town?"

Dad got real busy cleaning the grill.

"Any port in the storm will do."

Dad scraped the grill some more and then said:

"We got a law."

"A law against sleepin'?" Two-Sax chuckled. "Now, *that's* a hard law."

"Against ... colored sleepin' in town."

The grin fell from Two-Sax's face.

"It's a stupid law," Dad said, still not looking up.

Two-Sax didn't say a word. He loaded his musicians into the two cars they came in and headed into the night.

I watched as the three couples who'd paid the freight to dance to an all white, five-piece band finished their beers and staggered into the night. Dad emptied the cash register to pay the musicians, closed the door, turned out the lights, and ended the most ambitious dream of his life.

The Nightclub Casa Loma died at 2:10 AM, Sunday, January 11, 1948.

Dad sold his half of the Casa Loma back to Slim, who was happy to forgo all this big band stuff and just go back to running a beer bar. He paid Dad cash, and three days later John and Sam were stashed at Aunt Mary Kathryn's and I was placed under the wing of Rodge's mother. Dad, Mom, Uncle Buck and Aunt Nadine bid adieu to the biting wind of a north-Missouri winter and headed for the sunny climes of Houston. I figured they deserved the get-away. They'd worked really hard, and it'd all come to nothing. I knew Mom wouldn't miss the booze-fed clamor of the place at all.

The question was, would the Phantom ever whisper to Dad again?

Part II

▼

Fumbling and Stumbling

CHAPTER 20

▼

PRESIDENT NO PANTS

I heard Dad tell Mom something truly frightening. They'd returned from their three-week holiday in Houston and were in the loft talking. I hid on the stairway to listen. Dad said the money Slim had paid him for his half of the Casa Loma was gone; he'd spent it all on the trip. Mom said nothing. Then Dad added something really scary. He said that after next week we had no place to live.

I sneaked back down the stairs and went into the bar. Slim swished glasses in the disinfectant tank while a couple of customers talked about last Sunday's Demolition Derby. One of our Unionville boys had won again. Slim smiled at the news. You could tell that he didn't miss Dad's nightclub fuss at all. I went to the far corner of the bar and sat down by the window. The world outside was gray and cold; bits of sleet spit against the window; and I blew my breath on a portion of the glass and made it cloudy; then, with my finger, drew a picture of a tent. *Were we going to live in a tent again, like we did in Texas? Missouri got colder than Texas—we'd freeze to death.*

The day before we were supposed to move, Dad took us to our new home. Sweet, gentle Grandma Jackson lived in a ten-dollar-a-month house that was so small that in any room two fat people made a crowd. The linoleum-covered floor in the living room slanted so much that when you lay on the couch you had to brace yourself to keep from rolling off it. Grandma retained her tiny bedroom downstairs, while John and Sam slept upstairs in the landing outside the eight by ten foot bedroom shared by Mom, Dad, and me. If you didn't go to sleep fast, you heard the nightly serenade of tiny rodent feet scampering through crumbling plaster walls. The coal stove in the living room struggled mightily, but failed to warm anything beyond ten feet away. The house boasted electricity, but no running water and no bathroom. A large bowl and water pitcher in the kitchen provided washing facilities, but on winter mornings you first had to chip the ice out of the pitcher to pour the water.

Saturday night baths provided adventure: a dip in the round, galvanized-metal tub placed in the middle of the kitchen. I liked bathing, but dreaded that tub. Closing the kitchen door meant nothing. Little brothers John and Sam would fling it open, race around the tub taunting and giggling, throw my clothes into the water, dodge my openhanded swats, and rush out like the James boys making a fast escape. Of course, they left the door wide open for God and everybody to see.

Going to the bathroom proved to be no joy, either. At age thirteen, I didn't find it acceptable to squat behind the bed on a little white pot. My facility of choice became the outhouse about forty feet from the back door. It exuded luxury, two holes—in case you wanted to invite a friend—and a Sears catalog for both reading and wiping. The bitter bite of winter mornings didn't encourage loitering, and come summer a maneuver of no more than thirty seconds became quite common, because just when you were most vulnerable, angry wasps darted out of the holes like German Messerschmitts. On the pretense of playing with cousins Jimmy and Janice, I took many a hurried stroll the two and a half blocks to their house just to use the vitreous-china bathroom Uncle Buck the plumber had installed.

That fall, shortly after school started, all the classes met one morning and elected officers, and my freshman classmates did the unbelievable. They elected *me* president. The results of the elections spread, and I wandered the halls with a big, dopey grin plastered on my face as kids I didn't even know called my new title and waved.

Then came lunch hour. Cousins Cook and Paddy Joe depantsed me and ran their trophy up the schoolyard flagpole. A mere hour following my ascension to high office, I was darting from bush to busy in my skivvies while the president's pants waved majestically just under Old Glory.

Gerald Dean Carr retrieved my pants and tried to cheer me up.

"Guess what, Mr. President."

"What?" I asked forlornly.

"Even the girls voted for you."

I peered from behind a spirea bush.

"Even Dorothy?"

"Yes, even Dorothy."

I slowly let out a long breath. My shameful debasement had been forgiven.

Delighted with Dorothy's pardon, I pulled on my pants and walked back into the school building already planning my presidential agenda.

That first meeting of the Freshmen Class, I expressed thanks for my election and immediately announced my first objective.

"We'll go to Hannibal and see The Cave!"

My fellow freshmen applauded; Rodge even stood up and whistled. "Hannibal," everyone knew, was Hannibal, Missouri, Mark Twain's home on the Mississippi River, about a morning's drive east of Unionville. Twain had written a lot about Hannibal's famous cave, and Rodge and I pretended a zillion times to be Tom Sawyer and Huck Finn hiding in its dark passageways from the infamous Indian Joe.

"How we gonna pay for it?" asked the ever practical Gerald Dean Carr.

Rodge yelled, "Car washes and bake sales!" like a seasoned fund raiser.

Everybody murmured approval, and I nodded like I'd thought out the answer days ago. After that first meeting, classmates smiled, flashed the V-for-victory sign, and called out, "The Cave! The Cave!"

A few days later, the principal's secretary appeared in the doorway of the freshman English class. She called to the teacher, Harold Wellman, to send Bill Ray Jackson to Mr. Neil's office "right now." The class broke into a frenzy of whispers. Their president was being hauled to the principal's office! What shameful trespass had he committed now?

The secretary preceded me to the office door and motioned me to enter. Mr. Neil sat behind his desk in a Sears-gray suit, fiddling with a note on his desk. A plump man, he usually walked around school with a slightly bemused smile on his face, sort of like Alfred Hitchcock's kindlier cousin. But Mr. Neil wasn't bald. He had a full head of gray hair closely cropped on the sides, military style. I had always avoided him, like you do the sheriff, but now I was so close he could reach out and smack me. The secretary left the room, closing the door behind her.

Mr. Neil looked up from the note he held and gave a soft smile that surprised me.

"You're Tramp Jackson's boy, aren't you?"

"Yes sir."

"Don't you think you're a tad young to start the day drinking beer? It'll mess up your math scores in a hurry."

"I don't drink beer," I protested.

Mr. Neil waved the note at me. "One of our teachers says she sees you going into this bar every morning before school, the, uh …" he checked his note again, "ah, yes, …, the Friendly Tavern."

"My Dad owns it," I said. "I have to clean it."

"That little hole just off the Square?"

I nodded. Where Dad had gotten the money to buy the bar, I don't know— maybe another loan from "Uncle" Albert at the bank or Uncle Buck, who liked to stop in on his way home from work.

Mr. Neil said, "I, uh, ahem, have never frequented the establishment. Tell me about it."

I thought I'd try to make Mr. Neil laugh. It's hard to punish somebody while you're laughing.

"Well, it's grungy and loud and some of the customers act real weird."

"Weird?"

"Well, like this little, glassy-eyed guy, Poker Bill Hayes. He's bald and scroungy and giggles after everything he says and comes out of the donicker with his pants wet."

"Donicker?" Mr. Neil chuckled.

"Yeah, the toilet. One time he came out with his whachacallit hanging out. Dad said, 'Poker! Your thing's hanging out!' Poker said, 'I know it!' and crowed like a rooster."

Mr. Neil bit his lip.

"But the oddest character is this bony guy who wears a ball cap. His name is Edgar Spauvey. He sits at the end of the bar nearest the door and stares at his glass a long time; then grabs it in both hands and chugs down the beer. The trouble is, he's got a hole in his bottom lip, and half the beer runs down his chest."

"Fascinating," said Mr. Neil with his hand hiding his mouth. "And you clean up this place?"

"Yeah," I answered. "The toughest part is when I open the door in the morning. The blast of stale beer is enough to puke a maggot off a gut wagon."

Mr. Neil winced.

"Lots of farmers go there," I continued, "so first I scrape all the cow, uh, dung off the metal rungs of the bar chairs. Then I sweep the floor and mop up the tobacco spit. Then I dip the dirty beer glasses into a tank of disinfectant and fill the coolers with Muelbach, Falstaff, and Griesedick. The last thing I do is clean the toilet. Usually I just close my eyes and swish the brush around."

Mr. Neil sat in silence with his lips pursed real tight.

"You do this every morning?"

"Yes, sir."

He shook his head. "Go on back to class."

As I went out the door, he called, "You'd best study hard. You're going to need a better job."

The next morning I clomped to the tavern, unlocked the latch, and took a deep breath before turning the knob. The door swung open like a black mouth releasing a smelly belch. I flipped on the lights. I noticed a new hole in the juke box, and from the beer puddles on the bar and the overturned stools, it looked like those in attendance had a fine time last night. As I swept the floor I remembered what Mr. Neil had said about getting a better job. What was I going to do when I grew up, run a beer joint?

Dad was the smartest, most talented man in town. He could talk about Socrates; build a car from the ground up; and play banjo like he had twenty fingers. But follow his footsteps? His footsteps meandered all over the place and usually ended up on one side or the other of a bar. What a comedown he'd suffered with this smelly hole. Just months ago he'd created the fanciest roadhouse in northern Missouri. Now, instead of a live jazz band from Kansas City, he had Roy Acuff wailing *Great Speckled Bird* out of a juke box some music critic had bashed in with his fist.

After sweeping, I turned to the beer coolers. The cases of beer were stored behind the bar, and I slid open the metal cooler tops and placed the bottles down inside the way Dad had taught me: first a layer in one direction, then a layer in the other. I'd left the tavern door open to air out the stench and could see kids walking, riding bikes, calling to each other on their way to school.

Rodge stuck his head in the door and yelled, "C'mon, Mr. President, you're gonna be late!"

She was a blue-eyed blond and looked like Lana Turner. Okay, Lana Turner had brown eyes and was older and filled out her sweater more, but Rodge and I always thought the prettiest girls in school looked like famous movie stars—and Marilyn Berry was our Lana. And there she was, standing on this dock at the edge of the Mississippi, slightly squinting her pale blues, watching the big, powerful river lumber by. A soft breeze caressed a few loose strands of her blond hair and her faintly rouged lips wore an almost smile. She stood alone, lingering, savoring a last look before joining her classmates on the bus and heading home.

This trip to Hannibal was the crowning achievement of my freshman class presidency. Well, actually, it was the only achievement, and it wasn't mine it was the class's. And now, having stumbled and shrieked through the blackness of Indian Joe's cave and stocked up on miniature outhouses and corncob pipes at the tourist traps, we made our last stop a reverential look at this huge river that had been Huckleberry's highway.

Having rendered its homage, the class clamored aboard the bus like hungry geese, and called for Christy Hodges, our sainted driver of unending patience, to make tracks for the nearest hotdog stand. But Lana, I mean, Marilyn, had remained on the dock; and I stood, transfixed, but a few feet from her side. Supposedly admiring the river, I watched intensely with my peripheral vision her every move, her slightest expression.

Rodge called from the bus that he was saving me a seat. It was time to go home. But not for me. I stood frozen on the dock with a dozen doves inside my chest flapping their wings. I wanted to move closer—wink, smile, make my Lana laugh—but, my God, I couldn't move my mouth. My tongue was numb; I barely could breathe. What if I did say something, and she laughed at me the way girls do when they think you're stupid? No! No! I couldn't risk that! Better that I act nonchalant and look at the river like I'm having deep thoughts.

And yet ... there she stood, quiet, dreamy-eyed, hanging back, maybe, like me, *pretending* to look at the water. Was that a side-long glance I saw? My heart pounded like a jack hammer. I wanted to kiss her. Right there in broad daylight. A first-ever kiss by the roaring Mississippi.

Her girlfriends called from the bus, but Marilyn paid no heed. She stared at the river's flow and remained as still as a young doe on alert. Do it, Jackson. Just like in the movies. Errol Flynn time. Move boldly beside her. Slip your arm around her waist. Press your lips to hers! Oh, rapture of raptures! Feet move! Mouth talk! She's there! She's waiting!

My mouth opened and I was about to say, "That's quite a river, isn't it?"

But it was too late.

My Lana had turned away and was walking back to the bus. At the open door, she paused and, with a wistful smile, glanced at me over her shoulder and sighed, "Bashful Bill Ray."

Then she got on the bus.

CHAPTER 21

▼

THE SLAP

Dad had taught me to play poker when we were on the carnival. I was five-years-old, but we didn't bet matchsticks, we bet money, his and mine, and it didn't matter if I'd saved my dime all week, he took it. When I was eight or ten or thirteen and my dimes had grown to quarters and half dollars, he took those, too. Shuffling the cards with a chuckle, he'd deal and say, "A fool and his money are soon parted."

But this time I wasn't playing Dad. I was at the Country Club on a rainy afternoon playing Buddy Bramhall. That summer before my sophomore year, I'd gotten a job running the lunch counter on weekdays. The rain discouraged any attempt at golf, so the clubhouse was empty. Bramhall lived up a hill close by and had bicycled down packing a deck of cards. He came in dripping wet wanting to play five-card draw. I had almost two dollars on me, so I said sure. Three hands later, I choked back a giggle. Bramhall played worse than I did. He bluffed every hand he got. This time I had three Jacks to draw to, and I made my move. Pushing in my pile of nickels and dimes to the center of the table, I said, "Table stakes," in a fake nervous voice.

Ol' Bramhall took the bait. He figured *I* was bluffing. Grinning through his freckles, he shoved all of his money to the center of the table.

The back door flew open. Dad walked in, wet hair askew, eyes glassy-red, his breath arriving before he did. He'd sold the bar months ago and had been "on vacation" since then. Pulling up a chair, he tossed some change in front of him and said, "Deal me in."

"We've already started this hand," I said.

"I'll catch up," Dad said. "Give me five cards."

I lowered my head and dealt his five.

"It's table stakes, Dad."

"Good," he answered. He shoved his money to the center of the table.

He took two cards, Bramhall took four cards, and I took two. I fanned the cards out in my hand. *Holy smoke! I had four Jacks, the best hand of my life!*

"Showdown!" I called, and laid out my trophies.

Bramhall had a pair of nines.

Dad waited a moment, smiled, and laid down his hand.

Four Kings.

"Why do you come down here drunk?" I yelled. "We were doing fine until you horned in."

The slap knocked my head back. It had come out of nowhere and caught me on the side of the face. Dad glared across the table not saying a word.

Bramhall half whispered, "I'd better be going," and bolted out the back door.

Dad's eyes didn't leave me. He sat there, looking at me with more anger than I'd ever seen in him. Then without a word, he scooped his winnings into his pants pocket and left. I heard his car spit gravel all the way to the highway.

I sat stunned. My cheek stung from the impact, but my shame burned far hotter. I had done something I'd never done before; never, ever *considered* doing before. It had just blurted out. I had sassed my father. This man, who showed me how to fly a kite, ride a bike, hit a ball, catch a fish. This man, who had driven the countryside with me, teaching me about people and life. This special man. I had disrespected him.

I sat at the table for a long time.

CHAPTER 22

▼

SHORTY AND THE
PUTNAMS

Dad had been near drunk. Not staggering, slurring drunk, but those red eyes signaled pretty close. He used to drink without showing it much. Then he lost his castle. The Casa Loma would've been his crowning achievement. *Ladies and gentlemen, Tramp Jackson proudly presents the finest nightclub in northern Missouri.* When it folded, so did Dad. He'd scrounged money to buy that smelly tavern, but it was too noisy and grungy. No new dreams came in the night. His Phantom whispered no more.

Without a dream, Dad lost his laughter; no longer told his funny stories; didn't comb his hair much; looked different, unkempt. But it was his eyes that bothered me the most, booze red and vacant, like he was dead inside. Would that happen to me? Would I hit the skids if a big dream went bust?

The rain continued in fits and spurts, guaranteeing no golfers that day, so I closed the clubhouse early and headed my bike toward home. Rodge lived nearby, and I stood up to peddle the long, muddy hill to his house. When I got to his porch, he popped out the front door, then drew up short.

"What's wrong?" he asked, looking at me closely.

"Nothing," I answered. "Just wet from the rain."

"Yeah. Hey, I saw Bramhall go by. Was he down at the clubhouse?"

"Uh huh. We played some poker."

"Just the two of you?"

"Yup."

"Who won?"

"It was about even."

I figured telling him about Dad horning in and then slapping me made Dad sound like he whacked me a lot. He didn't whack me at all; he talked, told me what I'd done wrong. Except there wasn't even much talking after the Casa Loma. But hit me? Heck, he'd only given me a couple of whippings when I was a little kid. Used his razor strap, which scared the buh-Jesus out of me, but the whippings never really hurt.

"Guess what?" Rodge said.

"What?"

"The school's looking for a new coach."

"How do you know that?"

"Carr told me."

"Must be so, then."

Gerald Dean Carr, who lived up the hill before you got to Bramhall's, usually had the lowdown on everything.

"Going out for football this year?" I asked, glad for a change of subject.

"I dunno, maybe. You?"

"Think so. I'm getting bigger. Maybe I can be as good as Cook and Davis."

"In your dreams," Rodge snorted.

Rodge was right. Nobody played football like my cousins. I guess they got it from Uncle Joe and Uncle Bill. Uncle Joe had been a sledgehammer lineman and Uncle Bill a wily quarterback. Now they wanted to pass the baton.

This fall of 1950, cousins Cook and Davis (the latter no longer called Paddy Joe) would be high school juniors. Throughout their grade years, in backyards and vacant lots, the boys had devoured the teachings of the uncles. The subjects were blocking, tackling, passing, running with the ball, and any other skill that might ready these family princes for gridiron glory.

My uncles longed for a legacy, new blood from the family to return Unionville football to its halcyon days. But Unionville football had stunk up the place; it had been years since the town celebrated a winning season. The current coach, after slumping off the field a loser so many times, couldn't inspire a hot game of hopscotch. Cook and Davis' first two years had hissed and sputtered, but failed to catch fire. Now, with the uncle's protégés about to suit up for their junior year, there was no time to waste on what didn't work. Uncle Bill and Uncle Joe went to the Board of Education and demanded a new coach. The city fathers sitting around the table frowned and grumped. A new man would cost more money. The budget was short. They'd think about a replacement in a couple of years. The brothers jointly launched a *this year* pitch:

The best players Unionville had seen in ages would be taking the field *this year*. Therefore, the best chance in a decade for a winning team was *this year*. But only if "*this year's* fine crop of boys" had the right leader.

The old men groused some more, but finally they said to get the guy.

My uncles got a dynamo: Shorty Preston, a fast, feisty halfback fresh from mid-Missouri's Marshall College, home of "hide-'em" football.

That first day of school my sophomore year, Shorty, with thinning blond hair and winning smile, stood in the middle of the gym with two former teammates, one in front of him and one beside him. The new coach held the ball high for all to see. "Keep your eye on the ball," he called. He tossed the ball to his friend in front of him who bent over and hiked it back. Shorty took the ball in a crouch, covered it with his arms, spun sharply to his left, and handed off to his other buddy crossing in a crouch behind him. But wait, Shorty didn't hand it off. He still had the ball. Next time the ball was hiked to Shorty's buddy who faked a handoff to Shorty rushing by. No, it was a real handoff. Or was it? This game of "Who's Got It?" went on and on, baffling everyone in the gym. Finally, Shorty held the ball high and yelled, "We're going to tie Milan's jock straps into granny knots!"

The roar from the bleachers shook the building. I may have cheered the loudest, because just maybe this new coach would make me football dynamite like my cousins. Then Shorty gave his alter call, a firestorm invitation to every male student in the gym to follow him onto the field and be a part of Unionville High's new "hide-'em" football. Practically every boy in the building rushed outside, even small guys like Hibbs, Bramhall, and Pollock, all ready to tuck and spin for the glory of the Midgets.

Yes, "Midgets" was the name of our team.

Where other schools gave themselves burly names like Bears and Lions, we called ourselves something a bit more diminutive because the sorry fact was—we were. For ages the average male height in Unionville had been somewhere between five foot seven and five foot nine. Anyone five foot ten or over was a cloud banger. Town fathers had suggested a fitting name for our school's teams would be something small but heroic, like *The Napoleons*. But that sounded dumb. *The Napoleons are on the twenty yard line.* No way. People would giggle.

Finally, Unionville's celebrated attorney Clare Magee suggested we should accept our smaller stature and proudly call ourselves what we were: midgets. The Midgets we became.

However, a few of us were relatively tall. At fifteen, I was almost six foot, except I didn't have any heft, unless you counted my suitcase feet, which weighed fifty pounds a piece. At 145 pounds, I was a certified skinny; and Shorty's call to arms hadn't mentioned the tackling line. This sanctioned train wreck occurred near the end of every practice when Shorty fed us scrawny underclassmen to the brawny, slavering juniors and seniors. These burly cowboys slammed us to the ground like rodeo calves. Then they punctuated their dominance by lying on top of us and dripping drool in our faces.

Ah, but one afternoon early in the season, the answer to every underclassman's prayer trotted onto the field—actually, two answers—the raw-boned, stringy muscled, always-laughing Putnam twins. They were fellow sophomores, fresh from the recent school district consolidation that gathered all the farm kids from miles around. With their sun-bronzed skin and bone-white smiles, the boys looked like frolicking Indians that had emerged from deep within the heavy timber south of town for a day of play.

Robert and Richard were identical twins, so close in looks that a story circulated that shortly after Robert had started seeing his girlfriend Colleen, he couldn't make a date and sent Richard in his stead. Colleen couldn't tell the difference, except that her boyfriend grinned more than usual after their goodnight kiss.

The twins embraced life like bounding, overgrown pups and found this fandangle called football more fun than riding hogs. Principal Noble Neil spoke of one Monday morning when they showed up at his office asking if they could have some "costumes" so they could "play that game Coach Shorty's Midgets was playin'." Looking up from his desk at these cow-licked grain silos, Mr. Neil bit his lip and allowed that the couch would get them some "costumes."

The following afternoon the Putnams joined the Midgets on the practice field. The twins tugged at the cumbersome pads and wore their tight-fitting helmets back on their heads so they could see better. Shorty wanted to know what these rangy hill boys could do, so he put them into the B-team lineup to scrimmage the A-team. The twins showed not the slightest understanding of what "plays" were, especially the part called "blockin'." But they delighted in "tacklin';" and whether on offense or defense, when the ball was snapped, they tackled anyone in front of them.

Shorty watched with a half smile as the Putnams tackled almost everyone on the opposite team. Then he blew his whistle. If they liked to tackle, he'd give it to them. I shuddered. He was going to feed them to the tackling line. The coach had his biggest fullbacks, tackles, and guards form a single line and tossed the ball to the first one; then placed the twins a few yards across from the ball carrier.

"Now, Putnam," he addressed the nearest twin, "when I blow the whistle, the first guy is going to run at you with the ball. Bring him down."

First up was the biggest lineman we had, outweighing most everybody by twenty five pounds. The lineman slammed the ball from hand to hand and leered at this farm boy in pure delight. The whistle blew and he plowed into Putnam Number One like a truck, knocking him flat on his back. The A-team cheered.

Putnam Number One bounded up grinning.

"Haw! That was fun, Coach! Let's do it again!"

Shorty smiled and accommodated the request. Head low, the lineman charged like a leg-churning bull. They collided head on and both fell backward to the ground. Putnam Number One jumped up laughing.

"That felt *good!* Blow 'er again!"

Shorty blew the whistle. This time Putnam Number One grabbed the tiring lineman by the neck and threw him to the ground like a sack of feed.

The lineman got up slowly and handed the ball to the next hulk in line, who found to his dismay that Putnam Number Two also wanted to keep tackling again and again. I looked heavenward. *There was a God! The A-team had Cook, Davis, and the rest of its heroes, but, dear Lord, we sophomores had the Putnams.*

That Friday night, the Midgets traveled to nearby Princeton, Missouri, the first game the Putnams had ever seen. Princeton won the toss and chose to receive the ball. As our kick-off team took the field, Shorty held back a starter and sent in one of the twins, again not knowing which one. This Putnam ran onto the field whooping and hollering, then stopped abruptly and turned to the bench.

"Coach? What's my job?" he called.

"Putnam," Shorty yelled, "when we kick off, run down and tackle the guy with the ball. *That's* your job."

The Putnam grinned and lined up for the kick off with his fellow costume wearers. The kick was high and deep. The pride of the sophomores lowered his head like a hunting dog and raced a straight line for the receiver. Bam! He knocked a blocker aside. Bam! Bam! Another and another. Princeton's receiver looked downfield and froze like a deer in headlights. Galloping toward him was an obsessed moose, knocking would-be blockers left and right. The Putnam swooped in, grabbed the poor ball carrier, held him high, and slammed him to the ground. Then The Putnam turned back toward the Midget's bench, jumped up and down and waved his arms.

"I got 'im, Coach! I got 'im!"

The Putnam had no idea what his teammates were supposed to do, but he'd done *his* job.

CHAPTER 23

▼

FIRST KISS

Bicycles were out. I'd ridden my bike from one end of town to the other, but when I turned fifteen I dropped it like it was a dead horse. Girls would see you. And girls only were interested in guys with cars, so you walked everywhere pretending you had a car, but it was getting fixed or something.

Hi, there. I'm walking down this street, 'cause my Chevy's in the shop. Transmission trouble; had 'er doin' ninety down Blackbird Hill!

Dad taught me to drive when I was fourteen. We lived in Grandma Jackson's little lean-to with its ten-dollar-a-month rent, so maybe that's how he saved up the money to get the best car he ever owned: a black, 1946 Buick Roadmaster with a silver grill that smiled like a shark, and a visor perched atop the windshield like the shiny bill on a military cap. If I pestered him enough, he'd take me on country roads and let me get behind the wheel. After I could shift gears without grinding them, stay on my side of the road, and stop without throwing both of us into the windshield, he'd let me drive for five miles or so down the highway, never putting the speedometer over forty.

One afternoon I caught Dad just as he was settling down for a nap. I asked him if I could take the Buick for a short drive. Maybe down the hilly dirt road a few blocks away that ran through The Hollows, a rag-taggle dip in the hills where the Eckles family lived. Dad said okay, twenty minutes, and stretched out on the couch. I rushed outside and yelled across the street for Cook. He stuck his head out the door and saw me behind the wheel of the Buick revving the motor and waving for him to come aboard. He hopped in shotgun, I gave a war whoop, and we took off. Boy, I wanted to stay on the main road so some girls would see us, but I kept my word to Dad and pulled onto the rutted, dirt road leading to the desolation of The Hollows. The big ruts were rain drenched from last night's storm, and Cook and I grinned at the way the big car swerved through the mud. I came to a steep hill, gave the Buick the gas, and it wiggled like a giant tadpole up, up, and over the top. There the fun ended. We plunged down the other side toward pure disaster: a huge rain pond that had swamped the road. I slammed on the brakes and skidded to an abrupt stop five feet from the water, the right rear wheel resting in a shallow, but rain-filled ditch.

Cook pushed while I gunned the engine and jerked the gears from forward to reverse trying to rock free, but this only buried the wheel deeper. There was nothing to do but hang my head, walk back to the house, and tell Dad. Cook shot into his house and I slumped into mine. I woke Dad from his nap, stammered what had happened and braced for the volcano's wrath. But Dad seemed to sense how sorry I was. He rose up on one elbow and said, "Well, there's your lesson. You don't drive a wet road like you do a dry one." He borrowed Uncle Buck's black panel truck and a towing chain, and I steered the Buick while he pulled the big car backwards out of the ditch. Then, to give me a little extra experience, he had me continue driving backwards all the way home. A few blocks from the house, two girls stood at a street corner watching me with puzzled looks as the Buick fishtailed from one curb to the other. I think one of them was Marilyn. Oh, well, I was driving.

Not having a car became nigh unbearable when Cook started driving a '41 Pontiac 2-Door Torpedo that had been his father's. It was blue and white with a snazzy tapered rear end, and Cook drove around with his sleeves rolled high and his left arm crooked and resting out the window. If I were footing it down some road, he'd drive by sporting a bevy of beauties, spray gravel, and grin like stupid Tony Curtis.

Of course, with my Novocain tongue, it didn't really matter if I had a car or not.

Hi. Yuh wanna … maybe … uh …, by the time I finished the question, I'd be taking 'em to the nursing home instead of the movies.

Then Beverly smiled.

Well, she usually smiled at boys, but this time it was at *this* boy. Her full name, Beverly Lightfoot, sounded like she hung out with Pocahontas, but her hazel eyes and bobbed brown hair didn't look Indian at all. She was an eighth grader, and one day as I was going to class she gave me the eye and giggled to her girlfriend. Carr, the class oracle, watched me shuffle by her like a doofus, and then pulled me into a corner and gave me the message in words I could understand:

She likes you, dumb butt."

"She does?"

I couldn't believe it. Girls didn't like me. They liked slick guys like Shelby Dixon. The Shelb had wavy hair and pouty lips and sleepy eyes, and he said clever things like, "Hey, pretty thang, your momma know you're out?"

"Yeah, she likes you," Carr said. "She told me to tell you. So ask her for a date."

Good God, a date?

I started sweating and sucking air like I was back on the Mississippi boat dock with Lana.

"Calm down, Jackson," Carr said. "You can do this." He leaned close for emphasis. "It's time."

He was right. I looked back down the hall, and Beverly flashed me a killer smile and disappeared into the crowd. She'd signaled "yes!" I could ask her out for a date without stammering around looking at my big toe. I'd make a date for Saturday night, take her to the Royal, buy her popcorn, hold her hand, drive her home and, oh-ho-ho, kiss her goodnight. No I wouldn't. Little Billy Ray didn't have a car.

But Dad did.

It came with his new job. Dad had left bartending and swung a loan for a furniture store. After peddling dinette sets and coffee tables until it made him miserable, he sold the store at a loss. He was back on the customer side of the bar when Uncle Bill gave Dad a job selling used cars at Davis Chevrolet Garage, which was owned by three of Mom's brothers. Dad liked being around cars and won a little lapel pin for selling a bunch of them. And one of the perks to the job was that he got use of one of the cars on the lot.

It'd been a couple of months since that slap at the poker game. Mom didn't even know about it. Anyway, things had smoothed out; and if he was in a good mood when he got off work, I'd ask him if I could use the car. After school, I rushed home to await his arrival.

We'd moved to a worn, slightly larger house a straight shot from Grandma Jackson's front door, which later my brothers and I would refer to as "The House across the Street." Grandma had died, and in her last days her mind failed and her gentle soul filled with threatening, disembodied spirits seen only by her eyes.

Dad had become the Devil and the voices of demons hissed her name in the night. She would run off, and we'd find her in neighborhood bushes, frozen with fear. She wasn't about to come home with the Devil, so Dad would leave me with her alone to coax her back.

"C'mon, Grandma, it's Bill Ray. It's all right, let's go home. We'll make some cocoa."

I sometimes had trouble speaking as I remembered the love she bathed me in when I was small; nestling me in her lap; reading me the funnies by her kerosene lamp. Her eyes, once so lively and dark, had dimmed to watery tea and receded into the grayish sockets in her skin tight skull. She barely recognized me, but followed my reassuring voice back to the house that had become her nightmare. Finally, the demons spoke no more; and the family placed the sweetest soul God every created next to Grandpa Bill in the Pollock hill country where she was born.

Now we lived at "The House across the Street," and I sat in the living room waiting for Dad to come through the front door. He entered looking reasonably happy, but before I could say anything he headed out the back door. To Mom's dismay, Dad had built a still in the storm cellar under the house. I hustled down the cellar stairs to plead for the car, but Dad already had his ear up to a metal barrel listening to the mash work.

"Dad, I need a favor," I said nervously.

Dad looked at me. I was flushed and sweaty.

"Is this about a girl?" he asked.

I sank onto a wooden stool by the washing machine. "Uh, yeah … I want to ask her on a date, but …"

Dad held up his hand, then motioned for me to come stand by him. "I'm going to add to your education," he said.

Oh, Lordy, I thought. He's going to tell me about the birds and the bees.

He didn't. The education was of a quite different sort.

"I think this batch is ready," he said, "but it's got to be tested."

He held a coffee cup saucer at the bottom of the barrel and drained a small puddle of moonshine from the spigot. Then he pulled a wooden match out of his pocket.

"I'm going to light this," he said, "and if the flame burns blue, it's a good batch. If it burns yellow, it's a bad one."

He struck the match and ignited the puddle. Blue flame.

"Good batch!" He blew out the flame and gulped down the experiment.

While he drew a cupful for a bigger sample, I babbled about Beverly and my desperate need for a car; how I knew I didn't have a license, but I would be, oh, so careful....

"You can use the car ..." he said, sipping his cup.

"Wahooo!"

"... *providing* you only drive the back streets. You don't go over thirty. And you have the car back by ten o'clock. Leave one inch of black rubber on the road, and you won't be driving again."

"Thank you, Dad!"

I parked on a dark street two blocks off the Square, since I couldn't go pulling up in front of the Royal—Sheriff Stillman "Bub" Beary patrolled downtown like he was searching for escaped convicts. I turned to Beverly and mumbled something about liking to walk. Beverly just smiled. She was wearing extra lipstick and a beige sweater that matched her eyes.

As we started for the theater, I remembered Mom saying a gentleman took the side closest to the street to protect the lady from cars that might hop the curb. I didn't much like the idea of being a bumper, but I did it anyway. What about taking the girl's hand? Beverly's was there for the taking, but I feared being too forward and jammed my hands into my pockets and walked the two blocks like a cowboy sauntering to the bar.

I paid the dollar for two tickets and twenty cents for two popcorns, and we sat midway from the screen. Carr, Torrey, and Bramhall were there, but gave us lots of space. Dixon didn't. The Shelb came up, all smarmy and wavy-haired, and plopped right next to Beverly, and she smiled real big. He laughed, saying he was "just testing out seats," and drifted down front. Beverly's eyes followed him.

We ate our popcorn and Beverly talked. She was new to the school, and she said she liked it better in this town, "'cause the kids in the other town were snotty and Unionville kids were nice." My part of the conversation was to grin at everything she said and bob my head like I'd have a brain hemorrhage if she stopped.

When the lights dimmed for the movie, all I could think about was putting my arm around Beverly like The Shelb did all of his girls. But when I went to make my move, my hand turned traitor and welded itself to my popcorn sack. I stared at my fingers, silently cursed them; called them yellow, gutless chicken livers. They squeezed the sack tighter. Half way through Coming Attractions they finally uncurled and edged cautiously across the chair arm and touched Beverly's wrist. Without taking her eyes from the screen, she took my hand and gave it a little squeeze. Electric sparks shot out my ears. Hey, Carr! Torrey! Bramhall!

Look at me! I'm sitting here in the Royal holding a girl's hand! It wasn't a "Shelb" move, but it was a start.

When we came out of the movie, the courthouse clock said nine thirty. Back at the car, I held the door open for Beverly like classy David Niven, hustled to my side, and slide behind the wheel.

"I don't have to be home 'til ten," Beverly cooed.

Hot dog! I could make a fast run to make out heaven: the Old City Pond.

Naw, I didn't have the guts. Instead, I laid low, creeping up and down the back streets at about twenty miles an hour, pretending to show Beverly the town, which was pretty dumb since she'd been here for months. She smiled and acted like I was showing her Kansas City. Nearing the Kozy Corner gas station west of the Square, I spotted Sheriff Bub's '49 Ford idling in the shadows. I didn't want his red spotlight shining on this fifteen year old, so I turned short of the station, eased the car back to Beverly's, cut the engine and turned off the lights. I figured I had ten minutes before the car had to be in front of my house. Beverly lived only a few blocks from me, so that gave me at least eight minutes to work on a goodnight kiss. And the clock was ticking.

I turned toward her and the porch light hit me like a prison searchlight. Bobbing my head like an ostrich, I tried to dodge the glare, while Beverly told me she'd enjoyed the movie very much, especially the romantic parts, and, my, I certainly seemed fidgety. I slumped low in my seat, positioning Beverly's head between me and the light, and tried to talk about the movie, *King Solomon's* something. It had Stewart Granger strutting around with his shirt off and lots of oil glistening on his chest. I couldn't recall much more, because what I mostly remembered was cheetah-grinning Shelb turning around every five minutes and giving us a big wink.

"Well, I'd better go in," Beverly said. "You don't have to walk me to the door."

Good grief. I'd forgotten the walking to the door part.

"I had a very nice time," Beverly said, and turned directly toward me.

"Me, too," I answered.

Silence.

Beverly sat there looking at me. *It was time for the kiss.* I'd been thinking about it all night and now I was sweating bullets and could hardly swallow. Maybe we weren't supposed to kiss on the first date. She was only thirteen. I looked at her. Maybe we were. She kinda looked like we were. I'd better check. I swallowed a gallon of saliva and croaked, "Is it all right if I kiss you goodnight?"

"Ohhhh!" she groaned. I could tell from her look I wasn't supposed to ask.

"I'm sorry," I fumbled, "I just should've gone ahead and …"

She lunged across the car seat and laid a smacker on me that banged my head against the car door window. Then she sprinted to the house, gave a little wave and disappeared inside the front door. Off went the porch light, and I sat in the dark feeling the back of my head. This kissing stuff could be dangerous.

When I entered the house, the clock on the stand by the living room sofa read 9:59. No one was up and Dad was snoring. I tiptoed to my room, shucked my clothes and slid into bed. Hands behind my head, I stared up at the ceiling and let out a three mile sigh. What a knock-your-socks-off day this had been. First girlfriend. First date. First driving a car with a girl by my side.

And *wow-dee-dow-dow!* First kiss!

Smiling, I rubbed the bump on the back of my head and drifted to sleep.

CHAPTER 24

▼

ALL THINGS MALE

After that first date, I used Dad's loaner car to ferry Beverly down one dark street after another. She still smiled, but at school I saw her making eyes at older guys—guys with drivers' licenses. They drove their girls where couples could be seen, mostly around the Square honking and waving at each other like it was Old Home Week. It was early summer1950, and I wouldn't be sixteen for three months. Would Beverly wait that long for me to get us into the parade? No she wouldn't. After the school year ended, I spotted her snuggled close to a new and older boy friend as they drove the Square; Beverly waving gleefully at everyone she knew. But she didn't wave at me. For me she reserved a small, sad smile and leaned her head upon the shoulder of her new, older beau.

It was going to be a long summer. And come fall, when I got my license, I didn't want to be driving Dad's loaner; I wanted my own wheels. But even a junker cost fifty dollars. I needed a job; so did Cook; and we hoped Uncle Bill might give us each one.

After returning from the war to an empty nest, Uncle Bill divorced Aunt Kate, spent some healing time, and in November of 1946 married one of those cute McKay farm girls from north of town. An independent sort, Avis McKay had worked for some of Unionville's most influential men and was considered a bit worldly, having lived in San Francisco a spell. Although she disliked accounting, she came to work for Uncle Bill as a bookkeeper. He must've liked her figures, because he made her name rhyme. She became Avis Davis. Cook and I knew that when Uncle Bill was happy he rattled the keys in his front pants pocket; and since marrying Aunt Avis, he'd been jingling his keys like it was Christmas. We decided to try for the big time and hit him up for a job at the most revered business in town—the Davis Chevrolet Garage.

For the males of Unionville, the Garage reigned as the town's unofficial social center, the hub of discussion for all matters male: cars, sports, women, politics, you name it, and was owned by three of my four Davis uncles: Glen, Joe, and Bill. Uncle Virgil, the oldest—and the pride of the family—managed a three-story Woolworth's in Minneapolis. The remaining three uncles bought equal shares of the flagging Fowler Garage and turned it into Unionville's most compelling business emporium: a Chevy-Olds dealership.

Practically everyone in town stopped by to admire the marvels on display in the showroom: the 1950 Chevy Bel-Air and the 1950 Oldsmobile Ninety Eight. The Ninety Eight was a battleship, taking up so much display room you had to stand outside and look through the window to fully appreciate its mighty presence.

All three uncles drove new demo cars. Uncle Bill—the youngest of the three— sold cars and managed the repair shop and gasoline pumps. Happily jingling the keys in his right front pocket, he greeted customers like long-lost relation.

He drove a sporty Chevy Bel-Air.

Erudite Uncle Glen, the oldest of the partners, was a former naval officer and pioneer television engineer. He smoked his pipe, checked the books, and strolled daily to the post office for the mail.

Uncle Glen drove the conservative Chevy Styleline Deluxe.

Boisterous Uncle Joe, long on generosity, short on patience, was one of Unionville's movers and shakers. He laughed loud, growled louder, usually picked up the check, and ran the Parts Department.

He drove the gargantuan Olds Ninety Eight.

Uncle Joe was a rascal, and Uncle Bill told the story that proved it. He and Uncle Joe and a couple of cronies were in Joe's Ninety Eight headed for St. Louis to take in a Cardinals game. A few miles down the road a bottle was passed around the car to toast the Card's heavy hitter, Stan-the-Man Musial. Bill was driving and didn't partake; but soon the car reeked of many toasts to the great batter.

Bill looked in the rear-view mirror and saw a black car following closely behind them. Tailgaters irritated him, so he sped up. So did his pursuer. Bill nudged the accelerator; the black car stayed right with him. Bill pushed the accelerator hard.

A red light flashed.

"Good Lord, I'm racing a cop," Bill muttered. He pulled the car over and turned to his buddies.

"Now, just let me do the talking. I've never gotten a ticket before and I'll sugar us out of this one."

The police officer walked up to Bill's window with his ticket book already open.

"Afternoon, officer. What's the problem?"

"The problem is you've got a lead foot." The officer sniffed the air and crinkled his nose. "And we may have another problem. Where're you gentlemen from?"

"Oh, we're just some good old boys from Unionville goin' down to the ballgame in St. Louis. Want to see Stan-the-Man belt one. Isn't that Musial something? Must be battin' over .330." Flashing the pearly smile that had won Putnam County's heart, Bill said, "Listen, officer, I'm real sorry about this. We'll be extra careful from now on."

The cop looked in the back seat. No bottle was in sight; no one made a peep.

"All right," he said, closing his ticket book, "go see Stan-the-Man. Just watch your driving."

As the officer started back to his patrol car, Joe stuck his head out his side window.

"Whas' yer name?" he called.

The cop turned around. "Officer Davis."

Joe said, "Davis? Thas' my name. But now I'm gonna change it."

The officer flipped the book open, wrote the ticket, shoved it in Bill's face, and strode back to the patrol car.

Bill turned to his brother. "Why on earth did you do that for?"

Joe grinned.

"Well, you said you'd never hadda ticket before and I jus' want'd you to know what it felt like."

When Uncle Bill hired Cook and me to work at the garage; Uncle Joe already had hired his son Paddy Joe to work in the Parts Department. Paddy Joe always looked neat and clean; Cook and I did not. Cook changed oil and lubed cars on the grease rack, but I had the messier job; I washed cars. It sounded clean, but it wasn't. Farmers came in with these lunky old cars with about ten tons of manure globbed underneath them. It took a power hose to knock it loose. The trouble was that the manure splattered back at you, and I always looked like I'd been walking on the wrong end of a cow.

The power hose, called Blunderbuss, blasted water with such force that controlling it was like wrestling a python. One afternoon I was crouched by a car grappling this monster, knocking clods from the undercarriage, when I felt someone looking at me. I glanced over my shoulder and there was Cook wearing about five miles of smirk across his face. Now, first off, let me say that Uncle Bill should've known better than to hire us both under one roof anyway.

"You got poop freckles," Cook snickered.

I kept on blasting.

He smiled big like he'd thought of a real good one and said, "Hey, when you're done, let's play superheroes. I'll be Superman and you can be Pooperman."

He laughed like he was smarty Bob Hope. I said nothing.

A moment passed and then he said, "I'll bet you're afraid to shoot me with that."

Well, world, what was I to do?

I wheeled Blunderbuss around and blasted Cook right in the gut. The impact knocked him five feet backwards and flat on his can.

Well, that was it; he jumped up and lunged on me like a gorilla; and while the work clock ticked away, Cook and I rolled around the greasy garage floor, punching, kicking, gouging, and saying ever so sweet things to each other—just two devoted employees at the Davis Chevrolet Garage.

I was knocking manure off a pickup's rear end when *she* came into my life. My mind was filled with cars and girls and how good a Pepsi with some peanuts in it would taste when I heard this hushed, feminine voice.

"Excuse me, but are you a member of that wonderful organization, *The Working Men of America?*"

I looked around and there stood the cutest girl a fifteen-year-old boy could possibly hope to see. She looked eighteen, and was about five-foot-two and wore a white blouse with the shirt tails tied up so you could see the tan on her tummy. Her curly brown hair was tucked under a perky, short-billed cap, which was red like her shorts. And we're talking short shorts, a lot shorter than the girls in Unionville wore 'em. But what riveted my attention were her legs. They looked like Betty Grable's. I'm not lying. I just stood there, my mouth dry and hanging open. She gave an "ahem," and nodded upward. I had Blunderbuss knocking paint off the ceiling.

You *are* a working man of America, aren't you?" she asked, giving a sun-dazzling smile as she opened the black satchel slung over her shoulder.

"Oh, yeah!" I answered, shutting off the power hose. I was ready to be Hitler's uncle if she wanted me to be. She moved closer, and I smelled a perfume nobody's mother ever wore. She looked into my eyes and gave me this heart-stopping smile—all the while talking about how educated I looked, and how certainly I would want to "stay abreast of current events." When she said "abreast," I could swear she took a deep breath. I about died. I gritted my teeth and forced my eyes to stay focused somewhere around her nose. A paper and fountain pen appeared, and she made a little "x" at the bottom of the paper. Then she moved *real* close and her moist red lips said, "Sign here."

I signed.

She said, "Your year-long subscriptions to *Life, Look, Collier's,* and *The Saturday Evening Post* come to $49.50. Cash, please."

"Forty nine fifty?" I looked in my billfold. I only had three dollars. Miss Perky Cap didn't look so friendly anymore.

"Mr. Jackson, you've signed a legal contract for five subscriptions. You can go to the office and draw the money from your next paycheck."

"I don't *make* forty nine fifty a week."

"Then draw what you make and pay the rest later. I'll wait for you by the gas pumps," she said and walked outside.

Ask Uncle Bill for my paycheck? This was Monday!

I trudged to the showroom like I was going to the gas chamber. Uncle Bill, smiling his high spirits, was just finishing with a customer. I stood hangdog a few feet away. Here he'd given me a job so I could buy a car, and I was going to hit him for an advance to buy stupid magazines. I wanted to throw up. When the customer left, I shuffled to Uncle Bill and mumbled about magazines and my need for early pay, nodding toward the girl waiting at the pumps.

"You can't have it," he said matter-of-factly.

"But Uncle Bill, I signed ..."

"I'll handle this," he said.

I watched from behind the showroom door as Uncle Bill marched out to the girl and said something. She looked mad and showed him the paper I'd signed. He took it and tore it up. She waved her arms like a wild woman. Uncle Bill pointed down the street and the girl stalked off.

When he came back inside I said, "Oh, thank you!"

Uncle Bill said, "That's all right." Then he grinned. "She did have nice legs, didn't she?

CHAPTER 25

▼

COMES A PIPER

That spring of 1951, the men stopping by for coffee at Davis Chevrolet leap-frogged baseball and talked of nothing but the coming fall's Midget football. Uncle Bill's keys jingled faster and Uncle Joe's laughter boomed louder as the town fathers savored a most delicious prospect: revenge.

After years of humiliation inflicted by mammoth teams from bigger towns, this year's Midgets just might "rub there noses in it." Last year, peppery Shorty Preston had fired the team to its first winning season in years. This year, the town expected cousins Cook and Davis, now battle-savvy seniors, to fulfill an expected destiny: lead Unionville to football glory. Preston would be their Patton, the general who'd sweep them and their teammates to the school's first conference championship since 1904.

Then the shocker hit: "General Patton" headed for other battles.

He took a coaching job near Kansas City; and the town's plans for vengeance plummeted. We had to have an exceptional coach, because there was no ignoring one glaring fact: the Midgets were aptly named. Teams like Kirksville and Marceline, Trenton and Milan, were powerhouses. When the Midgets took the field against these big teams, they looked something like coyotes against grizzly bears. We needed a fire-eater coach, one who would inspire Cook & Company to play three sizes bigger than they were. But although the school board searched for dynamite, it only found firecrackers: coaches who'd grown content to merely win more than they lost.

That wouldn't do, not in this, the year of Cook and Davis.

Uncle Bill, Uncle Joe, and W. E. Ross, the ranking school board member, converged on Shorty just as he was leaving town. Could he think of anyone who might save Unionville's dream? Loading his bags into the car, Shorty left them one name: Ernie Piper.

And what a Pied Piper he was.

A former college teammate of Shorty's, Piper was tall and good-looking with cropped black hair, blue eyes, and a smile that fluttered every female heart within fifty feet. He accepted nothing but your best, and gave you nothing but his. Arriving in early summer, far ahead of schedule, he immediately called a meeting with Cook, Davis, and other senior classmen on the team.

Cook spoke of the meeting with awe. Piper, in resolute tones, designated this small band of seniors as the team leaders who would set the benchmark for the team. They were to "relentlessly hammer the giants until they fall." No bruise, no aching bone would prevent the Midgets from ramming the ball across the goal line. They would give their all and find strength to give even more.

The team leaders had never heard words like this. Coach Piper had ignited the torches, now it was their job to carry them forth.

Word spread that this would be the Midgets' finest hour. On the first day of practice in stifling mid-August heat, a full week prior to the normal first day of showing up and trying on your pads, eighty six wide-eyed, sweat-soaked, tongue-lolling teenage males jumped, shoved, blocked, tackled, and ran themselves to complete exhaustion. Football practice came as close to hell and any kid wanted to be. From the bottom of a pile of collided bodies, I looked across the field, wiped the sweat from my eyes, and looked again. There on the sidelines, that silent, silhouetted figure wearing the fedora was my father.

I was to catch his presence at several practices, but he never mentioned being there, never gave advice like the other fathers. Dad had been a baseball man, a sandlot pitcher, and he had tried his best to pass that talent on to me; but I was no good at it, no good at any position in the game. The truth was, baseballs scared me. They shot at you like rocks out of a cannon and hurt like hell if you misjudged their arrival. I misjudged a lot. And I couldn't hit 'em, either. The pitcher would wind up; and the next thing would be a *thunk* in the catcher's glove. No, I was better at running head-on into rhinos, so here I was, out for football; and seeing Dad on the sidelines once in a while made me feel like he still cared about what I did.

We played our first game sixty miles away at La Plata, Missouri. Piper kept the hide-the-ball, spinning-back formation that Shorty had introduced, and my cousins strutted their stuff. Cook, the quarterback, called the plays, but unlike quarterbacks in other formations, he rarely took the snap. Instead, he lined up to the right behind the center, charged out in front of the ball carrier and, despite his wiry stature, flung his body at would-be tacklers like Attila the Hun. Cook called such a mix-up of plays that he razzle-dazzled half the La Plata team into running the wrong direction; and his teammates dubbed him "The Brain."

Davis earned his own nickname. His legs churned and changed direction so fast, the lumbering La Plata Bulldogs could only grab at his wake. Piper watched his spinner back zigzag around the groping giants, turned to our bench and, giving a wink, said, "The Galloping Ghost." And from then on, Davis shared the nickname made famous by Red Grange, the three-time All-American.

Lined up in the backfield alongside Davis was Gary Grabosch, a fluid, natural athlete who did all the passing—lofting the ball long and drilling it short to lanky Willie Edmunds, our husky, catch-'em-one-handed end who played both offense and defense. Our 142 pound tailback, Billy Musgrove, darted downfield like a rabbit. And what about Carter? Dad had been right about his making touchdowns. When we neared the goal line, Cook called on bread 'n butter Carter. The backfield husky took the handoff, lowered his head, and barreled through would-be tacklers like a fixated bull.

I sat on the bench with the rest of the wannabes and cheered the A-team to victory. We had just kicked off after another easy touchdown when I heard a familiar name.

"Jackson!"

Good God, Piper was calling in the subs!

I grabbed my helmet, untangled my big feet from under the bench, and stumbled to the coach's side.

"Go in for Edmunds. Five man line, ends crashing."

I ran onto the field and thumbed Edmunds out before Coach changed his mind. "Five man, ends crashing," I hissed to my teammates and jammed on my helmet. When the Bulldog's quarterback looked over his center at the new defense, he spotted this greenie still fumbling with his helmet strap. He barked an audible that changed the play and leaned forward to take the snap.

"Hut, one!"

I gave up on the strap and let it hang.

"Hut, two!"

Ends crashing I was supposed to slant-charge by the tackle and catch the ball carrier by surprise.

"Hut, three!"

The quarterback slapped the ball into the fullback's midsection and he charged straight at me. Strap dangling, I braced to meet my destiny. My destiny had no neck and outweighed me by thirty pounds. We met, that is, his helmet met my nose—face guards didn't exit. The collision pancaked my snout, sent my helmet flying, and knocked me flat on my back.

When I got up, the Bulldogs' fullback stood smiling on the other side of the goal line. It was to be La Plata's only score; the game ended 40 to 6. Being as good as Cook and Davis might take a while.

Our next game was on a Friday night the following week with the Princeton Tigers. To make sure we were "fresh to fight," Coach Piper ordered the team to be in bed by nine o'clock the night before. Keeping his curfew would be a challenge. I'd turned sixteen and had bought my first car with the money I'd earned wrestling Blunderbuss for Uncle Bill. I'd gone to the car lot where Dad worked and asked him to help me pick out something sporty. He selected a gray hearse. Well, not exactly. It was a 4-door '37 Pontiac that looked like a hearse. Dad said a preacher had traded it in on a spiffy, red Chevy Bel-Air; swearing with "big, solemn eyes" that the old Pontiac was in perfect condition.

When Coach Piper gave the 9:00 PM. curfew, I still hadn't properly initiated my new wheels. To do so meant crossing into Iowa and dazzling the Centerville girls with your chariot. And because we never played Centerville, you could tell the girls you were a football hotshot from Unionville and they wouldn't know if you were or not. Promising ourselves to make Piper's deadline, Rodge and I left just after supper, crossed the state line and headed for the action: Centerville's town square. We circled it for an hour, but the evening refused to offer up any female under forty, so we grudgingly headed home.

Five miles north of Unionville, we started down the long descent to Blackbird Creek. In the rearview mirror, headlights appeared in the distance, closed rapidly and swerved to the left lane. It was a pickup I'd never seen, and it pulled even with me and honked. Hibbs was driving, and Johnny Bill Steele and Clark Carter were alongside him in the cab. The three of them and the two of us were on the football team—Steele and Carter were starters—Steele playing offensive guard even though he only weighed 124 pounds.

"Race you back!" Hibbs yelled.

Rodge and I howled like wolves and I tromped the gas. Hurtling down the hill, the big Pontiac became a rhino on wheels and lurched into the lead. As we crossed the valley floor, the creek's cement bridge loomed out of the darkness. I looked in the mirror and saw the pickup on top of me and starting to pass.

Sparks exploded in the mirror.

"Oh, my God!" yelled Rodge.

The sparks faded into the night like spent fireflies. I turned the car around and edged back, the Pontiac's headlights revealing an empty bridge. Heads out our windows, Rodge and I searched the darkness on each side of the highway and saw nothing. We looked at each other and feared the worst. *Teenage boys racing. A crash. Dead bodies.* I turned around and again slowly drove the bridge, both of us straining to hear any sound in the night's silence. Nothing. *Was the pickup under water? Were Hibbs, Steele, and Carter trapped in the cab … drowning?*

Carter, with a foolish grin, appeared in the glare of the headlights as he climbed out of the brush and onto the road. Steele, scowling, followed behind him; and, finally, a wan-looking Hibbs. I maneuvered the Pontiac so the lights would shine down the embankment. Near the creek, up to its door handles in weeds, was the pickup—right side up, roof caved in, fenders dented, and front bumper hanging loose.

"We rolled over," Carter said.

"You guys all right?" Rodge asked.

They checked themselves over. There was but one injury. The pickup had slammed the bridge railing and rolled over down a twenty foot embankment. You want a miracle? The only damage to the passengers was a small, moon-crescent cut on Johnny Bill's right knee.

I drove everyone home and pulled up to my house thirty minutes past Coach Piper's curfew. Getting back late was the least of my worries. Old Faithful roared from under the Pontiac's hood.

"The preacher lied," muttered Dad as he crawled out from under the car the next morning, "… said it ran like a top, but this car had a cracked engine block. Know what that preacher did? He stuffed the block with sawdust to stop the water leak. Well, this clunker's only good for the junkyard now." Dad gave me a close look. "You'd have to be running pretty hot to cause the sawdust to blow out."

I avoided Dad's eyes and mumbled something about just taking a little spin with Rodge. Dad said nothing, picked up his tool box, retrieved his half-smoked Chesterfield from the running board, and walked to the house. "You'd never make a lawyer," he called back, "that lie's written all over your face." He closed the door behind him.

That night, just minutes into the game, Carter, showing no wear and tear from the pickup's flip flop, bulled across the goal line for the Midgets' first score. Cook's surprise plays confused Princeton; Davis snaked for touchdowns; Grabosch scored; and The Putnams tackled everything in sight, taming the Tigers 33–6. Early in the rout, Piper sent in the subs, giving me another chance at gridiron stardom; but Grabosch passed only to Davis and Edmunds. However, I did show progress: I made a couple of tackles and could now find my chin strap.

CHAPTER 26

▼

THE JOB, THE CAR, THE NIGHT FROM HELL

Carr passed the word that Hibbs had "borrowed" the pickup from the auto repair shop where he worked; and we didn't see much of him after that—he was busy working to pay for the repair of what he'd borrowed. As for my car, Dad's diagnosis proved correct, the block was cracked and couldn't be sealed. I drove the Pontiac to Shields' junkyard, collected twenty dollars, and walked home.

The days that followed were humiliating. Here I was, sixteen, and had to walk everywhere. *Hi there, cutie-pie. Want to stroll around the Square? We can wave to all your friends as they drive by.* Not going to happen.

Then one Sunday afternoon I was walking home from the Royal, and The Shelb drove up. Shelby Dixon was in his folks' '47 Studebaker, the one where the front-end and the back-end looked the same—you couldn't tell if the car was coming or going.

"Wanna cruise?" The Shelb called out the car window.

I couldn't believe it. Cruising with the master himself! I hopped in and Dixon headed for the Square.

"I think there's some stuff on the west side," he said, giving a wink. Sure enough, two girls were walking real slow, looking in the display windows of the closed shops.

"Ah, Shirley Shuey and Donna Medlin," he said, "little freshmen baton twirlers. Let's see what we can get going."

Even though a fellow junior, the Shelb reigned as the lover boy of the whole school. I felt like a baby bird learning to fly. He pulled the car ahead of the girls and slowed, waiting for them to walk by.

"Call to 'em," said The Shelb.

Good grief, he'd put them on my side of the car! I was going to have to talk! I squinted my eyes and opened my mouth. Nothing came out.

The Shelb leaned across me and called, "Hey, pretty thangs, what'cha doin' out this late in the day?"

The girls stopped, looked at each other and giggled.

"We're jus' seein' the sights; why don'cha get in?" he continued, laying that puffy-lipped smile of his on them. The Shelb reeled them up to the car like fish on a line; and they stood less than a foot away, on *my* side. I could smell their perfume. Shirley was a brunette and Donna was a blonde—cute girls—cuter than I'd ever messed with. I swallowed; worked my mouth; tried to form words of at least two syllables.

"Is this your car, Shelb?" cooed Shirley.

"It is today," he replied. "Get in, girls, we'll cruise away the blues."

Shirley was looking at Dixon and Donna was looking at Dixon and I was looking at Donna. I thought she looked like Virginia Mayo the movie star, same blonde hair, same cheek bones, and especially, the same penetrating blue eyes. I wished they'd look at me.

Shirley gestured toward a car parked at the end of the block. "We can't. My mother's waiting to take us home."

"Bring 'er along," said The Shelb, giving a big wink. They both giggled like he'd said the cleverest thing in the world. I was still trying to say "hi."

"No, we really have to go," Shirley answered. The girls slowly walked toward momma's car, giggling, looking back at us every few moments. Well, they looked at The Shelb. He ran his comb through his hair and then wiggled the comb at them. They practically fell down laughing.

"Give 'em a wink and tell 'em we'll catch 'em next time," Dixon said as we slowly passed by.

I leaned my head out the window, closed one eye, and said:

"Catch it next time!"

I fell back into my seat. *Catch it? What were they supposed to catch, the mumps?* The Shelb shook his head and drove me home.

.

Carr gave me that knowing look of his when Donna went by. That meant I wasn't imagining things; this baton twirler girl liked me, at least some. A freshman, she'd passed me three times in the hall with that Virginia Mayo look, the one that tripled my heart beat. Carr leaned to my ear.

"Gonna take her to the show?" he asked.

"In what, my little red wagon?"

We watched Donna sashay down the hallway.

Without taking his eyes off her exit, Carr said, "Little man, you'd better get some wheels." He patted me on the shoulder and added, "Soon," and walked away.

Of course I needed a car *soon*, but when school started I could only wash cars for Uncle Bill on Saturdays. To get enough money, I needed to work during the week, and school took a big hunk out of a guy's day. During lunch break, Torrey, Bramhall, and I nursed our Pepsis at the counter of the Little Store, a grocery-café across from the school.

"Anyone know any magic?" I asked, sloshing the Pepsi around in my bottle.

"I can make money disappear," said Bramhall.

"Try making it *appear* once in a while; you owe me a quarter," said Torrey.

"I'm talking big magic," I said, "like how to go to school and still make enough money to buy a car."

Torrey and Bramhall, who didn't have cars either, sipped their drinks. The clock behind the counter showed that afternoon classes were about to start, and we tossed our nickels on the counter and headed for the door.

"Take ... D.O.," said a low voice.

I looked back at the counter. Down at the end was James Morrow, who, I'd been told, was born in a log cabin south of Hartford. Our freshman year, he'd come off the farm and promptly became wallpaper. Except for his blue eyes, he looked like Tonto with wider cheek bones; and I don't think I'd ever heard him talk before. I lingered as my buddies went outside.

"What's D. O.?" I asked.

Morrow drained his Pepsi; wiped his mouth with the back of his hand and then stared at the potato chip sacks on the ledge behind the counter. I thought he hadn't heard me; then he mumbled," Diversified ... Occupations," and fished in his pocket for some change.

Holy Toledo, here was a guy who talked even slower than I did.

Torrey called from outside. "Jackson, you're gonna be late."

Morrow counted the coins he placed on the counter. I figured this conversation would continue in about a week and headed for the door.

Morrow called after me:

"Mr. Neil … teaches it. But he … don't teach nothin'. He … lets you work and … gives you credit for it. He lets me … raise my own chickens."

Morrow looked exhausted, like it was the most he'd talked the whole year. I nodded my thanks and ran for class.

After school, I hustled to the principal's office and asked Mr. Neil about this D. O. class. Morrow talked slow, but he was dead on. You could work during school hours—*if you had a job before signing up for class.*

I hit every store in town, but the few places that had jobs wanted you there all day. I gave up on a car, dating Donna, anything approaching survival in a teenage world. Then Dell Rockwood, who ran a hatchery, stopped by Davis Chevrolet and mentioned to Uncle Bill the need for some part time help. Dell had a refined look and a quiet smile, someone who came to mind when the word "gentleman" came up. Co-owner of Loughridge Hatchery, which for years had sold chicks to farmers, Dell added a new venture, supplying fattened chickens, called broilers, to the burgeoning TV-dinner industry. He needed extra help because now, in addition to the fuzzy little incubator chicks, he had ten thousand big chickens to feed and clean up after. I'd cleaned a lot of dung off farmers' cars, so Uncle Bill recommended me for the job; and the following day I stood with shovel in hand, surrounded by thousands of bug-eyed birds larger than ravens and all demanding dinner.

Packed wing to wing into long, flat, airless buildings, these crazies were time bombs. One would twitch; causing two to jump; five to squawk; fifty to flap— and in a cat wink thousands of manic Henny Pennies plowed over one another like a dust and feather tornado. All you could do was stand stone still until they quieted down. And if the feathers made your nose itch, forget scratching it. That little motion would make some goggle-eyed darling nervous and the madness erupted all over again.

The hatchery had two other employees: the foreman Jack Maulsby, a shy man in his thirties, and his assistant Claude Hawkins, a year older than I and not shy at all. My education in the treachery of eggs began the day they showed me how to clean incubator trays. Taking fuzzy baby chicks out of the trays was fun, but what remained looked like the remains of a bad biology experiment. Some of the eggs hadn't hatched. Instead, foul-smelling, green and yellow glop had volcanically bubbled out of the shells and cemented the eggs to the trays. I tentatively nudged a big, warty egg that looked like it had erupted rotten oatmeal.

"How do you get these things loose?" I asked.

Before Jack could answer, Hawkins said, "Oh, just grab hold and give it a good yank."

I encircled the egg with my fingers and tugged. It didn't budge.

"Oh, ya gotta pull hard," Hawkins said, not looking up.

I didn't want to appear prissy, so I yanked hard.

Kaboom!

A grenade exploded. Yellow and brown mucilage splotched my white uniform like runny snot. Oozy stuff dripped off my nose. The stench took my breath.

At that inglorious moment, Dell stuck his head in the door. "How's it going?" he asked with a little smile.

"Baptism!" called Hawkins and he cackled like the demented. Jack held his observance to a quiet chuckle.

The hired help usually made the baby chick deliveries to the surrounding farms, but if we were busy, Dell had Roy handle some of them. Roy was never called Mr. Loughridge, even though no one would dream of calling Mrs. Loughridge by her first name—which I think was Myrtle. Unlike his no-nonsense spouse, Roy was as mild as yesterday's mashed potatoes; quite likable in his shuffling, lanky way, and at one time had been a discerning leader of education as County Superintendent of Schools. But the years had taking their toll, and he was not given to many stimulating thoughts these sunset days.

One morning around eleven o'clock, Dell sent him off in the panel truck with a load of baby chicks to be delivered to a nearby farm. Dell felt comfortable in sending him; it was only a fifteen minute drive, and the farmer had sons to help unload. Roy would be back by noon. He wasn't. Dell tried to call the farm, but there was no phone. Another half hour and still no Roy. Mrs. Loughridge, with worried eyes, came to the incubator room and asked if he had returned. No one had seen him. By one o'clock we feared the worst:

Roy'd had a heart attack. The truck was off in a ditch. He'd turned the wrong way and was in Kansas City. Something.

One by one we gathered outside the hatchery and stared down the road.

"I'll go look for him," Dell said with furrowed brow, and climbed into his car. As he backed out, the panel truck rolled into the driveway. Roy slowly unwound his long legs from behind the wheel and smiled sheepishly at his welcoming committee.

"Roy, where have you been?" barked Mrs. Loughridge.

Roy had a habit of interrupting his speech every few words and extending his upper lip a good inch while pondering the rest of his statement. With an embarrassed glint in his eye, he replied:

"Well, (lip), you know that, (lip), new traffic light, (lip), they put in at Kozy Corner?" (Lip, lip.)

We all knew it; it was a four-way stop light, the first traffic signal ever to grace Unionville.

"Well, a feller, (lip), can hardly stop, (lip), and get started 'tween flashes." (Lip, lip, lip!)

I think that was Roy's last run.

Now that I had a job, I could buy a car; and Uncle Bill came up with a beauty: a '47 five-passenger Chevy coupe, which he let me make payments on. He even threw in a shiny black paint job. Morrow, a whiz with cars, helped me bring the Chevy's look to absolute perfection. First, we added a Dynatone muffler with its sexy dual exhaust pipes. Duels were illegal, but Dynatone's second pipe was a dog-leg off the first; so although it was a single unit, you saw two exhausts protruding out the back that purred like panthers—pure girl bait. Morrow was just warming up; he had me add metal whitewalls that clamped around the hub caps, and attach black fender skirts in back. Then he added the perfect touch: a flashy spinner knob for the steering wheel.

Demonstrating in his black, '40 Chevy, he showed me how to crank the spinner knob fast to make hairpin turns. Morrow also had big, furry, white dice hanging from his rear view mirror, but I passed on that; preferring to wait for the "sign of the stud," a scarf or garter from a girlfriend. I hoped that girlfriend would be Donna; and one evening before supper, I headed for her house, figuring to drive by a couple of times honking like New Year's Eve. But on the way I had another thought: maybe I should first take another run at the Centerville girls; kind of a dry run for my Black Beauty.

Who was I kidding? My sawdust mouth would never get any girls in this car no matter how neat it looked. I needed backup—glib, talk-to-anything-in-a-skirt backup. The Shelb. But The Shelb lived way out in the country. On the other hand, good friend Rodge, who talked to and about girls all the time, lived just minutes away. I drove up in front of his house, honked, he came out, I pleaded for help. Rodge grinned his answer, slid into the front seat, and we headed for the state line.

It was a Thursday night, which proved to not be a heavy action time in Centerville, and we circled the square at least twenty times before I parked down a side street and shut off the motor. The drugstore clock said it was nearly 10:00 PM. A night watchman passed, shaking doors along his way, and disappeared into the darkness. Rodge and I glumly nodded our failure and I started the car.

From down the street came an unmistakable sound: girls' laughter.

Dozens of girls streamed from a stairway onto the sidewalk, dressed in flurries of pink and blue chiffon and crinoline, calling out their joy like canaries in concert.

"Rainbow!" Rodge exclaimed. "It's Rainbow girls, that thing the Masons have."

Three Rainbows ran our way like the law was after them. My mind swirled for words to call out; Rodge had no such problem. He jumped out of the car and gave a shrill whistle. "Hey, girls! In here!" he yelled. In they piled, the first two in back with Rodge and the third up front with me.

"They're after us!" yelled the girl up front.

I backed out, slammed into low, cranked the spinner knob Morrow style and hit the accelerator.

"Who's after you" I asked.

"Them," said the girl beside me, pointing behind us. I looked in the rear view mirror and saw something disturbing: a yellow pickup with big, drunk guys in it. Two were in the cab, the four others in back. They shook their fists and yelled that Missouri boys did bad things to their mothers. I headed for the town square hoping the presence of others would restrain their wrath. It didn't. Empty beer cans rained on the rear window. I headed east, a voice in my head telling me not to go south across the state line. The pickup followed. I pulled out of town and saw that I was on Highway 2; the pickup stayed behind me like I was pulling it with a rope.

No one in the car said a word. I drove mile after mile, gripping the steering wheel with both hands, and staring at whatever my headlights revealed, searching for escape. We passed a city limits sign for West Grove, and I prayed that this would be where these drunks would yell some foul farewell and head back home. They threw more beer cans. As we passed street lights, I could see the driver in my side mirror. He was huge and his face was red and contorted.

I came to Highway 63 and turned north. This really ticked them; the pickup lunged; bumped the Chevy; knocked it forward. *This couldn't be happening. I'd only had my beautiful Black Beauty a week, and these Iowa idiots were wrecking it!* I sped up to fifty. They caught up and bumped me again. I hit sixty. Another bump. Sixty five. Bump. That was it; I refused to go a mile faster. They passed, yelling, giving the finger; then Rage Face swung in front of me and tapped his brakes, flaring his brake lights. I hit the brake pedal, throwing us all forward. He slowed for me to catch up and hit his brakes again. *Certified insanity. These guys didn't care about the girls, they just wanted Missouri blood!*

We came to Ottumwa, fifty miles from Centerville. The pickup slowed. *Ottumwa's a bigger town; these guys are worried about the cops.* I stomped the gas and shot around them, heading straight for downtown. If these buttheads were going to wreck my car, I was going to have plenty of witnesses. We raced through red lights into the heart of town. Cars honked and swerved. Wheeling around a corner, I saw salvation: a police station with one empty parking space in front. I took it. The drunks screamed at us as the pickup sped by and turned right to go around the block.

I had second thoughts. Maybe two Missouri boys limping into the police station with three Iowa girls wasn't such a good idea. I backed out; raced to the end of the block; turned left and indiscriminately flew down one street and then another until I was out of town. Coming to a country road, I swerved onto it, killed the lights, and slid to a stop in a corn field. We waited. No lights appeared behind us. I let out my breath. We had lost the enemy.

I turned to my seat companion. Out of the darkness stared a mousey-haired girl with frightened eyes. I looked in the back seat. In one corner, Rodge was pressing a walrus kiss on one of the girls, who was giving as much as she got. In the darkness of the opposite corner was a girl who was very short.

"How old are you?" I asked.

"Nine."

The walrus kiss ended abruptly. Rodge and I looked at each other in panic; we had an ankle biter on board.

"I wanna come up front," wailed the nine-year-old.

"She's my little sister," said Mousey Hair.

Little sister plunged head first over the seat to the far side of her sister and scrunched against the passenger door. Hardly missing a beat, Rodge and his girl lunged into an embrace. After all the trouble we'd gone to, I thought Mousey Hair and I should make out, too. I kissed her. She kissed back, so I decided to make it a long one. Then I heard humming. With lips locked, I turned our heads slightly to my right to get a look at little sister. Her elbows were on the dash with her chin in her hands; and she was looking out at the cornfield humming *The Marine Hymn.*

I started the car and headed back for Centerville.

Early next morning, while Dad was still in the kitchen drinking his coffee, I sneaked outside to see if my car had suffered any damage from last night's madness. I crouched down and, inch by inch, examined the rear bumper. Amazing. Not a scratch. Dad's shadow fell across the trunk.

"Playing a little bumper tag last night?"

I jumped up and asked, "What do you mean?"

Dad gestured his coffee cup toward the license plate. "Looks like a little kiss between the "3" and the "6." Sure enough, the plate had a half-dollar dent between the numbers. Dad took a sip of his coffee and went inside. *That man knew everything I did.*

CHAPTER 27

▼

BILLY RAY FUMBLEPASS

With Centerville girls out of my system, I concentrated on Donna; but decided that driving by her place honking and yelling might not be the coolest form of courtship. I wanted to say something neat to her like The Shelb would come up with, and practiced "Hi there, pretty thang," all the way to school one day. But what I should've practiced was breathing, because when I met her in the hall, all I got out was, "Hi there," and ran out of air. Donna ignored my labored breathing and asked me to the Sadie Hawkins Dance. I remembered it was the annual dance in *L'il Abner* where the girls asked the boys. My head bobbed yes like a yo-yo on a short string.

That evening after supper, I edged up to Mom while she did the dishes and asked if she would teach me to dance.

She wiped her hands on a towel and smiled at me in a way both happy and sad.

"What's her name?" she asked.

"No name," I said. "I just might need to know how to dance sometime."

Mom knew the sometime was now. She dialed some slow music on the radio, Perry Como singing *Forever and Ever,* and held her right hand away from her body. "Take my hand," she said. I reached out. "No, in your *left* hand. Now put your right hand behind my waist. Good. Now, slide your left foot forward and bring up your right. Good. Do it again. Good. Now slide your right foot back and then your left. Good."

I had it. Two left-rights forward; one right-left backwards. Keep singing, Mr. Como, I can do this all night. Suddenly Mom stopped. I had backed her against the kitchen sink. I'd have to practice turning.

No reason was given, but school officials canceled the dance, and I sighed with relief at not having to glide across the dance floor like Frankenstein on roller skates. And now, knowing I wouldn't be rejected, I asked Donna to go to the show. The night of the date, I pulled up to her house with the coupe's black finish buffed to a shine you could shave in. No need to turn off the motor, she'd be out in seconds, except, of course, she wasn't; and the chilling realization came that I had to go into the house and meet her parents. I already knew her father, Clarence; he was the janitor at the high school—bald and hard-work bony—and usually favored most of us boys with a stern look. You want to get barked at, just leave a mark from your rubber-soled tootsies on his highly polished gymnasium floor.

I knocked lightly and Donna opened the door immediately. She was wearing lipstick and a little mascara and looked terrific. Her mother came out of the kitchen wearing an apron and a small, tentative smile. She was older than Mom, with gray hair and glasses. She had a nice face.

"Mom, this is Bill Ray," Donna said.

"Call me Winnie," her mom replied, the smile increasing only slightly. "Pleased to meet you," she said, wiping her hand on her apron before offering it. "What's your family's name?"

"Jackson," I answered, giving her hand a quick shake.

"What's your father's name?" she asked.

"Cecil."

She shook her head. "Don't know any Cecils."

I shifted uneasily.

"Tramp. Most people call him Tramp."

"Oh, yes …" She looked at me a bit closer.

"Daddy, this is Bill Ray," Donna called, leading me into the kitchen. Clarence sat at a little table eating some soup. He looked up and nodded, giving no sign of the hundred times he'd seen me in the gym. We shook hands with him still seated, and his hard, calloused skin spoke of years of hard work. He made it a short handshake.

"Well, we'd better go," said Donna.

We started for the front door.

"She's only fourteen," said Clarence in a low voice and went back to his soup.

I had her home real early.

After Donna and I had dated twice, Carr stopped by my locker and said, "Guess you two are jacketed." Carr's stamp of approval made it official. We were going steady, the perfect high school couple: she was a cheerleader and I was a football player. And, boy, did I want to give her something to cheer.

The problem was, I played end, and ends were supposed to catch passes. Grabosch, who threw to Edmunds, Davis, Musgrove, and Carter, would never throw me a pass. Time after time, I ran down the field and looked back to see the ball going to someone else, even if they weren't open. Then during one night game, he broke the pattern. He took the snap and ran right; I charged deep down the left sideline and was wide open. He heaved a long, beautiful spiral; I watched it streak toward me like a silhouetted missile; and following it, stared directly into an overhead light. The world went black, and the prize whistled over my head. Grabosch never threw to me again.

Not throwing to Jackson appeared no great loss; the Midgets became the talk of the conference. Piper's fired-up half pints were hammering the big guys. Coach played me some every game until the unbeaten Bloomfield Mustangs thundered into town. They had come south for a non-conference game to show this fancy, hide-the-ball Missouri team what football was all about. When Bloomfield came onto the field for pre-game warm up, the Midgets collectively took a sharp intake of breath. These Iowa farm boys were enormous—bull elephants doing calisthenics, far bigger than any team in our conference. Back in the locker room we sat in silence. Davis suddenly yelled, "Okay, so they're big! They put their pants on the same way we do, one leg at a time!"

Yeah, I thought, *but those are big legs.*

We received the kickoff and a load of trouble. These behemoths broke through our line before the spinner-backs could spin; slammed them to the ground; knocked down Grabosch's passes; stopped Carter cold; and just plain beat our butts. Cook & Company played hard—harder than the team had played all year—but at half-time the Midgets limped back to the locker room behind 12 to 7. I looked around the room at heads with purple knots, bloody noses, busted lips—our finest looked beat to hell. Their eyes radiated their thoughts: Bloomfield was too big for us. I thought, *Piper if you're ever going to yell and scream, now is the time.*

He did just the opposite.

He stood in the center of the room and waited for the fear-tinged voices to fall silent. When he spoke, we strained to hear.

"There's been talk around town about us winning the conference champion-ship this year. Maybe, maybe not. We have some tough games coming up; and I don't know how they're going to turn out, but I'll tell you this ...," here his voice fell to a whisper, "I'd rather lose the championship that go down to a team from out of state, a bunch of Iowa bohunks who think they can come down here and shove us around."

Everybody straightened. The words, "... from out of state ...," echoed in every mind. This was a battle for Missouri pride. Piper left the locker room. We stared, graveyard quiet, at the door he'd just existed. Then Davis jumped up and yelled, "Well, you bunch of Missouri mules, let's go out there and kick some Iowa ass!"

To start the second half, the Mustangs trotted slowly onto the field smiling their confidence. Their jaunty body language didn't just speak, it sneered; they were ready to finish off these little runts from south of the Iowa line. Cook and Davis lead the Midgets' charge onto the field like it was red meat day at the zoo. They pounded backs; shook fists; screamed into ears; and whipped the White and Blue into a frenzy. The Mustangs watched this display with condescension; and just to show who was boss, took the second-half kickoff and scored again.

But Unionville refused to give up. Cook called no long passes, no razzle-dazzle plays—the backfield simply battered forward, a few grim yards at a time. A ham-mering tackle by a huge Bloomfield linebacker knocked Davis unconscious. Piper revived him with smelling salts, and the Galloping Ghost rode again. Fourth down, two yards short of a first? Cook took the snap himself and plowed under the opposing tackle's legs. Repeatedly knocked to the ground, Edmunds sprang back into the air, high over the linebackers' heads and caught Grabosch's bullet passes.

And the defense: the defense threw their smaller bodies at these big Iowa jocks like enraged alley cats—snarling, clawing, grabbing anything available—making Bloomfield pay dearly for every yard gained. The game became a contest in con-ditioning, and Piper's early extra week of practice in the boiling heat of August paid off. By third quarter's end, Bloomfield's heavier boys gasped with chest-heaving pain. By mid-fourth quarter, Mustang starters were hobbling off the field bruised and exhausted. When the final whistle blew, Piper's half-time whisper had fanned a fire storm of pride and Unionville's little runts reigned 28 to 18.

I hadn't gotten to play, nor should I have. This wasn't a time for Billy Ray Fumble Pass. For this one, Coach could only send his very best.

CHAPTER 28

▼

MR. BARTLEY HAS LONG LEGS

I slid into the passenger's side of Morrow's car in a foul mood. My ego needed a recharge. Grabosch still hadn't thrown me any passes. My car had conked out. And Donna had broken our Saturday night date to show the town to her visiting cousin she had a crush on. Now Morrow and I sat in his car looking at an empty town square on Halloween night.

"Let's prank Bartley," I said.

Morrow looked at me like I'd gone brain dead. "Let's just … jump off … the courthouse," Morrow answered, "… nobody pranks Bartley."

He had a point; no one had yet succeeded in pulling a Halloween trick on the high school superintendent. What glorious infamy that would be.

"I said, "That's 'cause everybody rushes into it; he lays for them and spots 'em every time. We could really case the place; see where he's hiding; and then do a trick where he can't see us."

Morrow started the motor.

We cruised by Bartley's house, which was on the corner three blocks north of the high school. The street was empty; the house was dark. We passed again, slowly, studying the porch, then the backyard. Bartley was about 6 foot 2. A foot, maybe a knee, might stick out from his hiding place. Morrow edged the car down a side street two blocks away and parked the car far from the streetlights' glare.

We sneaked back on foot, darting in and out of shadows, tip-toeing across lawns to muffle our approach. Crossing through the superintendent's garden, we cautiously checked the backyard; then slowly circled the house, looking for any sign of a looming, angular man lurking around corners, crouching behind bushes. We even looked in the trees—Bartley was crafty. We saw nothing to alarm us.

Morrow pointed to the garage behind the house. Its open door served as an irresistible invitation. We could soap the window's of Bartley's car while he was in the house snoozing. But we didn't have any soap, so we gathered an armload of baby tomatoes left on the vine in the garden. We would smear them on the car. The car was a black four-door; and Morrow silently smooshed tomatoes on the passenger side while I did the same on the driver's side. Then I did something stupid. I eased the gas cap off and squeezed the juice from a couple of tomatoes into the gas tank Not to be outdone, Morrow crouched down and began letting the air out of the right rear tire. The escaping air made a hissing sound.

A light flashed on inside the car. Out of the back seat scrambled Bartley's long legs. I shot out of the garage like a rocket; ran to the front of the house; turned right and shot up the street. Morrow followed right behind me. Bartley's long legs had slowed his exit from the car, but now he closed on us like a track star. I ran faster, fueled by pure fear, darted up an alley and dove headlong into some bushes on the left. With Bartley just a long arm-grab behind him, Morrow shot by me and charged into a barn on the right and scrambled up the ladder to the haymow. Bartley's breath was on Morrow's butt. Then on this starry, moonlit night, a scene transpired that I will never forget:

Morrow burst forth from the haymow window, arms pumping and legs churning in the air like a fledgling in flight. He fell a good twelve feet, hit the ground, rolled a somersault and disappeared into the night.

Bartley looked out the haymow window a few moments; then descended the ladder, and, lost in thought, walked by my hiding place and headed home.

Two school days passed without a summons to the office, so Morrow and I rejoiced in the conclusion that the superintendent hadn't recognized us in the dark. Then Rodge stopped me in the hall and said:

"Crazy thing happened yesterday. Carr and I were coming back from Centerville, and Bartley was off to the side of the road peering under the hood of his car. We checked it for him and finally I unhooked the gas line and blew it out. Jackson, little things came out that looked like maggots."

Not maggots, I thought, *tomato seeds.* I felt awful.

The next day, a summons to the office arrived. Mr. Bartley's secretary appeared at the door in Mr. Tade's Social Studies class. "Bill Ray Jackson is to come to the superintendent's office immediately," she announced. My heart sank. *He'd discovered it wasn't maggots!* Then she added, "Roger Torrey is to come, too. And both of you bring any text books that have your drawings in them." Our lockers were side by side; and Rodge and I retrieved the books we'd drawn in, which, of course, was every book we had. Rodge hung his head. "Jackson, we're done for. We've drawn goofy-looking pictures of every teacher in school."

"Yeah," I said, "which is why the books get big bucks when we sell 'em. Somebody's showed Bartley one of them and now he's gonna expel us."

Lugging the evidence of our crime, we trudged up the steps to the superintendent's office. I paused outside the door and turned to Rodge.

"We'll say we've reformed. I haven't drawn anybody for a long time, have you?"

"Not really," Rodge answered. "The last one was of Suzy Grant, the Home Ec teacher."

"Yeah, I saw it. Looked like cantaloupes under that sweater."

Rodge grinned. "Got carried away."

Balancing my books in one arm, I opened the door. The secretary pointed toward Mr. Bartley's office. We entered, half hiding behind our stacks, and Mr. Bartley motioned for us the sit down opposite of him at his desk. He plucked my Social Studies book from my pile and flipped it open. Thumbing a few pages, he stopped at a drawing of Mr. Tade, the most respected teacher on the faculty. Since he was short, I had drawn him as a sleepy-eyed Napoleon standing on his desk going "blah-blah, zzzzzz, blah-blah." His right hand groped inside his dress coat and the words "ham sandwich" pointed to where he was reaching. Then our superintendent opened one of Rodge's books. Even with it upside down I recognized Suzy Grant doing the hula in a skimpy sarong. And there were those cantaloupes again. Rodge smiled feebly.

"These are first rate!" Bartley exclaimed.

Suzy Grant's cantaloupes? No, he'd flipped to other pages.

"If you boys would, I'd like for you to draw pictures today at the Rotary luncheon. We can get big drawing pads from the art department."

Rodge and I looked at each other in astonishment. We weren't getting kicked out of school; we were taking our show on the road.

The Torrey-Jackson show scored big. Unionville's business elite loved seeing their own caricatures drawn alongside the likes of General MacArthur, W.C. Fields, and F. D. R.—so much so that the drawings were displayed on the Country Club walls. I looked at Mr. Bartley with new eyes. No longer was he the stern prison warden I'd thought him to be; this guy had a sense of humor, and he liked our drawings so much he pulled Rodge and I out of school and showcased us to the town leaders. I began to think I might want to do something besides shovel chicken poop.

I *really* felt bad about those tomato seeds.

▼

CHAPTER 29

THE PASS, THE PLAY, THE BANQUET WITH DAD

Donna was impressed, mostly by the fact that Mr. Bartley had let me out of school to draw the pictures. She and I reunited after her cutie cousin left town, but I felt, given a choice of boyfriend, Donna would've picked Willie Edmunds, not me. Edmunds, dark, husky, recently from Hawaii, caught Grabosch's passes; made touchdowns; and even punted barefooted for crying out loud. Willie Jackson looked into the lights; lost the ball; and blew any chance of ever being thrown another one.

The last game of the season, the Midgets met arch-rival Milan in a night game on the Wildcat's turf. Practically every football fan in Unionville made the trip, hoping to see the demolition of the team the whole town hated. During warm-up before the game, I searched the Unionville sideline and spotted Dad standing by himself at one end of the bleachers. I couldn't tell if he was looking at me or not. Uncles Bill and Joe, hollering and pumping their fists, were in the middle of a huge, clamoring turnout of Midget fans. Unionville had tied Marceline, but a victory tonight over Milan would make the Midgets undefeated co-champions of the conference.

Cook & Company took the field and made Midget history—barreling over Milan and never letting them get within a smell of our goal line. With the final whistle just minutes away, we led 52–0; Piper left Cook in to call plays and sent in the subs to savor a touchdown of their own. But Milan's A-team refused to roll over for any B-team pansies and stopped us cold on our forty yard line with fourth down and six yards to go. Only ten seconds remained on the clock, and normally Piper would've had Cook take the snap and put his knee to the ground. Instead, Coach decided to send in Edmunds so the big end could thrill the crowd with one last barefooted punt. But when I went to the huddle for the final play, I heard the unbelievable:

"Jackson, would you like to catch a pass?"

Did Cook actually say that? Everyone in the huddle looked at him like he had lost his mind. *Would I like to catch a pass?* I practically nodded my head off.

"Go straight down twenty yards; look over your right shoulder. On three."

We broke from the huddle; Edmunds trotted back to the punter's position with his right shoe off, just like always. I lined up like I was going to block. My heart pounded like a truck piston. What was Cook doing? The game won; ten seconds to go; and he's throwing to Billy Ray Fumblepass on fourth down? If I drop it, Cook will be called "The Idiot" instead of "The Brain."

"Hut, one!"

Twenty yards. Run twenty yards and look over my right shoulder. *Do not look into the lights!*

"Hut, two!"

I almost jumped off sides. Clear your head, Jackson! Twenty yards. Look around. *Do not look into the lights!*

"Hut, three!"

I charged down the field. Five yards. Ten yards. Oh, come on feet, why are you so heavy? Fifteen. Milan had dropped back for the punt and I was in the clear. I looked into the night sky for the ball. No! A stadium light hit me in the eyes like a prison spot! Where was the ball? Was that it?" Black, spiraling, streaking toward me like a rocket shell? I reached up groping the air. I had it! I had this beauty! Bam! A guy slammed into me and the ball bobbled in my hands; I covered it with my arms. A second guy pounded my arms with his fists; I clamped the ball in a death grip. A third tackler hit my legs and I went down. I didn't fumble. The whistle blew. The game was over.

I lifted my face out of the grass and looked at the markers on the sideline. A thirty-yard gain. I looked for Dad but couldn't find him in the delirium. The Unionville Midgets were the undefeated co-champions of the conference. We had annihilated Milan and topped it off at the end with a sneak play from "The Brain." I looked at Cook like he was a god. He smiled his crooked grin, gave me a pat on the shoulder, and trotted off the field. He'd risked his reputation on that call; he could've made the last play of the year something really dumb, but he knew how badly I wanted to catch a pass. Grabosch wouldn't throw it; so he threw it himself. What a cousin.

In the locker room, Carr told me that Piper had watched the play with his mouth hanging open. When the whistle blew, he asked, "Who caught that?"

"Jackson," someone answered.

Carr said Piper smiled.

Coach smiled. I was on top of the world.

Then Carr added: "Donna didn't see you catch it."

"Why not?" I ask incredulously.

"Well, after we got so far ahead, some of the cheerleaders kinda took a break."

"She wasn't watching the game?"

"No."

"What the heck was she doing?"

"Necking … with Donald Butler in his pickup."

Kick in the gut! Butler was a wiry, blond-headed kid a couple of years older than I. Played baseball. Always wore that dumb baseball cap. Always had some flirty thing to say to the girls. My high flying euphoria plummeted like a fat, dead duck. Here I finally catch a pass, and my cheerleader girlfriend is making out with some guy in his pickup.

Dad never mentioned the catch, but he looked like he'd seen it; gave a little nod at me this next morning. I replayed that nod in my head a hundred times. However, I got no acknowledgement from Donna; we weren't speaking and it looked like our going steady days were kaput. However, honey bee Butler evidently had other nectar to nuzzle and didn't come buzzing around her. So, Donna beamed me those Virginia Mayo eyes; I grinned back like the village idiot; and we were going steady again.

Going to the movies became just an excuse for necking afterwards, and I prayed necking didn't show, because when I picked her up, her father always looked at me like I'd just escaped Alcatraz. Her mother was different. She liked me and would invite me into the kitchen for a piece of pie and ask about my work at the hatchery and if I was drawing any more cartoons at the Rotary meetings.

Then the bushwhacking began.

We'd be tucked into some dark place after the show; when the glare of headlights filled the car. Donna's older sister, Dorothy, and her blank-faced husband,

Howard, cruised by. Dorothy had a favorite expression for people who smiled big—"grinning like a Cheshire cat"—and that was Dorothy peering out the passenger-side window. They gleefully showed up on every date until I found farm roads even the farmers didn't know they had.

When the season ended, I discovered that there was something I was better at than playing football. Acting. Of course my acting wasn't all that good; I just mugged better than I caught passes. Mae Hunt had moved from breaking up grade school fights to teaching high school theater, and to my delight cast me in the Junior Play. Titled *The Improper Henry Proper*, it was a comedy about a mixed-up wedding in which my character, Henry Proper, the groom, weds his mother-in-law—or at least thinks he has. In the tryouts, my buddy Morrow, normally a molasses mouth, made a real effort to fire off more than five words a minute and won the role of the preacher. A key early scene came when my betrothed is revealed to be my bride's mother, and I faint into the preacher's arms.

"Play it broadly," Mae counseled.

"Like Charlie Chaplin?," I said.

She nodded.

When my cue came, I let my body go limp and toppled backwards like a felled redwood. Caught by surprise, Morrow didn't even put his arms out; and I bounced a foot off the stage floor. Mae giggled.

"Maybe not that broad, Charlie," she said.

The faint in the first act was cake compared to the kiss in the third. My co-star was Winona McCollom, a cute, chatterbox blonde, who, at the outset of rehearsal, admonished me that the kissing scene was strictly for art, and that I wasn't to get any "funny ideas." The only idea I had was that kissing a girl in front of an audience would be pure hell; and as the rehearsal loomed closer to the big moment, my breath left me, and I started delivering my lines with great gulps of air. Winona drew back. From the look in her saucer eyes, she must've thought she was facing some panting sex maniac. When the cue came to kiss, I sucked in air; closed my eyes; puckered up; and leaned forward. An ominous feeling swept over me. I opened one eye and looked over Winona's shoulder. Lurking offstage was Winona's boyfriend, football star Billy Musgrove, staring out of the darkness like Count Dracula. The intensity of his eyes so rattled me I lurched off target and kissed my co-star's nose. Winona gasped; Mae giggled; the cast laughed; and Musgrove hooted, seeing that obviously I wasn't any threat to his own romantic capabilities.

The night of the play, prior to curtain time, the cast took turns peeking at the audience to check out who'd paid a dollar a head to see the future John Barrymores and Tallulah Bankheads. To my delight, I spotted both Mom and Dad seated in the back row. When the final curtain came down, the audience burst into prolonged applause followed by excited murmuring; the parents no doubt relieved that their children hadn't embarrassed the family name. Still wearing stage makeup as a badge of honor, the cast scampered from the stage to receive their huzzahs. Mom stood up and waved, but the seat next to her was empty. She gushed as mothers do: I had looked so handsome and been so funny. I soaked up the praise, but I kept looking around for my real critic.

"Where's Dad?" I asked.

"Oh, he went to the car."

I knew what that meant: he'd been two hours without a drink.

Two days passed, and I still hadn't heard a word from Dad about the play, let alone what he thought of my performance. I could've asked him straight out, but, of course, like my catching the pass, that would've waved a flag about how much his opinion meant to me. I acted like I didn't give a fig, which was a fat one, because deep down I craved his praise more than anyone's.

The morning of the third day after the play, Mom was cleaning the kitchen while I sat at the table eating a bowl of Wheaties. Dad had repaired to the back stoop to smoke a roll-your-own and study the occasional cat roaming the back alley. I couldn't wait any longer to find out, so when I brought my empty bowl to the sink I asked Mom in a hushed voice what Dad had thought of the play.

"Oh, he laughed all the way through it," she said, "especially your part."

Dad never did mention the play.

In fact, he didn't talk to me much at all anymore; which was one reason I didn't bother asking him to go with me to the Lettermen's Father and Son Banquet. Piper had played me enough to letter, and, boy, I would've loved to be sitting next to my father with all the other guys and their fathers. But I knew Dad hated group functions, especially ones where you sat down; nibbled a salad; and cut up little pieces of masqueraded chicken while you made polite chitchat. Dad had no patience with chitchat, especially if you were drinking ice tea. No, he wouldn't go. And neither would I. Being the only kid there without a dad would be too embarrassing.

Two weeks before the banquet, Mom announced at the supper table that Eddie Griste was going with Cook. Then Mom looked directly at Dad. You could read her thoughts: this dinner was so important that her sister's boyfriend was standing in for Cook's deceased father. Dad said nothing, finished his potato soup, and went onto the back porch to smoke. I didn't hear Mom mention the event to Dad again, but out of my earshot she must've mounted a battle nothing short of the Normandy Invasion. Two days before the big dinner, she greeted me at the door smiling and clapping her hands. Dad had agreed to go.

I swept her into a bear hug and swirled her around the room. Then I put her down slowly.

"Mom, it's dress up; I don't have enough money for a suit."

"I've already got you one."

"What? Where'd you get it?"

"Husted's Funeral Home. I'm Mrs. Husted's second cousin. They had an extra your size."

"Mom, that's the suit they put on dead bodies!"

Well, as they say, beggars can't be choosers, and, by Jove, I had a new pavement gray suit for the dinner; and you hardly could smell the formaldehyde at all.

In the gymnasium, the fathers each sat next to an empty seat at long tables covered with white party paper. In front of each place setting for two was a tiny, blue cardboard "U" sprayed with glitter and stuck into a white Styrofoam base. Sweetly smiling mothers emerged from the back kitchen and filled the tables with huge trays of fried chicken and bowls of potato salad, green beans, and little squares of red Jell-O. Once the food was on the tables, Coach Piper called for the entrance of this year's lettermen. We entered in a single file; the fathers stood, greeting their sons with vigorous applause. And there in the midst of all this paternal pride stood *my* father, Tramp Jackson, his hands coming together slowly; his eyes hollow; his face glistening with sweat; uneasiness oozing from his every pore.

But he was there … for me.

CHAPTER 30

▼

TIME TO SHINE

Goodbye, cousins. Hello, spotlight. It was the start of football my senior year, and Cook and Davis were gone. I hadn't exactly electrified the fans last year, but this new season would be my redemption. If determination brought success, then look out, my body throbbed with it. I would put on the pads, hit the field, and dazzle Dad, my uncles, and every football fan in the county.

But first I had to dazzle the new coach. After his short, unparalleled reign, Ernie Piper had made his pasture greener at Brookfield; and the town fathers brought in Dean Nelson, another football star from Missouri State University. Unlike Piper's arrival in early summer the previous year, Nelson appeared just before school started. Aware of the fiery exhortation Piper had given Cook & Company the year before, we new seniors anxiously awaited our own call to arms. No call came. Finally, the day before first practice, five or six of us knocked at the door of the new coach's apartment just north of the Square. Presently the door opened and Coach Nelson, blond, lanky, somber as an undertaker, looked us over like we were a bunch of Fuller Brush salesmen.

We introduced ourselves; and I did most of the talking, babbling nonstop about how excited we were to be his senior players and how lucky Marceline had been to tie us last year and how we'd show 'em this time.

Nelson said nothing.

I edged forward and said, "I'm a returning letterman."

The new coach looked at me with ice-gray eyes.

"I'll pick the team," he said. "See you at practice."

He closed the door.

We practiced; he picked. On our first game, which was at home, we ran onto the field whooping and hollering, ready to flatten the team that last year had put the "co" in co-champions. Marceline kicked off, and three plays later we had ground out three yards to our own twenty-nine yard line. I left my end position and went back to punt; a job I got because my big feet, at least my right one, could kick the ball a great distance. Unfortunately, that distance was mostly straight up. When Nelson picked me, he must've prayed that a strong wind would blow the ball downfield. The half-back protecting me from carnage was my pre-school boxing nemesis, Don Clark Pollock. The Terror of the Hilltop hadn't grown much; in fact he could barely peek above his shoulder pads.

I called for the hike. What happened next is remembered in slow motion. The ball spiraled high above my head. I lunged into the air and caught it. A big Marceline linebacker broke through the line. Pollock crouched forward, legs dancing nervously. I turned the laces of the ball upwards. The linebacker charged toward Pollock. Pollock backed up a step. I held the ball out to kick. Pollock backed up two steps. I swung my right foot into the ball as hard as I could—and kicked it square into Pollock's butt. The ball bounced twenty yards back over my head.

First and goal, Marceline.

But Marceline had lost even more of last year's A-team than we had, and although the Midgets had no "Brain" or "Galloping Ghost," we rallied from my butt kick and won the game. However, without Piper we had no spark, no fire in the belly to play beyond our abilities; and we went on to lose about as many games as we won. I'd see Dad on the sidelines, standing apart from Uncle Bill and Uncle Joe, always silent; and afterwards, as before, never mentioning the games at all. I hadn't given him much to cheer, yet I wondered what he thought of Nelson. Unlike Piper, Nelson coached like he *expected* you to screw up, and we fulfilled his expectations.

Near season's end, Piper brought his Brookfield Bulldogs to Unionville, and we stoked ourselves into a frenzy to avenge his abandonment. Our backfield didn't run, it galloped; our line didn't block, it bulldozed; and our defense—ah, our defense, led by the fabulous Putnams—did more than tackle, it demolished Brookfield's will. At game's end, our locker room resounded with jeers and gloating; we'd wiped the field with Piper's new darlings. He should've stayed with us; Brookfield was a bunch of pantywaists. Nelson congratulated our win and left the locker room. We resumed whooping and hollering.

Piper came down the stairs.

The room fell silent. His gaze swept the entire team and in a firm, quiet voice he said, "If you'd played like this the whole season, you'd have never lost a game." He turned away and trotted back up the stairs.

But we'd spent our fire; and we stumbled through the remainder of the season sluggish and uninspired, until we faced the final game—Homecoming against our arch enemy, the lowly, despicable Milan Wildcats. The week prior to the game, we pushed and polished our abilities to new heights, performing the sport with a level of competence unseen except for the Brookfield game Our confidence soared; we would conclude the season with a crisp, dazzling display of football executed at our absolute best.

Milan received the opening kickoff, and a Putnam immediately stopped the return dead in its tracks. I lined up as defensive left end, ready to display my vastly improved tackling ability. At the snap of the ball, I charged forward intent on shoving the quarter back's blocker aside and nailing Milan for a loss. But the blocker didn't throw a block; he threw a punch that smacked me full on the nose. All reason left me; left the whole team. Milan, always rough and rowdy, hadn't come to honor the game. it had come to brawl; and it had sucker-punched practically our entire defense that first play. Gone were our thoughts of the clean block, crisp tackle, leaping catch, and finely executed play—the game exploded into a raging froth of punching, cursing, gouging and kicking.

By the end of the first quarter, the game had plummeted to the most unacceptable dirty play the conference could remember witnessing. Flags fell like confetti and whistles blew without end as the referees called more penalties in this one game than they had the entire season. And, when all the punches were punched and the gouges gouged and this foul frolic had ended, the score reflected not the better team, but the better alley fighters. Milan had won, 19 to 6.

Basketball proved worse than football. Under Nelson's glum tutelage the Midgets lost every game that season but one. That giddy victory was against Gorin, a dinky village that could only muster six players for its basketball team, and two of them fouled out in the fourth quarter. With five players on the court to Gorin's four, Unionville managed to squeak out a victory.

Early in the season, I quit for the best of all possible reasons: my playing stunk. I clopped down the court like I was wearing water skis and dribbled the ball like I was trying to slap it awake. But shooting the ball defined my athletic ineptness, especially when I raced down the court with the ball, shot, and missed the entire backboard. I had stepped out of my cousins' shadow only to face the glare of reality. Some of us have athletic ability and some of us do not—at least in my case, not especially—and I probably should stick to drawing goofy pictures.

I don't think Dad cared much when I quit basketball; he never came to any of the games. He probably didn't like sitting in the bleachers and having to walk in front of a bunch of people to go for a nip. I didn't know that; I just guessed. He drank a lot lately.

PART III

▼

FLYING SOLO

CHAPTER 31

▼

DAD'S DEAL

"What's wrong, Mom?"

I'd walked in the door and found Mom sitting on the front room couch in the dark, her hands in her lap. She looked like someone had died.

"Mom? Are you okay?"

"Your Uncle Bill came by today."

She chewed her lip and looked down at her hands.

"He said … they … had to let your dad go. Too much drinking. People would come on the lot to buy cars, and your dad wouldn't be there. Your Uncle Bill would have to go down to the tavern to get him."

I sat down beside her and put my hand over hers.

"What's Dad going to do?"

"Bill and Joe are setting him up with a small radiator repair shop in our garage. They'll send him all of their business."

"Has he been home, yet?"

"No."

She got up slowly and went into the kitchen and began setting a place for me at the table. It was potato soup again. I wasn't complaining; I ate free. My hatchery money went for clothes, movies, gas for the car, everything except meals at home. And Mom always managed to put something on the table, with Uncle Buck's prowess at catching catfish often coming to the rescue. Folks thought he was the best fisherman in the county. It was said that when Buck Jackson walked the banks of the Chariton, catfish just gave up and flopped onto the bank. He was no slouch of a hunter, either. When times got tough in the winter, Uncle Buck would appear with his trusty gunnysack stuffed with rabbit, squirrel, pheasant, or quail; and Mom prepared a feast.

But tonight it was potato soup.

My little brothers had eaten and were playing cars on the kitchen floor. At sixteen, I was nine years older than John, eleven years older than Sam; but I wanted to grab a toy and get down on the floor with them, forget all about Dad losing his job—and why. The "why" was written all over Mom's face. She was worn out from his drinking.

Saying something about putting the wash away, she left me at the kitchen table slowly stirring my soup, thinking about Dad. He'd hit bottom. Somebody needed to talk to him—maybe Uncle Cleo or Uncle Buck. No, Dad had been sliding downhill for a long time; if either of his brothers were going to say something, they would've said it by now. *I* had to do it. Sure didn't want to.

I listened to the radio a while waiting for Dad to come home; then around midnight I fell asleep on the couch. I awoke at about six thirty in the morning to sounds of Dad fixing coffee in the kitchen. His eyes were red; his face somber. Not a good time to talk. Mom stayed in the bedroom and John and Sam were still asleep. I washed up, ate some cereal, and checked Dad again. He was sitting on the back porch smoking a cigarette, not looking at anything, just wearing that "thinking" expression he got. I saw out the front window that he still had the loaner car from the garage. The clutch had gone out of my car yesterday, and I hoped he'd give me a ride to work. And maybe on the way we could talk.

When I asked him for the ride, he gave a small nod, finished his coffee, and we left the house. When he slid behind the wheel, he looked back to see if Mom was watching, then reached under the front seat and brought out a half pint of Old Crow.

The time to talk was now. I took a breath.

"Dad, why do you do that?"

"Do what?" he asked.

I pointed at the bottle.

"To forget I'm not God," he answered.

He unscrewed the cap and chugged a couple of big swallows, coughed and, like always, pretended he was faking it and hacked even harder. After way overdoing it, he wiped his mouth with the back of his hand and said, "Damn, that's good!"

"Dad, it's seven thirty in the morning. You just lost your job for …"

"Hold it." he interrupted. He stared at me for a moment and then said, "I'll make you a deal."

His tone took my breath. I sat very still.

"You leave me alone and I'll leave you alone."

A chill swept my body. Dad was leaving me; casting me adrift. The man I'd followed all my life didn't want me any more.

He started the car and headed for the hatchery with me slightly rocking back and forth, barely breathing, looking out the window, seeing nothing but blurs. My father had handed me every sixteen-year-old boy's dream: permission to do as I pleased; come and go as I pleased; wreck the car if I pleased; jump off a cliff if I pleased. But I didn't want to do as I pleased. I wanted him a part of my life, telling me his opinion on what I was doing. Was I getting too serious about Donna? What about after high school? Feed chickens? Work at a factory?

I looked at him as we crossed the Square. He sat crouched over the wheel chewing gum to knock the whisky smell and staring down the road with the eyes of the dead; like nothing this day or any day was ever going to make him laugh or dance again. We came to the hatchery and he let me out near the big broiler house at the bottom of the hill; I slid out without a goodbye, and Dad drove away.

When I opened the broiler house door, the odor hit me like a blast furnace. The dumb chickens had done it again: clogged their long water troughs by kicking wood shavings into them. The water had overflowed, mixed with their droppings, and now there was a small, stinking pond in the middle of the broiler house. I got the big cart and started shoveling.

Leave me alone and I'll leave you alone. Dad's words haunted me. He'd meant it. Go your way, I'll go mine. Well, who'd give a hang what I did with my life? Mom, of course; she thought everything I did was wonderful. But the truth was folks in town didn't expect much from Tramp Jackson's boy. When I passed by the old-timers on the courthouse steps, I could guess what they said and how they said it:

"Yeah, he can draw them pictures, but that don't amount to pittle. The boy's cow-dumb about important things like fixin' cars and raisin' hogs. S'pose he could drive truck or shovel feed, but he's kinda skinny. His best bet's a factory job in Tri-Cities fastenin' bolts to somethin'."

I filled the cart with the wet, fouled wood shavings; emptied them behind the broiler house, and waded into the room for more. It was a cinch I didn't want to shovel this stuff for the rest of my life. And I didn't want to drive truck or fasten handles to pots on some assembly line.

What did I want to be? What I wanted was to be someone people admired, maybe somebody like Doc Judd, who'd brought practically every kid in the county into the world. He stopped by Davis Chevrolet nearly everyday looking sharper than anybody in town: black-rimmed glasses, gray tweed jacket with a vest, black shoes shined to a high gloss. And he walked erect, confident. Just looking at him you knew he was smart—smarter than just about anybody. But I didn't want to be a doctor. Too much looking at people's insides.

Maybe I'd be a smooth talking lawyer like Clare Magee. I'd heard that once he shot a man the sheriff had handcuffed, shot him right on the Town Square; then handed over the gun, pleaded self defense and got off free as a bird. No, I'd make a terrible lawyer. A lawyer sometimes fiddles with the truth, and Dad said every lie I ever told was written all over my face.

What about a writer? Yeah, that's more like it. I loved to create things. I could write stories, maybe even draw pictures to go with 'em. A cartooning writer. *Perfect.* But there was a problem: I could draw some, but I didn't know sickum about writing.

Then I heard a whisper in my head. It was like Dad said he heard. But this voice whispered to me. *It was my own Phantom.* What it directed me to do was incredible.

Standing ankle deep in the waste of five thousand manic chickens, I raised my shovel to the heavens and swore aloud the Phantom's bidding:

"I, Bill Ray Jackson, will do what no Unionville Jackson has done before. *Go to college.*"

Knowing I'd have to raise the money myself, I hit Dell up later in the day for extra hours. I just said I needed the extra money and didn't mention the college part, in case I didn't make it.

"Sure," Dell said. "We need some extra help. Let's go to the office and inform Mrs. Loughridge."

"Inform" meant getting her approval, and Mrs. Loughridge carried a scowl that could drop an elephant. Son-in-law Dell was co-owner and ran the store, but the old lady kept a hawk eye on the books. When we entered the office, she was standing behind the counter frowning through wire-rimmed glasses at her bookkeeping ledger. Dell approached his mother-in-law with a smile.

"Myrtle," he said softly, "since we have so many more broilers than last year, wouldn't you agree we need more help? Bill Ray can work Saturdays."

Mrs. Loughridge looked up from the ledger like bankruptcy would be the topic at dinner that night.

"Humph," she replied.

Taking this as hearty approval, Dell left the two of us to fill out the paper work.

Mrs. Loughridge began an entry in the ledger. "Well, young man, what are you going to do with all of this extra money?"

I hesitated before answering. "Something special," I mumbled.

"Hmm, a trip around the world?" she asked distractedly. It was a joke her expression didn't acknowledge.

"No ... something else."

I studied her as she continued writing in the ledger. She was the most intimidating woman I had ever known. Deep creases framed a doubting mouth; piercing eyes bore right into your brain. And yet, I sensed that under her flinty exterior, she harbored a streak of compassion—the no-nonsense variety—but compassion nevertheless. Maybe, if I told her my dream, she wouldn't snicker. Lord, I hoped she wouldn't.

"College," I half whispered.

Mrs. Loughridge stopped writing and cast a look that said she didn't suffer fools easily. She turned the ledger toward me and pointed her pencil to what she'd written.

"You make sixty five cents an hour. You'll be working twenty three hours a week. That's $14.95 a payday. You drive that shiny black car parked outside, which I'm sure comes with a girlfriend. That means gas, movies, soda pop, presents. And you're going to save *part* of your wages for college. Obviously, your folks are sending you. Who's your father?"

"Tramp ... Cecil Jackson."

Mrs. Loughridge looked at me and said nothing. I could hear myself breathing.

"Are we all done here, ma'am?" I asked.

She slowly closed the ledger. "What do you want to learn?"

"Uh, writing, I guess."

"You guess. What have you written?"

"Um, some high school skits with my friend Roger Torrey, and, uh, a play."

Her eyebrows arched. "A play?"

"In sixth grade."

"Do tell. What was the play about?"

I chewed my lower lip. "Well, about this ... deaf prize fighter called Deefy Comeback. See, he would come out swinging before the bell rang, and ..."

"… They always had to call him back," she finished dryly. "Well, it's a start. What college are you attending?"

"I thought maybe Kirksville, ma'am."

She tossed the ledger aside.

"No, not Kirksville. Kirksville is for teachers, musicians, osteopaths. If you want to write, you go to journalism school. The finest in the world is right here in our state, The University of Missouri."

"Journalism school?"

"Yes. Go down to Columbia and check it out. Check out the grants, too. Unless your father struck oil setting up his still, you're going to need one."

With that, she left the office.

Two days later, Mr. Bartley called me out of study hall. He sat at his desk looking at a file with my name on it.

"I hear you plan to go to college," he said.

"Yes," I replied.

How did he know that? I hadn't told anyone … except … Mrs. Loughridge.

The superintendent fished a paper from my file. I recognized it as the sign-up sheet for my final semester classes. He glanced over it, shaking his head.

"Bill Ray, you've taken all of the requirements necessary to graduate, but this last semester is nothing but creampuff stuff. More art? Speech? You can walk through those blindfolded. Journalism school is it? Sit down."

I sat.

"Before Missouri's journalism school will even *consider* you, you must stuff into your head two years of liberal arts—*hard* courses: foreign language, economics, business law; history, *European* history. And you won't get in then if you don't maintain at least a B average. The best school wants only the best students."

He placed my registration paper on the desk and tapped it with his finger.

"And you're taking *shop*? You're not going down there to make bird houses. Bill Ray, you made good grades all through school without taking a book home; yes, I was watching. You'd spend twenty minutes in the library doing your homework and the rest of the time drawing nude pictures of poor Mrs. Aeschliman. Well, twenty minutes isn't going to cut it. Now you're going to learn how to study."

He pushed the paper across his desk. "*Then* you can go to college."

I nodded, scooped up the paper and headed back to study hall. Before going in, I leaned against a nearby locker and looked at my sign-up sheet. What a bloody thing it was. Red gashes slashed through all of my soft classes and above them written Physics, Advanced English, Advanced History ... good grief, advanced everything. Goodbye Mrs. Aeschliman; hello, books.

"You know I can't help you."

Dad's grizzled face appeared over my shoulder in the mirror. I continued shaving.

"I know you can't."

"What are you taking?"

"Journalism."

God, I liked how that trickled off my tongue.

Dad studied my reflection for a moment, then just before his face disappeared in the mirror, he delivered the last advice he would ever give me.

"Know what you should be?"

"What, Dad?"

"A big fish in a small pond."

▼

Blue Blazer, Gray Slacks

I didn't know why Dad said what he did. Maybe he thought I was putting on airs. Jacksons didn't go to college—at least any from Unionville. He probably wondered why I didn't want to do the things he did. Well, I was God-awful wretched at them, that's why. I played clarinet like it was a kazoo, and a wrench in my hand was darned near dangerous. I liked creating funny things like cartoons and skits where I could use my imagination. Compared to Dad's world of carnivals, beer joints, and dance bands, I came from Mars. The door to this creative world I wanted was college. The trouble was, it cost a lot of money to get the door open.

The first thing I did was cut down on going to the show. Donna was great about it, and instead of watching Tab Hunter at the Royal, we hid from her entertainment starved sister and necked. And talked. Most of the talk was about how I would come back when I could and she wouldn't date—just go out with her girlfriends. It didn't occur to us that she was fifteen and I was seventeen, and we were talking about doing this for four years.

My savings plan cruised along perfectly until it smacked into a big wall: the prom. I might not be taking Donna to see Tab wink and grin, but I darn well would be escorting her to the school's biggest social event of the year. The major expense was the corsage, a small clump of flowers that cost more than I made a week. The prom caught Morrow short on cash, too, but not for long. He sniffed out jobs like a coon dog.

"Your hand ... fit a mop?" he asked.

"Sure," I said.

"Well ... Bailey's Café is lookin' ... for moppers."

Saturday nights around ten o'clock we mopped out Bailey's Café, a gummy-floored, grease haven truckers liked. A ritual developed. After receiving five bucks each, Morrow and I drove our separate cars to the late-night liquor store west of town. It also carried grocery items, and we each bought a package of cinnamon rolls and a quart of milk. Then we parked our cars on the west side of the Square. One of us would settle into the other's car; and with the courthouse clock showing midnight we would feast upon our end-of-the-week treat and talk of girls, cars, and dreams of the future. James wanted to be something that Dad would've liked me to be: a master mechanic.

With money for the corsage tucked away, I thought I had the prom covered, until the official announcement appeared on the school bulletin board. One line leaped at me: "Male attire will be suits or sport coats." My heart sank; I had a suit all right—the formaldehyde suit Mom had gotten me from the funeral home.

"Gonna wear Ol' Smelly?" Rodge asked. He was reading over my shoulder.

"Guess so," I answered.

Rodge nodded down the hall at Shelby Dixon making a couple of girls giggle.

"Of course The Shelb will be dressed to the nines."

"Yeah, probably look like fancy David Niven," I muttered. "You *know* he's gonna take Shirley Shuey, Donna's friend. He'll be wearing some fancy cummerbund, and I'll look like I crawled out of a casket."

"Well, you'll smell like it," Rodge chuckled.

"Oh, thanks a bunch. Who you taking?" I asked.

"Irene McHenry."

I whistled. "She only dates older guys."

"Still is. Her boyfriend from Kansas City can't make it, so she's on 'platonic' loan."

"No making out, eh?"

"None, but at least I'm gonna have one knockout mama on my arm."

We looked down the hall at The Shelb again. Now, he had four girls giggling.

Rodge said, "Remember those college guys in Kirksville we saw at that restaurant?"

"Yeah," I answered, "blue blazers, gray slacks. Sharp. Every girl in the place had her tongue hanging out."

Now, The Shelb had six girls giggling.

"I've saved some money," Rodge said.

"Yeah, me, too." A sickly, guilty feeling crept over me. I'd just gotten started on saving for college.

"Blue blazers and gray slacks?"

I let my breath out and said, "Yep."

Top-of-the-line male attire at our local department store consisted of what the well dressed duck hunter would wear; so Rodge and I drove to Centerville. The clerk at their only men's store trotted out plenty of suits, but no blazers.

"Maybe we should just go to Kirksville," I grumbled.

"Aw, we'd have to backtrack," Rodge said, "Ottumwa's closer."

"You wanna go back there?" I asked.

"You want our dates drooling over The Shelb?"

At the third and last men's clothier in Ottumwa, we still hadn't found the snazzy blue-gray combo the Kirksville college boys wore. As we started for the door, the owner called, "Tell you what. I got two blue suits and two gray suits. I'll split them up and give you each a blue jacket and gray pants."

Close enough.

Rodge and I coordinated our arrivals so that we drove up in front of the gym at the same time. I opened the passenger door of my freshly-waxed, black '47 Chevy Coupe for Donna, who looked spectacular in a light blue, off-the-shoulder gown with the twenty dollar white corsage. Rodge opened the passenger door of a nifty, powder blue '51 Ford convertible he'd smooth-talked from a friend. Irene, one of the best looking girls in our class, flashed Rodge a smile, and he looked mighty pleased her Kansas City boyfriend had to work that night.

Confident of the splash our entrance would make, Rodge and I offered our well-tailored arms to our dates and strolled toward the gymnasium entrance. We stopped short. Just right of the doorway stood Carr and Pollock—both wearing blue blazers and gray slacks. And very toothy grins. I looked accusingly at Rodge, who raised his eyebrows, but I knew. Rodge could never keep a secret. He'd blabbed our plan to steal The Shelb's thunder, and our buddies had stolen ours. Irene managed a straight face, but Donna had to cover her mouth with the little purse she carried.

The gymnasium had undergone a magical transformation. Normally brightly lit and smelling faintly of sweat, it had been darkened and freshened—decorated with swooping ribbons of blue crepe and stars of glittery silver reflecting that perennial prom theme, *Stardust.* Rodge left Irene with some of her friends and headed to the kitchen, having promised to help Mrs. Aeschliman with the snacks and punch. A smooth, seven-piece band from Kirksville held forth on the stage, the members looking sharp in matching maroon sport coats. I waved at friends, stalling for time before I treated Donna to the joy of dancing with a camel. The Shelb, resplendent in a soft, beige sport coat with burgundy bow tie, but no cummerbund, danced toward us with Shirley. In mid swirl, he looked me over and said, "Hmm, half a blue suit, half a gray one. Interesting, Jackson."

Rodge brought out a huge bowl of fruit-laden punch and returned to the kitchen. From the bandstand drifted the soothing notes of *I'm Yours,* and Donna slowly swayed to the beat, obviously wanting to dance. With elaborate formality, I poured us each a cup of punch, handed Donna hers, made a ceremonial nod, and tasted Mrs. Aeschliman's efforts for the evening. *Mmmm, Mrs. Aeschliman had outdone herself; a delightfully interesting blend of fruits and carbonation and ... something else.* When I'd finished my cup, the band was playing *Sentimental Journey* nice and slow; so I led Donna onto the dance floor. *Slide left foot forward, then the right. Slide left foot forward, then the right; then right foot back, then the left. Repeat. I had it. Just like Mom taught me.* Surprised at my ability, I actually glided Donna around the dance floor as if I knew what I was doing. When the music ended, I took us back for more punch.

Rodge came by, wiggled his cup and gave a big wink.

I took another sip. Of course! The mystery ingredient was vodka. That rascal had spiked the punch. How had he gotten away with it? The teachers watched for such shenanigans like guards on a prison wall. But, then, Rodge looked so innocent. With big, choir-boy eyes, he'd volunteered to help in the kitchen. Somebody needed to carry that heavy punch bowl out to the table. He just made a slight detour on the way. And here that darling came with another bowlful. I downed two more cups, pulled Donna into the middle of the dance floor; made up my own steps; and tore up *Kansas City.* My new bravado delighted Donna; she didn't care if I bobbed around like a happy ostrich, at least I was moving.

The farm house was dark, but pole lights lit up the grounds. The barn shivered with music and voices. Rodge and I had taken our dates home and driven in my car to the secret, guys only, after-the-prom party thrown by the Peek brothers. Jim and his year-older brother, Dean, had invited their buddies to a big bash at a vacant farm usually rented out by their unsuspecting parents who lived half a mile away. Still dressed in our blue-and-grays, Rodge and I rushed into the barn, grabbed beers from a tub of ice, and melded into the throng of laughing, yelling, already intoxicated, teenage males.

Rodge got into a chug-a-lug contest with Jim Peek, who was drowning his sorrows. Between chugs, Jim, who'd been elected "best looking boy in school," told of expressing his love to two sisters—separately—but as sisters do, they compared notes and jointly rejected him.

I drifted through several clusters of Don't Talk When You Can Yell; accepted some generous slugs of hard stuff; and finally settled for leaning against a far wall and sipping my beer. The barn rippled with heat; arm waving young males shoved and shouted their delight in showing the world they were having a hell of a time. Somebody laughed at the beer I was drinking and stuck a bottle of Jim Beam in my face. I drank the Beam and the beer. Somebody pushed me, and booze slopped down the front of my dress shirt.

Then in the sweat and shoving, jokes turned to insults; bodies stiffened, fists clenched, and bile bubbled like hot lava. My eyes searched the barn for buddy Rodge. He and Jim Peek were in a far corner singing a duet, serenely oblivious to the madness building around them. I waved a high sign. Rodge made his way through the crowd doing his Jersey Joe Walcott impersonation, bobbing and weaving from imaginary punches. Then, again, maybe he was just drunk. I was. As he neared the door, he bobbed at the right time—an empty whisky bottle whistled by his head and shattered against the wall.

We'd barely made it outside when the uproar broke through the barn doors. In the eye of the storm was a not-so-big football halfback slandering the manhood of those around him. As we climbed into the car, Not-So-Big waved a fist and yelled that we were "a couple a' queers." To my horror, Rodge, who never raised his voice, let alone his fists, slid out of the car and started toward him. A big football lineman moved between them and told Not-So-Big to shut up. Not-So-Big told Big to shut up himself. Big knocked down Not-So-Big, jumped on top of him, and pounded his face with a huge fist like it was a meat tenderizer. I pulled Rodge into the car and drove into the night.

"You feelin' a little woozy?" I asked, trying not to slur my words.

"No. I'm feeling a *lot* woozy. And sick."

"Me, too … can't go home like this."

"Cozad. Go to Cozad," Rodge mumbled and rested his forehead on the dash.

I drove north of town to Cozad Park. A road circled the park, and we drove round and round for at least twenty minutes—windows down, heads hanging out, sucking in air trying to sober up. The circling made us dizzier.

Rodge said, "Somebody puked."

I answered, "I think it was me ... I mean 'I ... I'm goin' to journeylizzum school, ya know."

I awoke with sunshine searing my eyes and a truck piston hammering inside my head. Turning slowly, I looked at Rodge looking at me with a face resembling month-old pie dough. If I looked like that, I was in real trouble, 'cause I had to go to work this morning. I looked in the rearview mirror. I was in real trouble.

At Rodge's house, I managed a feeble wave as he trudged wordlessly to the front door. The last thing I wanted was for Mom to see me, so I decided to not go home and change into my white hatchery uniform. Instead, I drove directly to work, easing into the driveway, intent on disappearing into the camouflage of a thousand chickens. Leaving my jacket and tie in the car, I spit in my hand, patted down my hair, and plodded, somewhat unsteadily, toward the broiler house in my whiskey-stained white shirt and accordion-wrinkled slacks.

Out of the house bustled Mrs. Loughridge heading for the office. She stopped dead still. So did I. Looking at me from head to toe, her penetrating eyes said there wasn't a thing I'd done in the last twenty four hours that she didn't know about. When her searchlight eyes finally settled on my own, I braced myself for the scathing death sentence that would end my employment.

All she said was, "Lot's of work today, *college boy*."

CHAPTER 33

▼

FALLING DOWN

We filed into the gym, an army in black mortarboards and massive gowns; and sat with heads high and eyes fixed upon the magisterial speaker behind the podium. Hibbs, Pollock, Bramhall, Carr, Torrey, all of the grade school gang had made it the full twelve years; and now we sat respectfully upright, fighting nearly uncontrollable urges to contort our faces and mimic bowel sounds. Duly inspired to gird our loins, draw our swords, and lay waste the word's tyrannies; we passed by Mr. Bartley, received our parchments, tossed tassels to the left, and triumphantly marched out of the building.

Barely through the doors, we laughed, whooped, danced, threw graduation caps into the air; and fell to speaking in what we believed to be the deeper, more authoritative voices of adults. Donna beamed a smile. Mom gave me a long hug. Dad stood back, nodded congratulations, and headed to the car, probably for something stashed under the front seat.

Mom gave me another squeeze and went to the car; Donna knew I wanted to be with my buddies and joined her girl friends; and I hung around touching base with the old gang. We didn't bunch together; we saw each other in ones and twos; exchanged wisecracks; joked about past adventures: Mae Hunt breaking up the cloak room fights; the city hall cap gun fights; the magic of the Pickle Factory; and once again Torrey bragged how he'd climbed on my shoulders and changed the Royal's marquee from "starring Gary Cooper" to "starring Gary Pooper." At each remembrance, we laughed louder than needed and longer than necessary, hastening from story to story to mask our loss. Finally, the memories dwindled; the voices softened; and we quietly walked away from high school and each other.

Conspicuously absent from the gang's farewells had been James Morrow; but as I drove away from school, he pulled alongside and motioned for me to follow him. He headed for the Square and parked at our old meeting place on the west side of the courthouse. When I pulled beside him, he stuck his head out his window and drawled:

"Thought we might … celebrate old times."

It was bright mid-day and a long time since our Saturday nights mopping Bailey's Cafe, but Morrow held up two packages of cinnamon rolls and two quarts of milk. I slid in beside him. We ate. We drank. We talked our adventures—especially the time Bartley chased Morrow out of the hay mow—and we laughed. A lot. Then I returned to my car; we started our engines; gave each other a wave; and headed in opposite directions.

That summer, Donna and I drove to dark places; necked; and talked about how, come fall, she'd be referring to me as her "college boyfriend." She liked the sound of that; and I proudly displayed the brochures I'd received with their impressive pictures of the University of Missouri's two, sprawling campuses. I no longer walked, I strutted. I was going down to Mizzou; going to "J-School;" going to become a writer; maybe even write stuff for *Esquire Magazine* right alongside the Petty Girl pinup.

At home I'd make sure my bedroom door was closed, and then gaze into my dresser mirror and say, "Oh, hello there. Yes, I'm a college man. What school? Why, thank you for asking, the University of Missouri, School of Journalism."

Words of pure poetry.

About mid-summer, Cook and Edmunds returned home on leave, spectacular in their new, soft blue Air Force uniforms. Boy, did they turn heads. Hats with shiny black bills; trim-cut jackets; clip-on ties; pleated pants; and black shoes spit-polished to a diamond sparkle. Girls went gaga.

I was in uniform, too, a wrinkled white one with yellowish brown battle ribbons from The Great Chicken Wars. Envying the swath cut by the returning heroes, I needed reassurance that I, also, would amount to something; so I dug out Shirlene. Shirlene was the cigar box under my bed that contained my savings for college. Rodge and I thought the sloe-eyed princess smiling on the underside of the lid looked like Shirlene Worley, our 1950 Homecoming Queen. Shirlene's smile could melt an Eskimo's igloo, and I liked it warming my money.

I hadn't counted my savings in a long time, just assuming that come September I would have stuffed enough money into the box. I dug to the bottom for the brochure listing Mizzou's fees for admission. All the different fees listed came to $920. That didn't include food, housing, and books. Well, I'd eat baloney; sleep on a cot; and figure out the books later. The big thing was to get in the door.

I sat on the edge of the bed and counted my stash. As I neared the bottom of the box, a icy sickness crawled through my stomach. When I counted the last bill, I could barely breathe. I recounted. The total didn't change. I'd only saved five hundred and thirty dollars. How could I have been so stupid? Walking around blowing about going to school and not even counting my money? Did I think it was going to grow in the box? Dear Lord, I needed a miracle; registration was next month.

Working after my hatchery hours, I took every tote, dig, and grunt job I could find; but sweat labor paid fifty cents an hour, tops. After three weeks, I'd only made an extra fourteen dollars.

I gave up. Just plain gave up.

My Phantom gave me a dream, but I blew it—just like Dad. I'd worked at the hatchery for two years, rarely taken Donna to the movies, and made a dollar's worth of gas last two weeks, so I could stuff most of my paycheck into the cigar box. Well, be honest, Jackson, you did splurge on two things: your flashy '47 Chevy and those spiffy clothes you bought for the prom. Face it, your commitment to save money was not a hundred percent.

On my way to Donna's for our customary Sunday afternoon date, I spotted Rodge walking toward Herrick's Drug Store. He was lugging a big suitcase. I called to him and pulled over, and he left the suitcase on the curb and crossed the street. Rodge usually looked happy, but today he was a Christmas tree.

"You leaving town?" I asked.

"Yeah," he said with a big grin, "catching the bus to Des Moines. Didn't have time to call. Go to work tomorrow."

"You got a job? Where?"

"Merideth Publishing, you know, they publish *Better Homes and Gardens.*"

"You're *writing* for *Better Homes and Gardens?*"

"Naw. I'm working at the warehouse. The wages beat the tar out of anything around here. But, can you believe it? I'll soon have enough to go to Drake!"

Roger Torrey going to Drake University? The rich kids' school? Home of the famous Drake Relays?

I pasted a smile on my face and said, "That's great!"

"Here comes the bus. Gotta run. I'll write when I get settled."

He trotted back, grabbed the suitcase with both hands and started for the bus, then, half way, looked back.

"You still going to Mizzou?"

I nodded a lie and drove off.

Three blocks before Donna's house I pulled off the road, leaned out the car door and had the dry heaves. I looked at the rearview mirror. Looking back was the face of pure failure. A voice spoke. It wasn't the Phantom; it was a voice I'd heard in my head a hundred times:

You piece of nothin'. You're Tramp Jackson's boy. You're not supposed to amount to anything.

I arrived at Donna's late; she ran out to the car, and I drove to the Square. Usually on Sundays we cruised around and waved at our friends, but this time I drove directly to the Royal.

"Want to see *Roman Holiday?* I hear it's pretty good."

Donna looked puzzled.

"And I think *Calamity Jane's* on next week. You like Doris Day."

Donna stared at the crowd going into the theater for a moment, then shifted her eyes toward me.

"You're not going to college," she said in a quiet voice.

I forced a smile. "Aw, it takes too much money. Besides, now we'll get to see lots of shows like all our friends."

Donna said nothing.

The line to the movie slowly dwindled, and after a while I started the car and drove to the Tasty Freeze. But Donna didn't want anything, and we drove back to her house in silence. Driving home, I troubled over her reaction. *Why wasn't she happy that I was staying home? I'd be taking her to a lot more movies. Then it dawned on me that maybe it was because she'd been proud of me going to college. I'd been her "college boyfriend." Now, I was just "boyfriend."*

Chapter 34

▼

Getting Up

That next week at the hatchery, I plodded through chickens like I had chains around my ankles. When payday arrived, I slumped into the office and stood at the counter, defeated and forlorn, like an animal realizing it can't escape its cage. Paying no notice, Mrs. Loughridge made out my check and handed it to me. "Well, you have one more week with us, and then you'll be a college boy, right?"

I looked at the floor.

She recorded the payment in the ledger, and then looked up at me with her penetrating eyes. "Come up a little short on funds?"

I nodded and started for the door.

"You're giving up? Just going to stay with us chickens?"

I continued moving.

"Bill Ray …"

I stopped in the doorway. It was the first time she'd ever really said my name. I looked back.

"A late start beats no start."

All the way home my mind kept repeating "a late start beats no start." I rushed into my room and dug out Shirlene. Sure enough, the admissions brochure said you could enroll in the first *or* second semester of each school year—the second semester starting in mid-January. I calculated what I could save in three months, but I still was two hundred dollars short. Odd jobs paid piddle; I'd never raise that much money. Then I remembered something Dad told me when I was eight-years-old—back when he shared life with me. I had tagged along as he serviced the juke box route, and as usual we were sitting at a bar, taking a rest from the rigors of collecting nickels—I playing with the peanuts floating in my Pepsi, and Dad silently sipping a glass of Muelbach.

Suddenly he blurted, "Specialize!" causing me to spill my Pepsi. He set his glass down and turned toward me. "*Specialize* is what you need to do today."

"Today?" I asked.

"No, when you grow up."

"Oh," I said.

Dad returned to his beer, and I mopped up the counter with a napkin and went back to swirling peanuts. After a few moments, I asked, "Dad, what's 'specialize' mean?"

Dad made little wet rings on the counter with his glass. He looked at the pattern like he was decoding drawings on an Egyptian wall. Finally, in a quiet voice he said, "Doing something not everyone else does. Anybody can shovel manure. Invent a better shovel; that'll get you *big* money." He tapped his glass on the bar for a refill.

Now, nine years later, I sat in my room wondering how I could invent a better shovel. What could I do that any other stumblebum couldn't do? Draw cartoons? Not much call in Unionville for goofy pictures.

Then it came to me. There was one specialty I could do. I hated it. It bored me to death; took me three days to do what should take a half an hour. But I could do it, and since no one else in town did it, I could make money at it.

Paint signs.

My first job wasn't too painful. It was a sign for a pheasant farm; and along with the lettering, I painted a male pheasant in shimmering plumage of gold and red and green, and threw in a little gold glitter for no extra charge. The next job was even better—it was on a large mirror—a cartoon of a husky, ball-toting football player in the Midgets' blue and white uniform. The mirror was behind the counter of the new teen hangout opened by the mother of a friend of mine, Larry Bertini. Larry's step-father, Slim Robinson—formerly Dad's Casa Loma partner and the previously mentioned naked surprise at Mutt's Barbershop—tended the place. When I'd finished, Slim asked how much he owed me. I'd spent six hours on it and figured that painting people was more specialized than painting letters; plus I was two bucks out for the paint; so I said, "fifteen dollars."

Slim's face darkened.

"Should've been five," he muttered. He punched the cash register's "open" key and shoved the money at me like I was Jesse James.

From there I went to my old scoutmaster, Oren Lee Halley, and painted announcements on his market windows proclaiming prodigious savings on ham hocks, sauerkraut and black-eyed peas. When Thanksgiving approached, I decorated store fronts with grinning pilgrims and unsuspecting turkeys. Two weeks before Christmas, I filled windows around the Square with fat Santas and deer with enlarged red noses.

Then nothing.

Three weeks before I had to slide my money across the counter at Mizzou, the jobs ended. No one wanted a sign about anything. No "Hamburger, fifteen cents a pound;" no "Dresses Half Off;" no "Everything Must Go" signs. And Shirlene said I was at least a hundred dollars short.

Then the miracle happened: a gasoline price war.

Bantam, short-fused Red Cullum was the dealer for DX gasoline, a popular brand in northern Missouri. For all of 1953, Red had set the price of DX gasoline at an unwavering 21.9 cents a gallon; and Standard and Sinclair and all the other gas stations around followed suit. But in mid-December, an off-brand upstart lowered its price to 19.9.

Red blew his auburn stack. He stormed into Davis Chevrolet and announced to one and all that "you don't mess around with the big guys," and he, a bona fide representative of DX, Incorporated, would "lower the hammer on 'em." Red dropped DX gas to 18.9. Without missing a beat, Off-Brand countered with 17.9.

The war was on.

Every morning, DX was a penny lower. Every evening, Off Brand was a penny lower than that. People began to go out after supper to buy gas. Finally, Red roared into the garage and bellowed, "I'm through pussyfootin' around! From now on we're playin' hardball!"

DX plunged the price to 11.9.

After supper that day, Off-Brand hadn't lowered its price at all. It closed its doors.

And who benefited from all of Red's spit and spite besides the car owners? Why, the little ol' gas painter, me. Red set me up in one of his warehouses, and every time he lowered the price of DX gasoline I painted a new sign for every station he supplied—of which there were many. After my workday at the hatchery, I'd grab a sandwich and a Pepsi, go to the warehouse and labor until midnight. I painted two's and five's and nine's until my humming turned to screaming, but when the gas war was over, I'd filled Shirlene to the brim.

Sitting on the edge of the bed, I slowly counted the contents. I had the admissions fee, plus money for books. I got up and nodded to myself in the mirror. "Hi, there. Bill Jackson here, University of Missouri School of Journalism."

I wasn't Bill Ray anymore. I was Bill.

CHAPTER 35

▼

A RASPY VOICE

The day before I left for college I saw a ghost. My last day at the hatchery, a Saturday, Dell was issuing our assignments when the phone rang. When he hung up, he said, "That was a farmer in Albia. His chickens have coccidiosis."

"Chickens get venereal disease?" I asked.

Jack Maulsby grinned; Claude Hawkins snorted; Dell covered a smile by stroking his chin.

"No, it's a chicken ailment," Dell explained, trying not to embarrass me.

Hawkins had no such compunction. "There's a sex education movie at the Royal. Maybe Jackson should go see it."

Jack and Dell laughed, but Dell recovered quickly and said to me, "I'm taking them some medication. It's your last day; you can come with me and see what coccidiosis looks like."

Now, there's a treat. I hoped medicating them didn't involve anything kinky. It turned out to be medicated feed, several fifty pound sacks of it, which I loaded into the panel truck. I rode shotgun as we drove the forty miles to Albia, Iowa. Dell was his usual quiet self, but after about fifteen minutes he broke the silence. "It's good you're going to school at Mizzou," he said.

"Mrs. Loughridge pointed me there," I replied.

"Mrs. Loughridge points well," he said.

I realized that I'd been fortunate that she had taken an interest in me. And I realized something else: the hatchery had been a special place, a port in the storm giving me work when there was none and financially helping me open a door to a new life. I didn't know a Plymouth Rock from the Rock of Gibraltar, but I knew the people of the hatchery were of exceptional value. Jack Maulsby, soft-spoken and pleasant, my immediate boss who was never bossy. Claude Hawkins, a cackling prankster who became my friend, taught me my job, which kept me employed. Roy Loughridge, the kindly, quiet co-owner, whose twinkling eyes and gentle humor exemplified the grace of growing old. Mrs. Loughridge, a much needed, dead-on compass, who not only selected the race, but picked the horse I needed to ride. And Dell Rockwood: one of the finest men in Unionville—formally a flight instructor in World War II—placid, compassionate, a benchmark for everything decent. On this, my final day at the hatchery, riding through the Iowa countryside with Dell, did I look across and share my feelings? I'm sorry to say I did not.

The farmer had been waiting by his mail box and we followed in the panel truck as he walked down a short road adjacent to his house. We came to a weathered broiler house; Dell poked his head inside the door; then motioned for me to join him.

"Look," he said, "*that's* coccidiousis."

Inside the building, from wall to wall, chickens stumbled around wan and dopey with their feathers sticking up like Alfalfa's hair. Dell talked with the farmer while I began unloading the sacks of feed.

"I'll fetch you some help," said the farmer. He whistled through his fingers and beckoned to a bent figure at the far end of a truck garden several yards away. The figure approached, hobbling on short, bowed legs. It was an old man. He wore a gray, short-billed cloth cap pulled low over his eyes; and the exertion of the walk made his chest heave. When he got to the truck, he glanced at me with shadowed, watery-blue eyes.

"Hi, kid," he said in a raspy voice.

That voice! I knew that voice from somewhere long ago. He grabbed a feed sack and hoisted it to his shoulder, giving a grunt I'd heard a hundred times.

It was Sealy.

My God, it was Sealy, my Gorilla Man hero from the carnival The years had not been kind. He was so much smaller, his body bent forward like it carried an invisible burden of immense weight. He removed his cap to wipe away the sweat, revealing a head as round and bald as ever; but his face showed a ravage of roads going in all directions. His greeting was just courtesy. He hadn't recognized me.

Should I tell him who I was: that little boy hanging around his tent whose saucer eyes had idolized his every move? I watched him limp from the truck to the feed shed, arms grappling the heavy sack like an old opponent. He had been so marvelous—bounding onto the platform; roaring his savage gorilla scream; baring his huge, square teeth; taunting the farmers beyond endurance. Then wrapping the big rope around his neck; bracing against the might of two of the crowd's biggest as they pulled on each end of the rope trying to kill him.

No, it would shame him to know I saw him like this: bent and shuffling; wheezing like air escaping from an old tire. I said nothing.

Sealy and I finished unloading, and Dell and I got back into the panel truck and started down the long road leading to the highway. I looked back at my old hero. He trudged slowly to the far end of the truck garden, his shoulders weary, his head down, the roar that had rocked the midway now a whisper. I was glad Dell's attention was on the road. He didn't see the tears in my eyes.

CHAPTER 36

▼

MY GRAND EXIT

<bf>

Her arms clutched me like I was life itself. Finally, she gave a sigh and stepped back, her eyes wet and her mouth an attempted smile.

"My son, going to college. I'm so proud of you," she said.

"Thanks, Mom."

I put my hands on her shoulders. How worn she looked, this Virginia Lee, "the prettiest girl ever to come out of Putnam County." Now, recently forty, she stood shivering in the chill of a January morning, her face pale and drawn from traveling a road of ruts, rocks, and detours. This past year her smile had grown weary and her eyes dull and she took to bed a lot. The doctor, after several examinations, decided she had rheumatic fever; and this nebulous disease became the official explanation of her weakened condition. But I never bought it. I thought what really was wrong was that she had *the worries*: worries about when Dad was coming home; worries about the rent, food, clothing for John and Sam—a flood of concerns that had swamped her life after Dad scuttled the Casa Loma.

I gave Mom one last hug and waved across the street to brothers John and Sam happily playing Dog Pile with the Webber boys. Sam, the youngest, didn't see me; he was on the bottom. Sliding behind the wheel, I realized this would be the last time I'd drive my cherished '47 Chevy. Dad rode along so he could bring it back and sell it; I'd be needing the money for my second semester next fall.

The Square was Sunday-morning solemn, as gray as the Union soldier statue standing sentry at the courthouse. Where were the multitudes cheering my triumph? Bands should blare and streamers wave. *Hey, town. Tramp Jackson's boy is going to college!* But the streets stood empty and the store windows dark, and all that the Square offered was a stray dog sniffing the gutter for Saturday night's remains.

So, to celebrate my achievement, I called upon an old friend: my imagination.

A rocket soared over Unionville, exploded in a thunderous flash and blew away the winter. White doves streaked across a beautiful blue sky and morning sunshine bathed the buildings in gold. Standing at a podium on the courthouse lawn stood Mr. Meeks, the high school music instructor. He flashed his silver baton like a dueling sword as the high school band thundered "Stars and Stripes Forever." Townspeople, lauding my achievement, flooded the Square, laughing, weeping, cheering their joy; many grasping my extended hand as I motored by. A wave from Mr. Meeks' magic baton and the band segued to the tinny notes of a merry-go-round calliope. "Hey, kid!" rang out from the courthouse steps; and atop them waved Sealy, Delmar, and that rascal Peck Brooks holding Hydra, The Two-Headed Goat. Abruptly, the calliope music switched to "Rag Mop," and the street became a frenzied ballroom. Half crouched and snapping their fingers, teachers Harold Wellman and Suzy Grant bobbed to the beat like demons; Miss Hunt, wearing her Minnie Pearl hat, boogied her way to the car; followed by a shucking, jiving Miss Hill peeking through one of the half-dollar holes in Old Betsy. Close by, in a huge circle formed by the crowd, lanky Mr. Bartley twirled tubby Mrs. Aeschliman like a top.

"Rag Mop" became "Happy Trails to You;" the Royal's marquee read "Hi-O, Paint, Let's Get Where We Aint;" and alongside the car on golden palominos rode Uncle Bill, Uncle Cleo, and Dell Rockwood waving ten gallon hats.

The music faded as I edged eastward out of town and headed into the morning sun. The crowd dwindled, then disappeared, until all that remained was silence and a lone figure hunched in silhouette by the city limits sign. The figure looked up and smiled. It was Mrs. Loughridge.

Reality returned just beyond Shields' Junk Yard. The sky grayed and January's fields returned to their rolling dullness spotted with occasional patches of dirty snow. I stole a glance at Dad. A cigarette dangled from his mouth, and the smoke made his eyes squint as he took in the bleakness of north-Missouri winter.

"Hope you get a lot for the car, Dad."

He nodded and said nothing.

My thoughts drifted to last night with Donna. I'd picked the Old City Pond for our goodbye, no longer caring if her sister bushwhacked us down or not. We'd been there about five minutes, when I said, "I need to tell you something."

Donna looked at me closely.

"I won't be able to come home much."

"Not weekends?" Her voice sounded hurt.

"Well, I'm going to need a lot of money for next year ... so I took two jobs.

"*Two* jobs?"

"One's cleaning bathrooms at the boarding house where I'm staying ..."

Donna wrinkled her nose.

"... and the other's plopping mashed potatoes on plates at the student cafeteria."

Donna remained silent.

I rushed on. "Dad always said that when times are tough, get a job around food. Guess who'll go to class with a couple of pork chops in his pocket?" I laughed.

Donna scrunched down in the seat.

"Hey, but I get spring vacation. It's a whole week."

She sat up. "Then we'll drive around and see all of our friends, and ..."

"Uh, no—I'm selling the car."

"*This* car?" she asked, feeling the upholstery.

"I'll need the money for next year. But, hey, maybe we can double with Claude and Roxy. He saved his money from the hatchery and bought a new car. I talked to him; he invited us to double."

Donna stared at the blackness of the pond.

This wasn't going well at all. She was only sixteen and had two years of school left: two years of parties and proms and cruising the Square. Dumb Donald Butler probably had gassed up his pickup just waiting for me to leave town. We'd both said we'd be true to each other, but I needed to hear the vow again.

"I won't be dating anybody ... will you?" I asked.

She looked at me with those Virginia Mayo eyes. "No," she whispered, "I won't go out with anyone, just my girlfriends."

Later, as I drove Donna home, I turned on one of the music stations, and Nat King Cole was singing *Too Young*—a song about how the adults felt that this teenage boy and girl were too young to be in love, but the kids knew they were. I put an arm around Donna and drove slower. It was our song.

I turned south on highway 63 and my mind returned to two weeks ago when I had taken a day off from the hatchery and driven the 135 miles to Columbia in search of a room and part time work. The brochure pictures of the University had been impressive, but I wasn't prepared for the real thing. Once in the town, I turned a corner and this magnificent foreign city loomed before me, huge and sprawling with majestic architecture over two campuses: the Red with its rich russet brick, and the White with its imperial blanched stone.

And then I saw a building that took my breath: Jesse Hall, the cornerstone of Red Campus, rose like a dark red palace radiating authority over all that surrounded it. An immense quadrangle lay just beyond, and in the middle of it stretched a huge, grassy courtyard where six Corinthian columns towered like ancient Greek sentries. Surrounding the courtyard were red-hued mansions— monuments to the mind—with chiseled inscriptions over the entryways announcing learned subjects like Philosophy, Science, and Literature. And there it stood at the far end of the quadrangle, my quest: the venerable Journalism School. It looked small compared to the other schools, and no ivy climbed its walls, but I knew that in its basement the faculty and students created, not some flippy college handout, but the city of Columbia's leading newspaper. But as Mr. Bartley and the brochures had said, I'd have to wait a couple of years before I could be part of the action.

White campus was a quarter of a mile away, anchored by the cream-stoned Student Union building with its Big Ben-style clock tower. I planned to seek a job where I could filch some food, perhaps at the Student Union cafeteria; but first I'd look for a place to stay.

A block south of Jesse Hall, I found a withered, two-story house with a "Rooms for Rent" sign on the porch. A drawn hawk of a woman said she had one room left, but unfortunately I wouldn't be able to see it, because she had misplaced the key. The rent was thirty dollars a month, but she had a deal. She and her brother also owned the rooming house next door and wanted the hallways and bathrooms of both places cleaned Mondays and Thursdays. If her brother thought I could do the job, she would take ten dollars off the rent. I accepted immediately.

"Well, let's see what Brother thinks," she said.

She led me into a dimly lit hallway, gesturing with her thumb at a dark door on the right. "That's the room," she said. A few steps away, a stairway wound its way to the second floor. A door stood slightly ajar under the stairs. "That's the downstairs bathroom you'll share. The lock doesn't work, so don't go in if the door's closed and leave it open a little when you go out." *The house seemed to have a problem with locks and keys.* In the darkest recesses of the hallway, she opened a door that appeared to be ornately carved out of hardened brown mud, and invited me into her living quarters.

The living room was a study in Musty Strange: golden, dust-laden drapes edged with sickly tassels; a black leather couch that had to have been Freud's; and gnarled lamps fit for a voodoo séance. Across the room in semi-darkness rested Brother. He looked older than God, a withered, corn-stalk of a man with an erratic shock of white hair crowning his head. He sat in a wheelchair, and draped across his legs was an old, peach-colored blanket that smelled like it had come from a dog's bed. In his lap he held a Raggedy Ann doll.

Hawk Lady turned her brother's head in my direction and leaned close to the old man's ear.

She shouted, "He wants the job. What do you think?"

Brother peered at me with wavering, watery eyes; then held up Raggedy Ann and made her head nod yes.

With this approval, I left the hiring committee and headed for what I hoped would be my source of food. When I got to the Student Union Cafeteria, I entered a horde of students voicing their hunger, and I couldn't tell who was running the place. A white-jacketed busboy sensed I was looking for work and said, "The supervisor's over there," nodding toward a large woman with the biggest bosom I'd ever seen. I quickly rehearsed a speech about my extensive food serving experience and cautiously approached her. The closer I got, the bigger her bosom became; and by the time I reached them, *her,* I'd lost the ability to speak. She observed my approach with Mae West worldliness.

"What is it, honey?" she asked in a husky voice.

"I, uh, uh, need a job," I stammered.

She leaned real close, her enormities inches from my chin.

"You ever work around food?"

I swallowed hard and answered much too loudly, "Yes, ma'am. I was fry cook at the Unionville Country Club."

She gave me a small smile and said, "Sweetie, the only thing fried around here is me on Saturday night. You work two hours lunch, two hours dinner, six days a week. Pays sixty five cents an hour, no freebie meals. Want it?

"Want it."

CHAPTER 37

▼

FAREWELL, MY FATHER

Fifty miles south on 63 the snow patches disappeared and trees proudly clutched a few diehard leaves. Dad hadn't said much, except that he'd noticed that the right rear tire was getting bald and the car would need better rubber if he was going to get a decent price for it. I nodded, not wanting to think about saying goodbye to my cherished black Chevy coupe.

As we neared Columbia the sun came out, the traffic picked up, and rich people's houses crowded both sides of the highway. In the heart of downtown, cars honked their presence and well-attired shoppers scurried along the streets. Then I turned a corner and the magnificence of my new world loomed before us. I proudly pointed out Jesse Hall to Dad, drove by a row of elegant fraternity houses with shiny convertibles parked in front, and turned onto the decidedly less glamorous street where I would live. The rooming house looked more decrepit than I remembered and closed blinds secured the secrets within.

When I handed Dad the keys to the car, a deep sorrow flooded over me. What a gem she had been. I fought off an impulse to plant a wet kiss on her shiny hood. Dad already had one suitcase; I grabbed the other; and we entered the darkened house. From behind the door at the end of the hall, Hawk Lady's voice scolded Brother for not eating his oatmeal. I assumed that Raggedy Ann hadn't eaten hers, either. Luckily, I didn't have to disturb this quaint family—the elusive key was taped to my door.

"I've never actually seen the place," I said, fitting the large key in the lock.

"You rented this room sight unseen?" Dad asked.

"Well, yeah, but I got a real good deal on it."

I swung the door open.

We entered dark stuffiness and I stumbled over a chair groping my way to the Venetian blinds. Light streaming through dusty slats unveiled my treasure: a rock-hard kitchen chair at a heavy wooden table; a patched easy chair alongside a pale-green dresser with a cracked mirror; and a sagging daybed covered with a lumpy, faded spread, probably from Hawk Lady's grandmother. However, the walls took first prize in the mournful category with their rough, swirled plaster painted dark maroon.

We put the suitcases down and I pulled off my jacket, but Dad kept his on. He stood by the table and ran his fingers over its grain like he was grading wood or something. After an awkward silence, he asked, "What classes are you taking?"

My heart jumped. He'd never asked me anything about school, and my answer spilled out like a dam had burst.

"Oh, English, of course. You have to take lots of English for journalism. And history: European, American—teeth-grinding stuff. And a foreign language, three semesters of it. Girls like to hear that voulez-vous stuff, so think I'll take French."

Dad moved toward the door. My mind raced for some way to detain him, maybe talk old stories.

"Wish they offered Carny," I joked. "I'd breeze that."

Dad turned toward me.

"You still speak Carny?" he asked.

"She-uh-zure," I answered with a grin.

His eyes lit up. "You were only four when you learned it."

"The only kid on the carnival," I said.

"Your mother and I used to talk it when we didn't want you to know what we were saying. One day she said she wanted to get some 'ee-uh-zice cree-uh-zeem ...'"

"... and I yelled, 'Me, too!'"

We both laughed.

God, it felt good to hear him laugh.

My mind raced for more stories to share, but Dad had moved into the hallway. I followed, and he paused a few steps from the front door and looked back at me. It was time to hug, but Dad never hugged. I don't think his father had, nor the fathers before him. But I wanted to run to him, throw my arms around his neck and tell him I loved him. I searched his eyes for a sign that he wouldn't rebuff me, and for a moment, a flickering second, I thought it was there ... but then it was gone and his eyes sought exit.

"Better hit the road," he mumbled, moving onto the porch.

"G'bye, Dad."

He did not look back.

I watched him from the front door as he walked to the car, his once erect body now bent, his former brisk stride now slow.

What had happened to this man of remarkable gifts—the freight-hopping genius who trod the boards with the great Palmer, made a banjo sing, caressed a keyboard like a lover? The alchemist who turned kerosene into gasoline? The Barnum who brought jazz to Unionville? The father who built kites that soared like eagles and told stories so marvelous and alive, that a boy would carry their magic with him forever?

Gone. Eyes dead, smile buried, a slouched soul anxious to hit the door and at least two bars on the way home. Oh, Dad, what was this black, despicable cancer that devoured your spirit and destroyed your dreams? If I could but find it, I would kill it. Bash it. Smash it. Hammer it to death with a sledgehammer like it was a snake.

Dad started the car and slowly pulled away. I waved. He wasn't looking.

I watched until the car disappeared, and then I turned back toward my room. But I wasn't ready for maroon walls just yet, so I walked down the street toward Red Campus. As I drew closer, I could feel an electric charge in the air as students in bright colors swooped back from Christmas break, flying from their parents like birds escaping a cage—squawking, laughing, calling to each other from blocks away. In the midst of this bustle strolled a tall, professor-looking man dressed in a gray suit and carrying a briefcase. He walked up the steps to Jesse Hall and entered its massive doors. I took a deep breath. Tomorrow morning I would enter those doors, too, and change my life forever.

Epilogue
Wednesday, April 5, 1995

The audience roared its delight. People stood whistling, waving, pumping their fists like a favorite uncle had returned from the war. I stood center stage for *An Evening with Bill Jackson,* a tribute presented by the Chicago Museum of Broadcast Communications. In the front row, beaming her five star smile, sat my beautiful wife, Jo, flanked on both sides by a dozen extraordinary people who had endowed my shows with their special talents. People unable to get seats stood crowded against the back wall.

My God, I thought, the kid who drew Deefy Comeback has standing room only. I marveled at the journey that had brought me here tonight: from carnival to college to creating children's television some called "the best of the best." The audience's love overwhelmed me, stunned me, caught me completely by surprise. In show business, the dictum is "you're only as good as your last performance." Well, my last performance had been sixteen years ago, after which I had entered the academic world in California—and these wonderful people acted as if I'd dazzled their pants off this morning. Having introduced me in the most glowing of terms, the *Evening's* host, children's television historian Jim Engel, left me to the audience.

Microphone in hand, I forced my lips to move, tried to speak, say something, didn't matter what, just get my tongue launched and hope my brain caught up down the line. My words tumbled out in some jumbled mess about my delight in being back in Chicago, and heads nodded as if it didn't matter if I spoke Chinese, they were just happy to see me. The occasion cried out for a well-written speech, words of eloquence expressing my heartfelt appreciation for this special tribute, but all I could think of were two words: thank you. So I said them. The audience responded with applause and fell silent.

Now what?

I groped in my pocket for my prop. I hadn't prepared a speech, but I'd always been big on visuals, and in this case it was a huge set of fake sideburns. Back in the sixties and seventies big hair was in, and like Elvis, I grew sizable mutton chops, which became my trade mark. Now, my hair didn't cover the top of my head, let alone the sides. Turning away from the audience, I said, "Some of you may be thinking you wandered into the wrong room tonight, but this may help you recognize me." I faced the audience with big clumps of fake black hair stuck on each side of my head. That was it. I had my first laugh. Now, I could get on with the show.

Jim Engle, an outstanding cartoonist and a leading expert on Chicago' children's television, roamed the aisles with a microphone, and I took questions from the audience. Not surprisingly, many questions were about my puppets: large, latex creations, resembling three-dimensional cartoons. During the course of my shows, I had created over thirty characters with names like Dirty Dragon, Mother Plumtree, Wally and Weird, and Dr. Doompuss,

And I learned to make them in a very curious place.

After graduating from the University of Missouri, I became a copywriter, art director, and cartooning weatherman for KTVO-TV in Ottumwa, Iowa. One year later, with my name at the top of Putnam County's draft list, I joined the Army. At the conclusion of basic training, which I'd spent crawling over Colorado rocks, I received an astonishing assignment: Hollywood—The Land of La La and Elizabeth Taylor. There, as a lowly PFC at the Armed Forces Radio & Television Service, I served my country as a television writer, director, and staff artist. Young and full of untried ideas, I found our "military related public service announcements" as boring as their name. To liven up things, I asked Walker Edmiston, a highly talented Los Angeles based kid show performer, to do some spots for us using his hilarious puppets. Walker declined, but gave me an address where I could learn to make my own characters. I found myself at a bizarre "monster" factory, and learned the craft of making latex puppets while seated next to a conveyer belt of Frankenstein heads. My first puppets were Fergy and Morty Martian, operated by Hollywood voice actors Dawes Butler and Don Messick, and although I directed the films, I really was a student absorbing everything I could from these masters.

And tonight some of my creations would be encased just down the hall from my favorite plank of wood, Charlie McCarthy. The road to Charlie's neighborhood had been bumpy and rutted, but along the way I'd created three separate series that both the kids and critics liked: *Cartoon Town, BJ & Dirty Dragon,* and *The Gigglesnort Hotel.* Recognition from the Museum stemmed in part from my shows winning four Chicago Emmys and twice being acclaimed as "The Best Major Market Children's Television in America." Appearing in more than seventy markets across the nation, *The Gigglesnort Hotel* also entertained children in such diverse places as Canada, Italy, Singapore, and Saudi Arabia. And now, long after the studio lights had dimmed and the cameras had faded to black, Chicago told me in a loud and loving way that it remembered both the puppets and me.

After signing the last autograph, I took Jo's hand and we exited into the crisp Chicago night. As we strolled toward a late-hours diner, we talked about how delighted the audience had been, the showstopper being the surprise entrance of my most unusual character, not a puppet at all, but a big lump of clay. The audience had stomped and hollered when Town Monument Blob entered on his pedestal greeting everyone with his memorable "mood talk"—in this case some industrial grade moaning. Blob's lumpy, bandaged head showed the wear of his long absence from the small screen. But he was back, and I quickly sculpted his pliable features into a toothy-grinning, "Happy Boy." With a top hat on his head, and a "Home Again!" sign in his hand, Blob bellowed a guffaw and made the grandest exit a lump of clay could possibly make.

The people who had braved the congested streets, paid the exorbitant parking, and spent the grocery money on tickets had received something in return. For this short time, that flower garden called their childhood had bloomed again. Looking at the stars above the city lights, I thought of Dad. How would he have felt about this evening's hoopla? Would he have been proud of me?

I think he would have liked the Blob.

Biography

Born in 1935, the mid-ground of the Great Depression, Bill Ray Jackson spent his pre-school years on traveling carnivals. In 1940, the family returned to its hometown, Unionville, Missouri, where Bill Ray attended school. Painting signs for a gas war, he raised the money to enroll at the University of Missouri, and in 1957graduated Dean's List from the university's School of Journalism. Jackson then became the cartooning weatherman at KTVO-TV, Ottumwa, Iowa. In 1958, he joined the Army, and as a PFC was assigned as a writer, director, and staff artist at Armed Forces Radio and Television in Hollywood. While there, Jackson created his first puppets—large, latex, cartoon-looking characters—and worked with the great animation voice actors Dawes Butler and Don Messick. Returning to civilian life, Jackson launched a career in children's television that began in Fort Wayne, Indiana, continued to Indianapolis, and propelled him to Chicago, where he wrote, produced, and performed three highly imaginative series: *Cartoon Town, The BJ & Dirty Dragon Show,* and *The Gigglesnort Hotel*

These programs brought praise from innumerable critics. Pulitzer Prize winner Ron Powers made note of their "violence free" entertainment. Dr. Sammy R. Danna, Loyola University, proclaimed the *Gigglesnort* series "the best overall examples of children's programming I have seen since television began." Author Ted Okuda wrote in his book, *The Golden Age of Chicago Television,* "Of all the Chicago kid-show hosts, no one was more creative or more resourceful than Bill Jackson." Children's television historian Jim Engel summed up his view of Jackson's creations for children as "the best of the best." Awards included four Chicago Emmys and two national Iris Awards for the Best Major Market Children's Television in America. *The Gigglesnort Hotel* aired in over seventy television markets throughout the nation, plus Canada, Italy, Singapore, and Saudi Arabia.

Jackson is featured in the books *TvParty, Children's Television-Part II,* and *The Golden Age of Chicago Children's Television.*

After leaving children's television, Jackson joined the Disney-founded California Institute of the Arts as an administrator and teacher. He retired in 1989 and he and his wife, Jo, live in central California where he draws goofy pictures for his grandchildren.